THE INNER KINGDOM

Volume 1 of the Collected Works

THE COLLECTED WORKS
VOLUME I

The Inner Kingdom

by

BISHOP KALLISTOS WARE

ST VLADIMIR'S SEMINARY PRESS
CRESTWOOD, NEW YORK
2004

℘

*The publication of this book has been underwritten
through a grant provided by the*

Virginia H. Farah Foundation

LIBRARY OF CONGRESS CATALOGING-IN-PUBLICATION DATA

Ware, Kallistos, 1934-
    The inner kingdom / by Kallistos Ware.
       p. cm. — (The collected works; vol. 1)
    Includes bibliographical references (p.) and index.
    ISBN 0-88141-210-4 — ISBN 0-88141-209-0 (pbk.)
      1. Orthodox Eastern Church—Liturgy. 2. Spiritual life—Orthodox Eastern
Church. 3. Orthodox Eastern Church—Doctrines. I. Title.

BX395.W37 2000
230'19—dc21
                                           00-039008

THE INNER KINGDOM
Volume 1 of the Collected Works

ST VLADIMIR'S SEMINARY PRESS
575 Scarsdale Road • Crestwood • New York 10707-1699
1-800-204-2665

ISBN 0-88141-209-0 (paper)
ISBN 0-88141-210-4 (hard)

First printed 2000, reprinted 2001, 2004

PRINTED IN THE UNITED STATES OF AMERICA

CONTENTS

ABBREVIATIONS

AP	*Apophthegmata Patrum* (*The Sayings of the Desert Fathers*).
Avgoustinos	Avgoustinos Monachos, ed., *Abba Isaias: Logoi.* Jerusalem: Holy Sepulchre Press, 1911.
Baehrens	W. A. Baehrens, ed., *Origenes Werke: Homilien zu Samuel I, zum Hohenlied und zu den Propheten, Kommentar zum Hohenlied, in Rufins und Hieronymus' Übersetzungen.* Die Griechischen Christlichen Schriftsteller der ersten drei Jahrhunderte 33. Leipzig: J. C. Hinrichs, 1925.
Berthold	Heinz Berthold, ed., *Makarios/Symeon: Reden und Briefe.* 2 vols. Berlin: Akademie-Verlag, 1973.
Brock	Sebastian Brock, tr., *Isaac of Nineveh (Isaac the Syrian): "The Second Part", Chapters IV-XLI.* Corpus Scriptorum Christianorum Orientalium 555, Scriptores Syri 225. Louvain: Peeters, 1995.
Butler	Cuthbert Butler, ed., *The Lausiac History of Palladius: The Greek text.* Cambridge, England: Cambridge University Press, 1904.
Butterworth	G. W. Butterworth, tr., *Origen: On First Principles.* New York: Harper Torchbooks, 1966.
Chadwick	Henry Chadwick, tr., *Origen: Contra Celsum.* Cambridge, England: Cambridge University Press, 1965.
Coleman-Norton	P. R. Coleman-Norton, ed., *Palladii Dialogvs de Vita S. Joannis Chrysostomi,* Cambridge, England: Cambridge University Press, 1928.
Darrouzès	Jean Darrouzès, ed., *Syméon le Nouveau Théologien: Chapitres théologiques, gnostiques et pratiques.* Sources Chrétiennes 51. Paris: Cerf, 1957.
deCatanzaro	C. J. deCatanzaro, tr., *Symeon the New Theologian: The Discourses.* The Classics of Western Spirituality. New York/Ramsey/Toronto: Paulist Press, 1980.
des Places	E. des Places, ed., *Diadoque de Photicé: Oeuvres Spirituelles.* Sources Chrétiennes 5 bis. Paris: Cerf, 1955.
Dörries	Hermann Dörries, Erich Klostermann and Matthias Kroeger, eds., *Die 50 Geistlichen Homilien des Makarios.* Patristische Texte und Studien 4. Berlin: Walter de Gruyter, 1964.
DS	M. Viller, F. Cavallera, J. de Guibert *et al.,* eds., *Dictionnaire de spiritualité ascétique et mystique, doctrine et histoire.* 16 vols. Paris: Beauchesne, 1937-95.
Greer	Rowan A. Greer, ed., *Origen: An Exhortation to Martyrdom, On Prayer, On First Principles: Book IV, Prologue to the Commentary on the Song of Songs, Homily XXVII on Numbers.* The Classics of Western Spirituality. New York/Ramsey/Toronto: Paulist Press, 1979.

Gregg	Robert C. Gregg, ed., *Athanasius: The Life of Antony and the Letter to Marcellinus*. The Classics of Western Spirituality. New York/Ramsey/Toronto: Paulist Press, 1980.
Guy	J.-C. Guy, tr., *Les Apophtegmes des Pères du Désert*. Spiritualité Orientale 1. Bégrolles: Abbaye de Bellefontaine, 1966.
Halkin	François Halkin, ed., *Sancti Pachomii Vitae Graecae*. Subsidia Hagiographica 19. Brussels: Société des Bollandistes, 1932.
Henry & Schwyzer	P. Henry and H.-R. Schwyzer, eds., *Plotini Opera*. 3 vols. Museum Lessianum, Section Philosophique, 33-35. Paris: Desclée de Brouwer, 1951-73.
Kelley	C. F. Kelley, tr., *The Book of the Poor in Spirit*. London: Longmans Green, 1954.
Krivochéine	Archbishop Basile Krivochéine, ed., *Syméon le Nouveau Théologien: Catéchèses*. 3 vols. Sources Chrétiennes 96, 104, 113. Paris: Cerf, 1963-65.
Langerbeck	Hermann Langerbeck, ed., *In Canticum Canticorum*. Gregorii Nysseni Opera 6. Leiden: E. J. Brill, 1960.
Luibheid & Russell	Colm Luibheid and Norman Russell, trs., *John Climacus: The Ladder of Divine Ascent*. The Classics of Western Spirituality. New York/Ramsey/Toronto: Paulist Press, 1982.
Maloney	George A. Maloney, tr., *Pseudo-Macarius: The Fifty Spiritual Homilies and the Great Letter*. The Classics of Western Spirituality. New York/Mahwah: Paulist Press, 1992.
McGuckin	Paul McGuckin, tr., *Symeon the New Theologian: The Practical and Theological Chapters and the Three Theological Discourses*. Cistercian Studies Series 41. Kalamazoo, MI: Cistercian Publications, 1982.
Meyendorff	Jean Meyendorff, ed., *Grégoire Palamas: Défense des saints hésychastes*. 2 vols. Spicilegium Sacrum Lovaniense 30-31. Louvain: Université Catholique, 1959.
Miller	Dana Miller, tr., *The Ascetical Homilies of Saint Isaac the Syrian*. Boston: Holy Transfiguration Monastery, 1984.
Mühlenberg	E. Mühlenberg, ed., *Oratio catechetica*. Gregorii Nysseni Opera 3:4. Leiden: E. J. Brill, 1996.
Nau, *ROC*	F. Nau, ed., "Histoire des solitaires égyptiens (MS Coislin 126, fol. 158f.)," *Revue de l'orient chrétien* 12 (1907), 48-68, 171-81, 393-404; 13 (1908), 47-57, 266-83; 14 (1909), 357-79; 17 (1912), 204-11, 294-301; 18 (1913), 137-46. [Greek text of *Apophthegmata Patrum*, anonymous collection]
Novellae	K. E. Zacharia von Lingenthal, ed., *Corpus juris civilis. Novellae constitutiones*. 2 vols. Leipzig: B. G. Teubner, 1881-84.
Philokalia	G. E. H. Palmer, Philip Sherrard and Kallistos Ware (eds.), *St Nikodimos of the Holy Mountain and St Makarios of Corinth, The Philokalia: The Complete Text*. 4 vols. (vol. 5 in preparation). London: Faber, 1979-.

PG	J. P. Migne, ed., *Patrologiae cursus completus, Series Graeca.* 161 vols. in 166. Paris: Migne, 1857-66.
PL	J. P. Migne, ed., *Patrologiae cursus completus, Series Latina.* 221 vols. in 212. Paris: Migne, 1844-91.
PO	R. Graffin and F. Nau, eds., *Patrologia Orientalis.* Paris: Firmin-Didot, 1904-.
Regnault & Lemaire	L. Regnault and P. Lemaire, trs., *Barsanuphe et Jean de Gaza: correspondance. Receuil complet traduit du grec par Lucien Regnault et Philippe Lemaire ou du georgien par Bernard Outtier.* Sablé-sur-Sarthe: Abbaye Saint-Pierre de Solesmes, 1972.
Roth	Catharine P. Roth, tr., *St Gregory of Nyssa: The Soul and the Resurrection.* Crestwood, NY: St Vladimir's Seminary Press, 1993.
Schwartz	Eduard Schwartz, ed., *Kyrillos von Skythopolis.* Texte und Untersuchungen 49:2. Leipzig: J. C. Hinrichs, 1939.
Schoinas	St Nicodemus the Hagiorite, ed., *Vivlos Psychophelestate: periechousa apokriseis, diaphorois hypothesesin anekousas, syngrapheisa men para ton hosion kai theophoron pateron hemon Varsanouphiou kai Ioannou.* Volos, Greece: Soterios N. Schoinas, 1960. [Greek text of Barsanuphius and John, *Questions and Answers*]
Spira	Andreas Spira, ed., *Oratio funebris in Flacillam Imperatorem.* Gregorii Nysseni Opera 9. Leiden: E. J. Brill, 1967.
Stählin	Otto Stählin, ed., *Clemens Alexandrinus: Stromata Buch I-VI,* 3rd edn., revised by Ludwig Früchtel. Die Griechischen Christlichen Schriftsteller der ersten drei Jahrhunderte 15. Berlin: Akademie-Verlag, 1960.
Suchla	Beate Regina Suchla, ed., *Corpus Dionysiacum, I. Pseudo-Dionysius Areopagita: De Divinis Nominibus.* Patristische Texte und Studien 33. Berlin/ New York: Walter de Gruyter, 1990.
Ward, *Sayings*	Sister Benedicta Ward, SLG, tr., *The Sayings of the Desert Fathers. The Alphabetical Collection.* 2nd rev. edn., London/Oxford: Mowbray, 1981.
Ward, *Wisdom*	Sister Benedicta Ward, SLG, tr., *The Wisdom of the Desert Fathers. Apophthegmata Patrum from the Anonymous Series.* Fairacres Publication 48. Oxford: SLG Press, 1975.
Wensinck	A. J. Wensinck, tr., *Mystic Treatises by Isaac of Nineveh.* Amsterdam: Koninklijke Akademie van Wetenschappen, 1923.
Wortley	John Wortley, tr., *John Moschus: The Spiritual Meadow.* Cistercian Studies Series 139. Kalamazoo, MI: Cistercian Publications, 1992.

FOREWORD

*Enter eagerly into the treasure house that is within you, and so you will
see the things that are in heaven—for there is but one single entry to them
both. The ladder that leads to the Kingdom is hidden within your soul.
Flee from sin, dive into yourself, and in your soul you will discover the
stairs by which to ascend.*

So writes St Isaac the Syrian.[1] His purpose is to assure us that there exists,
hidden within each one of us, a secret treasure house, an inner Kingdom,
that is amazing in its depth and variety. It is a place of wonder and joy, a place
of glory, a place of encounter and dialogue. If only we will "dive" into ourself,
then we shall each discover eternity within our own heart. Jacob's ladder starts
from the point where I am at this very moment; the gate of heaven is everywhere. And this inner Kingdom, present within me here and now, is at the
same time the Kingdom of the Age to come; as St Philotheus of Sinai affirms,
the same path leads simultaneously to both of them.[2]

The articles contained in this volume were written over a period of thirty
years, for widely differing audiences; but they all relate, in one way or another, to this theme of the inner Kingdom. I speak here about the repentance
or "change of mind" with which we begin the journey inwards (chapter 3),
about the sense of wonder and the silence which mark our prayer as we explore the Kingdom that is within (chapters 4-7), about the companionship of
the spiritual guide as we embark on our ascent (chapter 9), about the martyr
and the fool in Christ as privileged witnesses to the Kingdom that is not of
this world (chapters 8 and 10), about time as a sacrament of the eternity that
is the mark of this inner Kingdom (chapter 11). And, since the inner Kingdom and the Kingdom of the Age to come are one and the same, I speak also

1 *Homily* 2: tr. Wensinck, 8; tr. Miller, 11.
2 *Texts on Watchfulness* 3; tr. *Philokalia*, 3:17.

of death, resurrection, and the possibility of a final and all-embracing reconciliation (chapters 2 and 12).

On a somewhat different note, I have included at the beginning an account of how I came to enter the Orthodox Church. Here I stop short at the moment when I was received; perhaps in the future I shall have the opportunity to write about my later experiences as an Orthodox layman, priest and bishop.

While all the material in this book has previously appeared in print, in almost every chapter I have made revisions, sometimes wide ranging in their scope. Where there are reasonably accessible translations of the sources that I use, this is indicated in the footnotes; but the translation actually given in the text is often my own.

It is a genuine pleasure to express my gratitude to those who have helped me with this volume. In particular, Sister Nonna (Verna Harrison) carefully prepared the text for publication, and through her perceptive comments has enabled me to correct and clarify several important points. I always enjoy working with St Vladimir's Seminary Press; I wish as ever to thank Ted Bazil for his unfailing encouragement, and to thank also his two assistants Amber Schley Houx and Charlotte Rodziewicz for their patience and accuracy.

STRANGE YET FAMILIAR:
MY JOURNEY TO THE ORTHODOX
CHURCH

Heaven and earth are united today.

Hymn from the Vigil on Christmas Eve

O strange Orthodox Church!

Father Lev Gillet

An absence and a presence

I can remember exactly when my personal journey to Orthodoxy began. It happened quite unexpectedly one Saturday afternoon in the summer of 1952, when I was seventeen. I was walking along Buckingham Palace Road, close to Victoria Station in central London, when I passed a nine-teenth-century Gothic church, large and somewhat dilapidated, that I had never noticed before. There was no proper notice-board outside it—public relations have never been the strong point of Orthodoxy in the Western world!—but I recall that there was a brass plate which simply said "Russian Church."

As I entered St Philip's—for that was the name of the church—at first I thought that it was entirely empty. Outside in the street there had been brilliant sunshine, but inside it was cool, cavernous and dark. As my eyes grew accustomed to the gloom, the first thing that caught my attention was an absence. There were no pews, no chairs in neat rows; in front of me stretched a wide and vacant expanse of polished floor.

Then I realized that the church was not altogether empty. Scattered in the nave and aisles there were a few worshipers, most of them elderly. Along the walls there were icons, with flickering lamps in front of them, and at the east end there were burning candles in front of the icon screen. Somewhere out of sight a choir was singing. After a while a deacon came out from the sanctuary and went round the church censing the icons and the people, and I noticed that his brocade vestment was old and slightly torn.

My initial impression of an absence was now replaced, with a sudden rush, by an overwhelming sense of presence. I felt that the church, so far from being empty, was full—full of countless unseen worshipers, surrounding me on every side. Intuitively I realized that we, the visible congregation, were part of a much larger whole, and that as we prayed we were being taken up into an action far greater than ourselves, into an undivided, all-embracing celebration that united time and eternity, things below with things above.

Years later, with a strange shock of recognition, I came across the story of St Vladimir's conversion, recorded in the *Russian Primary Chronicle*. Returning to Kiev, the Russian envoys told the Prince about the Divine Liturgy which they had attended in Constantinople. "We knew not whether we were in heaven or on earth," they said. "For on earth there is no such splendor or such beauty, and we are at a loss how to describe it. We only know that God dwells there among men... For we cannot forget that beauty."[1] I started with amazement as I read those words, for such exactly had been my own experience at the Russian Vigil Service in St Philip's, Buckingham Palace Road. The outward setting lacked the splendor of tenth-century Byzantium, but like St Vladimir's emissaries I too had encountered "heaven on earth." I too had felt the immediacy of the celestial Liturgy, the closeness of the angels and the saints, the uncreated beauty of God's Kingdom. "Now the powers of heaven worship with us invisibly" (The Liturgy of the Presanctified Gifts).

Before the service had ended, I left the church; and as I emerged I was struck by two things. First, I found that I had no idea how long I had been inside. It might have been only twenty minutes, it might have been two hours; I could not say. I had been existing on a level at which clock-time was unimportant. Secondly, as I stepped out on the pavement the roar of the London traffic engulfed me all at once like a huge wave.

---

1   *The Russian Primary Chronicle*, tr. S. H. Cross and O. P. Sherbowitz-Wetzor (Cambridge, MA: The Mediaeval Academy of America, 1953), 111.

The sound must have been audible within the church, but I had not noticed it. I had been in another world where time and traffic had no meaning; a world that was more real—I would almost say more *solid*—than that of twentieth-century London to which I now abruptly returned.

Everything at the Vigil Service was in Slavonic, and so with my conscious brain I could understand not a single word. Yet, as I left the church, I said to myself with a clear sense of conviction: *This is where I belong; I have come home.* Sometimes it happens—is it not curious?—that, before we have learnt anything in detail about a person, place or subject, we know with certainty: *This* is the person that I shall love, *this* is the place where I need to go, *this* is the subject that, above all others, I must spend my life exploring. From the moment of attending that service at St Philip's, Buckingham Palace Road, I felt deep in my heart that I was marked out for the Orthodox Church. (The church, incidentally, has long since disappeared; it was demolished about four years after my visit.)

I am grateful that my initial contact with Orthodoxy was not through reading books, nor yet through meeting members of the Orthodox Church in a social context, but through attending an act of worship. The Church, according to the Orthodox understanding, is primarily a liturgical community, which expresses its true self through invocation and doxology. Worship comes first, doctrine and discipline second. I was fortunate, then, to discover Orthodoxy first of all by participating in an act of corporate prayer. I encountered the Orthodox Church not as a theory or an ideology, but as a concrete and specific fact, as a worshiping presence.

"This is what I have always believed..."

In retrospect it is clear to me that my mind was already made up on that summer afternoon in 1952. Before being actually received, however, I waited for nearly six years. In Britain in the 1950s it was a highly unusual step for a Western person to seek entry into the Orthodox Church, and most of my English friends did their best to dissuade me. "You will be a lifelong eccentric," they objected. "God has set you culturally in the West; do not run away from the quandaries and the challenge of your historical inheritance." However beautiful Orthodox worship might be, was there not (they asked) a tragic gap between Orthodox principles and Orthodox practice? Was not my approach to Orthodoxy too idealized, too sentimental? Was I perhaps looking for a security and protection that we can never enjoy here on earth, and should not seek?

Less predictably, most of the Orthodox whose counsel I sought likewise offered me little encouragement. They were honest and realistic—and for this I remain grateful—in directing my attention to the historical shortcomings of the Orthodox Church, as well as to the particular difficulties it confronts in the Western world. There was much in Orthodoxy, so they warned me, that was very far from "heaven on earth"! When I approached the assistant bishop at the Greek Cathedral in London, Bishop James (Virvos) of Apamaea, he spoke to me kindly and at length, but urged me to remain a member of the Anglican Church in which I had been brought up. A Russian priest to whom I spoke in Paris gave me exactly the same advice.

At the time this puzzled me. In my reading about Orthodoxy I had quickly discovered that it claims to be, not just one among many alternative "denominations," but the true Church of Christ on earth. Yet it seemed as if the Orthodox themselves were telling me, "Yes, Orthodoxy is indeed the one true Church, but you should on no account join it. It is only for us Easterners, Greeks, Russians and the rest." Adherence to the saving truth appeared to depend on the accidents of birth and geography.

With hindsight I can appreciate better why Bishop James spoke as he did. Forty or fifty years ago there were many Orthodox, and also many Anglicans, who sincerely hoped that the Anglican communion would be reconciled to Orthodoxy in a corporate way. Individual conversions from Anglicanism to the Orthodox Church were therefore discouraged; Anglicans, it was felt, would do better to remain where they were, and to work for unity from within their present Church, acting as an "Anglo-Orthodox" leaven.

I fear that these hopes for corporate reunion were always unrealistic. But it has to be remembered that, during the first half of the twentieth century, the moderate "High Church" party within Anglicanism—which bases itself upon an appeal to the Ecumenical Councils and the Fathers—was far stronger than it is today, whereas the extreme "liberal" tendency, with its doctrinal and moral relativism, was much less pronounced, although already plainly in evidence. At any rate Bishop James was by no means alone in his dream that High Anglicanism might eventually develop into the nucleus of a native-grown Western Orthodoxy.

Bishop James also had pastoral reasons. None of his parishes at that time used any English in their Sunday worship, and only a few of his clergy spoke anything but Greek. He was unwilling to accept British people into his care, lacking as he did the resources to look after them. In this he was surely in large measure justified; it is grossly irresponsible for Orthodox clergy to receive converts, and after that to do nothing further about them. (I can think of many cases where this has in fact happened.) Converts need to be integrated into a living community; they should not just be thrown in at the deep end of the Orthodox swimming-pool, and then left to their own devices to sink or swim.

Besides this, as I now realize, Bishop James wished to test me. Seeing my eagerness to become Orthodox, he wanted me to look carefully at the arguments on the other side. He knew that, if I was serious, I would come back to him again. And so indeed it turned out.

Meanwhile, some time before I had gone to see Bishop James, I began to develop a variety of Orthodox contacts. Shortly after my first experience of Orthodox worship at the Russian church in London, I started my university course at Oxford. For four years I studied Classics—ancient Greek and Latin, with some modern philosophy—and then I stayed on at the university for two further years of theology. (Incidentally, I never went to an Anglican theological college, nor was I ordained in the Church of England.) At Oxford I had the chance to meet Orthodox Christians at first hand. In particular I came to know Nicolas Zernov, the University Lecturer in Eastern Orthodox Culture, and I still recall with pleasure the generous hospitality dispensed by him and his wife Militza, and the exhilarating and unpredictable conversations that they used to initiate with their many guests. I also met Father (later Archbishop) Basil Krivocheine, who officiated at the small Russian chapel in Oxford, and who was preparing his classic edition of the *Catecheses* of St Symeon the New Theologian. A new world opened up before me as I heard him read St Symeon's description of his visions of the divine and uncreated Light, and I began to appreciate the central place assigned in Orthodoxy to the mystery of Christ's Transfiguration.

While at Oxford, under the influence of my close friend from school days, Donald (A. M.) Allchin, I became an active member of the Fellowship of St Alban and St Sergius, whose aim is to promote *rapprochement* between Orthodoxy and Anglicanism. The summer conferences of the Fellowship had a decisive effect on me. Here I listened to such Anglicans as Archbishop Michael Ramsey, Father Derwas Chitty, and Professor H. A. Hodges, all of whom regarded Orthodoxy as the integral fullness of the Christian tradition, to which Anglicanism needed to return. As they saw it, Anglicans could hold the full Orthodox faith while still remaining in the Church of England, and in this manner we could help to bring our fellow-Anglicans nearer to Orthodoxy.

Their enthusiasm fired my imagination, but a part of me remained unsatisfied. I longed to be Orthodox in a total and visible way. The more I learnt about Orthodoxy, the more I realized: this is what I have always believed in my inmost self, but never before did I hear it so well expressed. I did not find Orthodoxy archaic, foreign or exotic. To me it was nothing other than simple Christianity.

The Church is One

My early contacts with the Orthodox world were for the most part Russian. I devoured such books as *A Treasury of Russian Spirituality* by G. P. Fedotov, and *With the Russian Pilgrims to Jerusalem* by Stephen Graham. I was immediately attracted to St Seraphim of Sarov, about whom I learnt from Iulia de Beausobre's slightly fictionalized but deeply moving account *Flame in the Snow*. On the more theological level a crucial landmark in my journey was Alexis Khomiakov's short essay "The Church is One." Here I found, verbally expressed, that vision of the communion of saints which I had first experienced as a living reality at the Russian church in London:

> The Church is one, notwithstanding her division, as it appears to a man who is still alive on earth... Those who are alive on earth, those who have finished their earthly course, those who, like the angels, were not created for a life on earth, those in future generations who have not yet begun their earthly course, are all united together in one Church, in one and the same grace of God... The Church visible, or upon earth, lives in complete communion and unity with the whole body of the Church, of which Christ is the head... The

Church, even upon earth, lives not an earthly life, but a life which is divine, and of grace... There is one God, and one Church.[2]

In later years, as I read more widely in Orthodox theology, I came to recognize the limitations of Khomiakov's Slavophil ecclesiology, but at the time he provided me with exactly what I needed. I was also greatly helped by Father Georges Florovsky's article, "*Sobornost:* the Catholicity of the Church," in which he emphasizes the essential nature of the Church as a unity-in-diversity after the image and likeness of God the Holy Trinity:

> The realm of the Church is unity. And of course this unity is no outward one, but is inner, intimate, organic. It is the unity of the living body, the unity of the organism. The Church is a unity not only in the sense that it is one and unique; it is a unity, first of all, because its very being consists in reuniting separated and divided mankind. *It is this unity which is the "sobornost" or catholicity of the Church.* In the Church humanity passes over into another plane, begins a new manner of existence. A new life becomes possible, a true, whole and complete life, a catholic life, "in the unity of the Spirit, in the bond of peace" (Eph 4:3). A new existence begins, a new principle of life, "even as Thou, Father, art in Me, and I in Thee, that they also may be in Us... that they may be one even as We are one" (Jn 17:21-23). This is the mystery of the final reunion in the image of the Unity of the Holy Trinity.[3]

Catholicity, Father Georges adds, "means seeing our own self in another, in the beloved one;"[4] and it is in the catholicity of the Church, and there alone, that "the painful duality and tension between freedom and authority is solved."[5] Throughout my later life I have constantly returned to this article, which says far more in twenty-one pages than most authors manage to say in whole volumes.

While it was chiefly from the Russians that I received my initial insight into Orthodoxy, during my first visit to Greece in 1954 the spiritual world of Byzantium also won my allegiance. As a Classicist my main purpose

---

2   Alexis Khomiakov, "The Church is One," in W. J. Birkbeck (ed.), *Russia and the English Church during the Last Fifty Years* (London: Eastern Church Association, 1895), 193-94, 211, 222.

3   Georges Florovsky, "*Sobornost:* the Catholicity of the Church," in E. L. Mascall (ed.), *The Church of God. An Anglo-Russian Symposium by Members of the Fellowship of St Alban and St Sergius* (London: SPCK, 1934), 55 (italics in the original). This article is reprinted in Vol. 1 of Florovsky's *Collected Works* (Belmont, MA: Nordland, 1972).

4   "*Sobornost,*" 59.

5   "*Sobornost,*" 73.

had been to look at the Acropolis, Olympia, Delphi and Knossos. So, when my traveling companions included Sparta in our itinerary, I protested. Were not the Spartans mere gymnasts and militarists, who had left behind them no monument worthy of a detour? In fact what my friends were taking me to visit was not Sparta itself but the Byzantine town of Mistra three miles beyond. Here I was delighted to see before me not just a few scattered ruins but an entire city rising up the hillside—streets, palaces, monasteries, many-domed churches—all set against the spectacular back-drop of the snow-covered Taygetus range. Looking at the frescoed saints alive on the church walls, like W. B. Yeats I found in them "the singing-masters of my soul."

Tradition, martyrdom, stillness

As I deepened my knowledge of Orthodoxy, three things in particular attracted me and held me fast. First, I perceived in the contemporary Orthodox Church—despite its internal tensions and its human failings—a living and unbroken continuity with the Church of the Apostles and Martyrs, of the Fathers and the Ecumenical Councils. This living continuity was summed up for me in the words *fullness* and *wholeness*, but most of all it was expressed by the term *Tradition*. Orthodoxy possesses, not through human merit but by God's grace, a fullness of faith and spiritual life, a fullness within which the elements of dogma and prayer, of theology and spirituality, constitute an integral and organic whole. It is in this sense the Church of Holy Tradition.

In this context I would like to put especial emphasis on the word "fullness." Orthodoxy has the plenitude of life in Christ, but it does not have an exclusive monopoly of the truth. I did not believe then, nor do I believe now, that there is a stark and unmitigated contrast between Orthodox "light" and non-Orthodox "darkness." We are not to imagine that, because Orthodoxy possesses the fullness of Holy Tradition, the other Christian bodies possess nothing at all. Far from it; I have never been convinced by the rigorist claim that sacramental life and the grace of the Holy Spirit can exist only within the visible limits of the Orthodox Church. Vladimir Lossky is surely right to maintain that, despite an outward separation, non-Orthodox communities still retain invisible links with the Orthodox Church:

Faithful to its vocation to assist the salvation of all, the Church of Christ values every "spark of life," however small, in the dissident communities. In this way it bears witness to the fact that, despite the separation, they still retain a certain link with the unique and life-giving center, a link that is—so far as we are concerned—"invisible and beyond our understanding." There is only one true Church, the sole bestower of sacramental grace; but there are several ways of being separated from that one true Church, and varying degrees of diminishing ecclesial reality outside its visible limits.[6]

Thus on Lossky's view, which I willingly made my own, non-Orthodox communities continue in varying degrees to participate in the Church's life of grace. Yet it still remains true that, while these non-Orthodox communities possess part of the saving and life-giving truth, in Orthodoxy alone is the *fullness* of that truth to be found.

I was particularly impressed by the manner in which Orthodox thinkers, when speaking of their Church as the Church of Holy Tradition, insist at the same time that Tradition is not static but dynamic, not defensive but exploratory, not closed and backward-facing but open to the future. Tradition, I learnt from the authors whom I studied, is not merely a formal repetition of what was stated in the past, but it is an active reexperiencing of the Christian message in the present. The only true Tradition is living and creative, formed from the union of human freedom with the grace of the Spirit. This vital dynamism was summed up for me in Vladimir Lossky's lapidary phrase: "Tradition…is the *life* of the Holy Spirit in the Church."[7] Emphasizing the point, he adds: "One can say that 'Tradition' represents the critical spirit of the Church."[8] We do not simply remain within the Tradition by inertia.

In the eyes of many non-Orthodox observers in the West, Orthodoxy appears as a Church of rigid immobility, oriented always towards the past.

---

6 Vladimir Lossky, introductory note to the article of Patriarch Sergius of Moscow, "L'Église du Christ et les communautés dissidentes," *Messager de l'Exarchat du Patriarche Russe en Europe Occidentale* 21 (Paris, 1955), 9-10.

7 My italics. See "Tradition and traditions," in Leonid Ouspensky and Vladimir Lossky, *The Meaning of Icons* (Olten, Switzerland: Urs Graf-Verlag, 1952), 17; in the revised edition (Crestwood, NY: St Vladimir's Seminary Press, 1982), 15. This essay is reprinted in Vladimir Lossky, *In the Image and Likeness of God* (Crestwood, NY: St Vladimir's Seminary Press, 1974), 141-68; see 152. Of course Lossky does not exclude the Christological dimension of Tradition, as is clear from the context in which this phrase occurs.

8 "Tradition and traditions," 19 (revised edition, 17).

That, however, was not my personal impression when first I came to know the Orthodox Church in the early 1950s, and it is certainly not my impression today after being Orthodox for over forty years. Although many aspects of Orthodox life are indeed characterized by a certain archaism, that is very far from being the whole story. On the contrary, what Sir Ernest Barker says of the twelve centuries of Byzantine history can be applied equally to the twenty centuries of Orthodox church life: "Conservatism is always mixed with change, and change is always impinging on conservatism, during the twelve hundred years of Byzantine history; and that is the essence and fascination of those years."[9]

As the life of the Holy Spirit within the Church, so I discovered, Tradition is all-embracing. In particular it includes the written word of the Bible, for there is no dichotomy between Scripture and Tradition. Scripture exists *within* Tradition, and by the same token Tradition is nothing else than the way in which Scripture has been understood and lived by the Church in every generation. Thus I came to see the Orthodox Church not only as "traditional" but also as Scriptural. It is not for nothing that the Book of the Gospels rests on the center of the Holy Table in every Orthodox place of worship. It is the Orthodox rather than the Protestants who are the true Evangelicals. (If only we Orthodox in practice studied the Bible as the Protestants do!)

As the life of the Spirit, so Lossky and Florovsky assured me in their writings,[10] Tradition is not only all-embracing but inexhaustible. In the words of Father Georges Florovsky:

> Tradition is the constant abiding of the Spirit and not only the memory of words. Tradition is a *charismatic*, not a historical principle... The grace-giving experience of the Church...in its catholic fullness...has not been exhausted either in Scripture, or in oral tradition, or in definitions. *It cannot, it must not, be exhausted.*[11]

While the period of the seven Ecumenical Councils possesses a pre-eminent importance for Orthodoxy, we are not for one moment to imagine that the "age of the Fathers" came to a close in the eighth century. On

---

9 *Social and Political Thought in Byzantium* (Oxford: Clarendon Press, 1957), 28.
10 I had the happiness of knowing both of them not just through their writings but personally: Vladimir Lossky before, and Father Georges after, my reception into the Orthodox Church.
11 "*Sobornost,*" 65, 67 (italics in original).

the contrary, the Patristic era is open-ended. There is no reason, apart from human sin, why there should not be in the third millennium further Ecumenical Councils and new Fathers of the Church, equal in authority to those in the early Christian centuries; for the Holy Spirit continues present and active in the Church as much today as ever He was in the past.

This vibrant and vivifying conception of Tradition that I discovered in Orthodoxy made increasing sense to me. More and more I found that the living continuity to which the Orthodox Church bore witness was lacking in the Anglicanism within which I had been brought up from early childhood. The continuity had been impaired, if not broken, by the developments within the Latin West during the Middle Ages. Even if, for many Anglicans from the sixteenth century onwards, the English Reformation represented an attempt to return to the Church of the Ecumenical Councils and the early Fathers, how far in actual fact could this attempt be reckoned a success? The "Orthodoxy" of the Church of England seemed at best implicit—an aspiration and a distant hope rather than an immediate and practical reality.

I shall never cease to be sincerely grateful for my Anglican upbringing. Never would I wish to engage in negative polemic against the communion where I first came to know Christ as my Savior. I remember with lasting happiness the beauty of the choral services in Westminster Abbey which I attended while a boy at Westminster School, and in particular I recall the great procession with cross, candles and banners at the Sung Eucharist on the feast of St Edward the Confessor. I am grateful also for the links which I formed, while at school and university, with members of the Society of St Francis such as Father Algy Robertson, the Father Guardian, and his young disciple Brother Peter. It was the Anglican Franciscans who taught me the place of mission within the Christian life and the value of sacramental confession.

I shall always regard my decision to embrace Orthodoxy as the crowning fulfillment of all that was best in my Anglican experience; as an affirmation, not a repudiation. Yet, for all my love and gratitude, I cannot in honesty remain silent about what troubled me in the 1950s, and today troubles me far more; and that is the extreme diversity of the conflicting beliefs and practices that coexist within the bounds of the Anglican communion. I was (and am) disturbed first of all by the contrasting views of Anglo-Catholics and Evangelicals concerning central articles of faith such as the real presence of Christ in the Eucharist and the Communion of Saints. Are the consecrated elements to be worshiped as the true Body and Blood of the Savior? May we intercede for the departed, and ask the Saints and the Mother of God to pray for us? These are not just marginal issues, over which Christians may legitimately agree to differ. They are fundamental to our life in Christ. How then could I continue in a Christian body which permitted its members to hold diametrically opposed views on these matters?

I was yet more disturbed by the existence within Anglicanism of a "liberal" wing that calls in doubt the Godhead of Christ, His Virgin Birth, His miracles and His bodily Resurrection. St Thomas's words rang in my ears: "My Lord *and my God!*" (Jn 20:28). I heard St Paul saying to me: "If Christ is not risen, then our preaching is in vain and your faith is also in vain" (1 Cor 15:14). For my own salvation I needed to belong to a Church which held fast with unwavering faithfulness to the primary Christian teachings concerning the Trinity and the Person of Christ. Where could I find such a Church? Not, alas! in Anglicanism. It did not have that continuity and fullness of living Tradition for which I was searching.

What, then, of Rome? In the 1950s, before the second Vatican Council, the obvious course—for any Catholic-minded member of the Church of England who was unhappy about Anglican "comprehensiveness"—was to become a Roman Catholic. Here is a Christian communion which, no less than the Orthodox Church, claims an unbroken continuity with the Apostles and the Martyrs, with the early Councils and the Fathers. What is more, here is a Church of Western culture. Why, then, look to Orthodoxy? Could not my search for living Tradition find its fulfillment much nearer at hand?

Yet, whenever I felt tempted to move Romewards, I hesitated. What held me back was not primarily the *Filioque*, although after reading Lossky I could see that this was important. The basic problem, however, was the papal claim to universal jurisdiction and infallibility. From my study of the early centuries of Christianity, it became clear to me that Eastern Fathers such as St Basil the Great and St John Chrysostom—and indeed Western Fathers such as St Cyprian and St Augustine—understood the nature of the Church on earth in a manner radically different from the viewpoint of the first Vatican Council. The developed doctrine of Roman primacy, as I saw it, was simply not true to history. Papal centralization, especially from the eleventh century onwards, had gravely impaired the continuity of Tradition within the Roman communion. Only in the Orthodox Church could I secure what I was seeking: the life-giving and undiminished presence of the past.

My conviction that only within Orthodoxy could I find in its fullness an unbroken continuity with the Church of the Apostles and the Fathers was reinforced by two other aspects of Orthodoxy that I began increasingly to notice. The first was the prevalence of persecution and martyrdom within recent Orthodox experience—first under the Turks and then, in the twentieth century, under Communism. Here was something that linked the Orthodox Church of modern times directly to the pre-Constantinian Church of the first three centuries. "My strength is made perfect in weakness," said Christ to St Paul (2 Cor 12:9); and I saw His words fulfilled again and again in Orthodox history since the fall of Byzantium.

Alongside those who underwent an outward and visible martyrdom of blood, there have also been countless others in Orthodoxy who have followed the humiliated Christ through a life of inner martyrdom: kenotic saints who displayed a gentle, generous and compassionate love, such as Xenia of St Petersburg, Seraphim of Sarov, John of Kronstadt, and Nektarios of Aegina. I found the same kenotic compassion in the writings of Dostoevsky and Tolstoy. Two saints who especially appealed to me—for I had been a pacifist since the age of seventeen—were the Passion-Bearers Boris and Gleb, brother Princes from eleventh-century Kiev. In their refusal to shed blood even in self-defense, in their repudiation of violence and in their innocent suffering, I saw exemplified the central message of Christ's Cross.

Another aspect of Orthodoxy which I came to value, alongside martyrdom, was the mystical theology of the Christian East. Tradition, I realized, signifies not just the handing-down of doctrinal definitions but equally the transmission of spirituality. There cannot be any separation, and still less any opposition, between the two; as Vladimir Lossky rightly states, "there is...no Christian mysticism without theology; but, above all, there is no theology without mysticism," for mysticism is to be seen "as the perfecting and crown of all theology: as theology *par excellence*."[12]

Whereas it had been the liturgical services with their rich symbolism and their music that originally drew me to Orthodoxy, I now saw how this "iconic" form of worship is counterbalanced in the Christian East by the "non-iconic" or apophatic practice of hesychastic prayer, with its "laying-aside" of images and thoughts. In *The Way of a Pilgrim* and the writings of "A Monk of the Eastern Church"—Archimandrite Lev Gillet, the Orthodox chaplain of the Fellowship of St Alban and St Sergius—I learnt how *hesychia*, stillness or silence of the heart, is attained through the constant repetition of the Jesus Prayer. St Isaac the Syrian showed me that all words find their fulfillment in stillness, just as servants fall silent when the master arrives in their midst:

> The movements of the tongue and heart during prayer are keys. What comes afterwards is the entering into the treasury. At this point let every mouth and every tongue become silent. Let the heart which is the treasury of our thoughts, and the intellect which is the ruler of our senses, and the mind, that swift-winged and daring bird, with all their resources and powers and persuasive intercessions—let all these now be still: for the Master of the house has come.[13]

The Church as communion

These three things—Tradition, martyrdom and stillness—were already sufficient to convince me of the truth and relevance of Orthodoxy. But the compelling need for me not only to contemplate Orthodoxy from the outside, but also to enter within, was brought home to me by words that I heard spoken in August 1956 at the summer conference of the Fellowship of St Alban and St Sergius. Father Lev Gillet was asked to define the term "Orthodoxy." He replied: "An Orthodox is one who accepts the Apostolic Tradition and *who lives in communion with the bishops* who are the appointed teachers of this Tradition."

The second half of this statement—the part which I have italicized—was of particular significance for me. I thought to myself: Yes, indeed, as an Anglican I am at liberty to hold the Apostolic Tradition of

12   *The Mystical Theology of the Eastern Church* (London: James Clarke, 1957), 9.
13   *Homily* 22(23): tr. Wensinck, 112; tr. Miller, 116.

Orthodoxy as my own private opinion. But can I honestly say that this Apostolic Tradition is taught unanimously by the Anglican bishops with whom I am in communion? Orthodoxy, so I recognized in a sudden flash of insight, is not merely a matter of personal belief; it also presupposes outward and visible communion in the sacraments with the bishops who are the divinely-commissioned witnesses to the truth. The question could not be avoided: If Orthodoxy means communion, was it possible for me to be truly Orthodox so long as I still remained an Anglican?

Those simple words spoken by Father Lev created no great stir in the conference at large, but for me they served as a critical turning-point. The idea which they planted in my mind—that Orthodox faith is inseparable from Eucharistic communion—was confirmed by two things which I read around this time. First, I came across the correspondence between Alexis Khomiakov and the Anglican (as he was then) William Palmer, Fellow of Magdalen College, Oxford. Palmer had sent Khomiakov a copy of his work *A Harmony of Anglican Doctrine with the Doctrine of the Catholic and Apostolic Church of the East.* Here Palmer took, phrase by phrase, the *Longer Russian Catechism* written by St Philaret of Moscow, and for every statement in the *Catechism* he cited passages from Anglican sources in which the same doctrine was affirmed. In his reply (November 28, 1846), Khomiakov pointed out that he could equally well have produced an alternative volume, quoting other Anglican writers—no less authoritative than those invoked by Palmer—who directly contradicted the teaching of Philaret's *Catechism*. In Khomiakov's words:

> Many Bishops and divines of your communion are and have been quite orthodox. But what of that? Their opinion is only *an individual opinion*, it is not *the Faith of the Community*. The Calvinist Ussher is an Anglican no less than the bishops (whom you quote) who hold quite Orthodox language. We may and do sympathize with the individuals; we cannot and dare not sympathize with a Church…which gives Communion to those *who declare* the Bread and Wine of the High Sacrifice to be mere bread and wine, as well as to those who declare it to be the Body and Blood of Christ. This for an example—and I could find hundreds more—but I go further. Suppose an impossibility—suppose all the Anglicans to be quite Orthodox; suppose their Creed and Faith quite concordant with ours; the mode and process by which that creed is or has been attained is a Protestant one; a simple logical act of the understanding… Were you to find all the truth, you would have found

nothing; for we alone can give you that without which all would be vain—the assurance of truth.[14]

Khomiakov's words, severe yet just, reinforced what Father Lev had said. By this time I had come to believe all that the Orthodox Church believed; yet the "mode and process" by which I had reached these beliefs was indeed a "Protestant one." My faith was "only *an individual opinion*," and not "*the Faith of the Community*;" for I could not say that all my fellow Anglicans believed the same as I did, or that mine was the faith taught by all the Anglican bishops with whom I was in communion. Only by becoming a full member of the Orthodox Church—by entering into full and visible communion with the Orthodox bishops who were the appointed teachers of the Orthodox faith—could I obtain "the assurance of truth."

A few months later I read in typescript an article on the ecclesiology of St Ignatius of Antioch by the Greek-American theologian Father John Romanides.[15] Here, for the first time in a fully developed form, I encountered the perspective of "Eucharistic ecclesiology" which has since been popularized by the writings of Father Nicolas Afanassieff[16] and Metropolitan John (Zizioulas) of Pergamum.[17] On a first reading Father John's interpretation of the letters of St Ignatius at once convinced me, and when I consulted the actual letters themselves my convictions were fully confirmed.

---

14 Birkbeck, *Russia and the English Church*, 70-71 (italics in the original).

15 This article, written while Romanides was studying under Afanassieff at the Orthodox Institute of St Sergius in Paris (1954-55), did not appear in print until several years later: see *The Greek Orthodox Theological Review* 7:1-2 (1961-62), 53-77. Subsequently Romanides became dissatisfied with the standpoint of Eucharistic ecclesiology: see Andrew J. Sopko, *Prophet of Roman Orthodoxy: The Theology of John Romanides* (Dewdney, BC, Canada: Synaxis Press, 1998), 150-53.

16 See N. Afanassieff, "The Church Which Presides in Love," in John Meyendorff and others, *The Primacy of Peter* (London: Faith Press, 1962), 57-110 (new edition [Crestwood, NY: St Vladimir's Seminary Press, 1992], 91-143). Cf. Aidan Nichols, *Theology in the Russian Diaspora: Church, Fathers, Eucharist in Nikolai Afanas'ev (1893-1966)* (Cambridge, England: Cambridge University Press, 1989).

17 See John D. Zizioulas, *Being As Communion: Studies in Personhood and the Church* (Crestwood, NY: St Vladimir's Seminary Press, 1985). Cf. Paul McPartlan, *The Eucharist Makes the Church: Henri du Lubac and John Zizioulas in Dialogue* (Edinburgh: T. & T. Clark, 1993).

The primary icon of the Church for St Ignatius, so I found, was precisely this: a table; on the table, a plate with bread and wine; around the table, the bishop, the presbyters and the deacons, along with all the Holy People of God, united together in the celebration of the Eucharist. As St Ignatius insisted, "Take care to participate in one Eucharist: for there is one flesh of our Lord Jesus Christ, and one cup for union in His blood, and one altar, just as there is one bishop."[18] The repetition of the word "one" is deliberate and striking: "one Eucharist...one flesh...one cup...one altar...one bishop." Such is St Ignatius' understanding of the Church and its unity: the Church is *local*, an assembly of all the faithful in the same place (*epi to avto*); the Church is *Eucharistic*, a gathering around the same altar, to share in a single loaf and a single cup; and the Church is *hierarchical*—it is not simply *any* kind of Eucharistic meeting, but it is that Eucharistic meeting which is convened under the presidency of the one local bishop.

Church unity, as the Bishop of Antioch envisages it, is not merely a theoretical ideal but a practical reality, established and made visible through the participation of each local community in the Holy Mysteries. Despite the central role exercised by the bishop, unity is not something imposed from outside by power of jurisdiction, but it is created from within through the act of receiving communion. The Church is above all else a Eucharistic organism, which becomes itself when celebrating the sacrament of the Lord's Supper "until He comes again" (1 Cor 11:26). In this way St Ignatius, as interpreted by Father John Romanides, supplied me with an all-essential missing link. Khomiakov had spoken about the organic unity of the Church, but he had not associated this with the Eucharist. Once I perceived the integral connection between ecclesial unity and sacramental communion, everything fell into place.

Yet where did this leave me, still (as I was) an outsider, unable to receive the Orthodox sacraments? At Easter 1957 for the first time I attended the Orthodox service at Paschal Midnight. I had intended to receive communion later in the morning at an Anglican church—in that year the dates of Orthodox and Western Easter coincided—but, emerging from the Orthodox celebration, I knew that this was an impossibility. I

18　*To the Philadelphians* 4.

had already kept Christ's Resurrection with the Orthodox Church, in a manner that was for me complete and unrepeatable. Had I afterwards received Holy Communion elsewhere, that would have been—for me personally—something unrealistic and untruthful.

Never thereafter did I make my communion at an Anglican altar. After remaining without the sacrament for some months, I was talking in September 1957 with Madeleine, the wife of Vladimir Lossky. She pointed out to me the peril of my situation, living as I was in no man's land. "You must not continue as you are," she insisted. "The Eucharist is our mystical food: without it, we starve."

Her words were confirmed a few days later by a strange incident that I have never been able fully to explain to myself. I went to the chapel in Versailles where the head of the Western European diocese of the Russian Church in Exile, Archbishop John (Maximovitch)—now glorified as a saint—was officiating at the Divine Liturgy. It was his custom to celebrate daily, and as it was a weekday there were very few present: only one or two monks, as I recall, and an old woman. I arrived near the end of the service, shortly before the moment when he emerged to give communion. No one came forward to receive the sacrament, but he remained standing with the chalice in his hand; and with his head on one side in his characteristic way, he stared fixedly and even fiercely in my direction (he had never seen me before). Only when I shook my head did he return to the sanctuary with the chalice.

After the conclusion of the Liturgy there was a service of intercession (*paraklesis, molieben*) in honor of the Saint whose day it was; and at the close the Archbishop anointed those present with oil from the lamp before the Saint's icon. I stayed where I was, not knowing if as a non-Orthodox it was appropriate for me to receive anointing. But this time he would accept no refusal. He beckoned firmly, and so I came forward and was anointed. Then I left the chapel, too shy to stay behind and speak with him (but we did meet and talk on future occasions).

St John's action at the moment of communion puzzled me. I knew that, according to the practice of the Russian Church in Exile, anyone intending to receive communion is required first to go to confession. Surely, then, the Archbishop would have been warned if there were going to be any communicants. In any case, a prospective communicant—at least in a Russian church—would not have arrived so late during the service. The Archbishop was gifted with the power to read the secrets of the human heart; had he perhaps some intimation that I was on the threshold of Orthodoxy, and was this his way of telling me not to delay any longer?

Whatever the truth of the matter, my experience at Versailles strengthened my feeling that the moment had come for action. If Orthodoxy is the one true Church, and if the Church is a communion in the sacraments, then I needed above all else to become an Orthodox communicant.

Look not at the things that are seen...

There remained, however, one powerful dissuasive. If Orthodoxy is really the one true Church of Christ on earth, how could it be (I asked myself) that the Orthodox Church in the West is so ethnic and nationalist in its outlook, so little interested in any form of missionary witness, so fragmented into parallel and often conflicting "jurisdictions"?

In principle, of course, Orthodoxy is indeed altogether clear about its claim to be the true Church. As I read in the message of the Orthodox delegates at the Assembly of the World Council of Churches in Evanston (1954):

> In conclusion we are bound to declare our profound conviction that the Holy Orthodox Church alone has preserved full and intact "the Faith once delivered to the saints." It is not because of our human merit, but because it pleases God to preserve "His treasure in earthen vessels, that the excellency of the power may be of God" (2 Cor 4:7).[19]

Yet there seemed to be a yawning gap between Orthodox principles and Orthodox practice. If the Orthodox really believed themselves to be the one true Church, why did they place such obstacles in the path of prospective converts? In what sense was Orthodoxy truly "one," when, for example, in North America there were at least nineteen different Orthodox "jurisdictions," with no less than thirteen bishops in the single city of New York?[20] Some of my Anglican friends argued that the Orthodox

---

19 In Constantin G. Patelos, *The Orthodox Church in the Ecumenical Movement. Documents and Statements 1902-1975* (Geneva: World Council of Churches, 1978), 96. I imagine that Father Georges Florovsky was closely involved in drafting this fine statement. What a pity that Orthodox delegates at recent meetings of the WCC have not spoken with so clear a voice!

20 I give the figures for the year 1960, as found in the brochure *Parishes and Clergy of the Orthodox, and Other Eastern Churches in North and South America together with the Parishes*

Church was no more unified than the Anglican communion, and in some respects less so; if I moved, it would be out of the frying pan into the fire!

At this point I was helped by some words of Vladimir Lossky:

> How many recognized in "the man of sorrows" the eternal Son of God? One must recognize the fullness there where the outward sense perceives only limitations and want... We must, in the words of St Paul, receive "not the spirit of the world, but the Spirit which is of God, that we may know the things that are freely given to us of God" (1 Cor 2:12), that we may be enabled to recognize victory beneath the outward appearance of failure, to discern the power of God fulfilling itself in weakness, the true Church within the historic reality.[21]

Looking at the empirical situation of twentieth-century Orthodoxy in the Western world, I was indeed confronted by apparent "failure" and "weakness;" and the Orthodox themselves did not deny this. But, looking more profoundly, I could also see "the true Church within the historical reality." The ethnic narrowness and intolerance of Orthodoxy, however deep-rooted, are not part of the essence of the Church, but they are a distortion and betrayal of its true nature (of course there are also positive aspects to Orthodox Christian nationalism). As for the jurisdictional pluralism of the Orthodox Church in the West, this has specific historical causes; and the more visionary among Orthodox leaders have always seen it as at best a provisional arrangement that is no more than temporary and transitional. Moreover, there is an evident difference between the divisions prevailing within Anglicanism and those found within Orthodoxy. The Anglicans are united (for the most part) in outward organization, but deeply divided in their beliefs and in their forms of public worship. The Orthodox, on the other hand, are divided only in outward organization, but firmly united in beliefs and worship.

At this juncture I received a powerfully-worded letter from an English Orthodox priest with whom I was in correspondence, Archimandrite Lazarus (Moore), at that time resident in India. With reference to the Orthodox Church, he wrote:

and Clergy of the Polish National Catholic Church, 1960-61, edited by Bishop Lauriston L. Scaife and issued by the Joint Commission on Cooperation with the Eastern Churches of the General Convention of the Protestant Episcopal Church. I have not included the non-Chalcedonians in my calculations. There are some splendid photographs in this publication.

21 The Mystical Theology of the Eastern Church, 245-46.

Here I must warn you that the outward form of the Church [i.e., the Orthodox Church] is desperately wretched, in a word crucified, with little cooperation or coordination between the various national bodies, little deep use and
appreciation of our spiritual riches, little missionary and apostolic spirit, little
grasp of the situation or of the needs of our times, little generosity or heroism
or real sanctity. My advice is: Look not at the things that are seen... [22]

I tried to follow Father Lazarus's guidance. Looking beyond the outward
and visible failings of Orthodoxy, I made an act of faith in "the things that
are not seen" (2 Cor 4:18)—in its fundamental oneness, and in the underlying wholeness of its doctrinal, liturgical and spiritual Tradition.

In order to enter the Orthodox house, I had to knock upon a particular door. Which "jurisdiction" should I choose? I felt strongly drawn to
the Russian Orthodox Church in Exile—the Russian Orthodox Church
Outside Russia (ROCOR), as it is today commonly styled. What I admired in particular was its fidelity to the liturgical, ascetic and monastic
heritage of Orthodoxy. While still sixteen I had come across Helen
Waddell's book *The Desert Fathers*, and from that moment I was fasci-
nated by the monastic history of the Christian East. I found that most of
the monasteries in the Orthodox emigration belonged to the Russian
Church in Exile. In Western Europe I visited two women's monasteries
under its care, the Convent of the Annunciation in London, and the
Convent of the Mother of God of Lesna outside Paris, and in both I was
given a warm welcome. I also admired the way in which the Russian
Church in Exile held in honor the New Martyrs and Confessors who had
suffered for the faith under the Soviet yoke. On the other hand, I was disturbed by the canonical isolation of the Exile Synod. In the 1950s this was
not so great as it has since become, for at that time there was still regular
concelebration between Russian Exile clergy and the bishops and priests
of the Ecumenical Patriarchate. But I saw that the Russian Church in
Exile was becoming increasingly cut off from worldwide Orthodoxy, and
that troubled me.

Had there existed in Britain a Russian diocese under the Ecumenical
Patriarchate, as there was in France, then I would probably have joined it.
As matters stood, the only Russian alternative to the Church in Exile was
the Moscow Patriarchate. This had some distinguished members in West-

22 Letter of April 11, 1957.

ern Europe, such as Vladimir Lossky in Paris, Father Basil Krivocheine in Oxford, and Father Anthony Bloom (now Metropolitan of Sourozh) in London. But I felt it impossible to belong to an Orthodox Church headed by bishops under Communist control who regularly praised Lenin and Stalin, and who were prevented from acknowledging the New Martyrs slain by the Bolsheviks. I did not wish in any way to pass judgment on the ordinary Russian faithful dwelling inside the Soviet Union; they were under bitter persecution and I was not, and I do not suppose that in their situation I would have shown anything of the heroic endurance which they displayed. But, living as I did outside the Communist world, I could not make my own the statements issued by leading hierarchs of the Moscow Patriarchate in the name of the Church. As one of the Russian Exile priests in London, Archpriest George Cheremeteff, said to me: "In a free country we must be free."

Despite my love of Russian spirituality, it became evident to me that my best course was to join the Greek diocese in Britain under the Patriarchate of Constantinople. As a Classicist, I had a good working knowledge of New Testament and Byzantine Greek, whereas at that time I had not studied Church Slavonic. If I became a member of the Ecumenical Patriarchate I would not have to take sides between the rival Russian groups, and I could maintain my personal friendships with members of both the Moscow Patriarchate and the Church in Exile. More importantly, Constantinople was the Mother Church from which Russia had received the Christian faith, and I felt it right in my quest for Orthodoxy to return to the source. Also I began to appreciate that, when eventually the Orthodox in Western Europe achieved organizational unity, this could only happen under the pastoral protection of the Ecumenical Throne.

So back I went to Bishop James of Apamaea, and much to my surprise I found him on this occasion willing to receive me almost at once. It is true that he warned me, "Please understand that we would never, under any circumstances, ordain you to the priesthood; we need only Greeks."[23] That did not worry me, for I was content to leave my future in the hands of God. I was only too delighted that the door had at last opened, and I entered without wishing to lay down any conditions. I saw my reception

---

23 In fact I was ordained priest in 1966, eight years after my reception, by Metropolitan (later Archbishop) Athenagoras II of Thyateira, who had arrived in Britain in 1963/64.

into Orthodoxy not as a "right," not as something that I was entitled to "demand," but simply as a free and unmerited gift of God's grace. It gave me quiet happiness when Bishop James appointed Father George Cheremeteff as my spiritual father, and so I was able to remain close to the Russian Church in Exile.

Thus I came to the end of my journey; or, more exactly, to a new and decisive stage on a journey which had begun in my earliest infancy and which, by the divine mercy, will continue into all eternity. Shortly after Pascha in 1958, on Friday in Bright Week—the Feast of the Life-Giving Source—I was chrismated by Bishop James at the Greek Cathedral of St Sophia in Bayswater, London. At last I had come home.

Father Lazarus had warned me that I would find in the Orthodox Church "little generosity or heroism or real sanctity." In retrospect, after more than four decades as an Orthodox, I can say that he was much too pessimistic. Doubtless I have been more fortunate than I deserve, but within Orthodoxy I have in fact found warm friendship and compassionate love almost everywhere that I have gone, and I have certainly enjoyed the privilege of meeting living saints. Those who predicted that, in becoming Orthodox, I would be cutting myself off from my own people and my national culture have been proved wrong. In embracing Orthodoxy, so I am convinced, I have become not less English but more genuinely so; I have rediscovered the ancient roots of my Englishness, for the Christian history of my nation extends back to a period long before the schism between East and West. I remember a conversation that I had with two Greeks soon after my reception. "How hard you must find it," remarked the first, "to have left the Church of your fathers." But the second said to me, "You did not leave the Church of your fathers: you returned to it." He spoke rightly.

Needless to say, my life as an Orthodox has not always been "heaven on earth." Repeatedly I have suffered deep discouragement; but did not Jesus Christ Himself foretell that discipleship means cross-bearing? Yet, forty-eight years later, I can affirm with all my heart that the vision of Orthodoxy which I saw at my first Vigil Service in 1952 was sure and true. I have not been disappointed.

I would make only one qualification: what I could not have appreciated back in 1952, but what today I see much more clearly, is the deeply enigmatic character of Orthodoxy, its many antitheses and polarities. The paradox of Orthodox life in the twentieth century is summed up by Father Lev Gillet, himself a Westerner who made the journey to Orthodoxy, in words which come closer to the heart of the matter than any others that I can recall:

> O strange Orthodox Church, so poor and so weak…maintained as if by a miracle through so many vicissitudes and struggles; Church of contrasts, so traditional and yet at the same time so free, so archaic and yet so alive, so ritualistic and yet so personally mystical; Church where the Evangelical pearl of great price is preciously safeguarded—yet often beneath a layer of dust… Church which has so frequently proved incapable of action—yet which knows, as does no other, how to sing the joy of Pascha![24]

---

24 Father Lev Gillet, in Vincent Bourne, *La Quête de Vérité d'Irénée Winnaert* (Geneva: Labor et Fides, 1966), 335.

2

"GO JOYFULLY": THE MYSTERY OF DEATH AND RESURRECTION

The end is where we start from.

T. S. Eliot

"I knew you would come..."

In the worship of the Russian Orthodox Church, while the prayers of preparation are being said before the start of the Eucharist, the doors in the center of the icon screen remain closed. Then comes the time for the Divine Liturgy itself to begin: the doors are opened, the sanctuary stands revealed, and the celebrant sings the initial blessing. It was precisely this moment that the religious philosopher Prince Evgeny Trubetskoy recalled as he lay dying. These were his last words: "The royal doors are opening! The Great Liturgy is about to begin."[1] For him death was not the closing but the opening of a door, not an end but a beginning. Like the early Christians, he saw his death-day as his birthday.

Let us think of our human existence as a book. Most people regard this present life as the actual text, the main story, and they see the future life—if, indeed, they believe that there is any future life—as no more than an appendix. But the genuinely Christian attitude is the exact reverse of this. Our present life is in reality no more than the preface, the introduction, while it is the future life that constitutes the main story. The moment of death signifies not the conclusion of the book but the start of Chapter One.

Two things, so obvious that they are easily overlooked, need to be said about this end-point which is in fact the starting-point. First, death is an unavoidable and certain fact; second, death is a mystery. This means that we are to view our coming death with contrasting feelings—with sober

---

1 Nicholas Arseniev, *Russian Piety* (London: Faith Press, 1964), 90.

realism on the one side, and at the same time with awe and wonder.

Death is an unavoidable and certain fact

In this life there is only one thing of which we can be sure: that we are all going to die (unless perchance the second coming of Christ should occur during our lifetime). Death is the one fixed, inevitable event to which every human must look forward. And if I try to forget about this fixed event and to hide its inevitability from myself, then it is I myself who am the loser. True humanism and the awareness of death are mutually dependent variables, for it is only by facing and accepting the reality of my coming death that I can become authentically alive. As D. H. Lawrence observed, "Without the song of death, the song of life becomes pointless and silly." By ignoring the dimension of death, we deprive life of its true grandeur.

This is a point that has been powerfully expressed by Metropolitan Anthony of Sourozh:

> Death is the touchstone of our attitude to life. People who are afraid of death are afraid of life. It is impossible not to be afraid of life with all its complexity and dangers if one is afraid of death... If we are afraid of death we will never be prepared to take ultimate risks; we will spend our life in a cowardly, careful and timid manner. It is only if we can face death, make sense of it, determine its place and our place in regard to it, that we will be able to live in a fearless way and to the fullness of our ability.[2]

Our realism, however, and our determination to "make sense" of death should not lead us to diminish the second truth: Death is a mystery. Despite all that we are told by our different religious traditions, we understand almost nothing about

> The undiscover'd country from whose bourn
> No traveller returns...

Truly, as Hamlet remarks, the dread of it "puzzles the will." We must resist the temptation to try and say too much. We are not to trivialize death. It is an unavoidable and certain fact, but it is also the great unknown.

The attitude of sober realism with which we are to confront the fact of death is well expressed by St Isaac the Syrian:

2   "On Death," *Sobornost* 1:2 (1979), 8.

Prepare your heart for your departure. If you are wise, you will expect it every hour. Each day say to yourself: "See, the messenger who comes to fetch me is already at the door. Why am I sitting idle? I must depart for ever. I cannot come back again." Go to sleep with these thoughts every night, and reflect on them throughout the day. And when the time of departure comes, go joyfully to meet it, saying: "Come in peace. I knew you would come, and I have not neglected anything that could help me on the journey."[3]

Deaths great and little

In determining death's place and our place in regard to it, there are three aspects to be kept constantly in view:

Death is closer to us than we imagine.

Death is deeply unnatural, contrary to the divine plan, and yet it is God's gift.

Death is a separation that is no separation.

Death is far closer to us than we imagine—not just a distant event at the conclusion of our earthly existence, but a present reality that is going on continually around us and within us.[4] "I die daily," said St Paul (1 Cor 15:31); in T. S. Eliot's words, "The time of death is every moment." All living is a kind of dying: we are dying all the time. But in this daily experience of dying, each death is followed by a new birth: all dying is also a kind of living. Life and death are not opposites, mutually exclusive, but they are intertwined. The whole of our human existence is a mixture of mortality and resurrection: "dying, and behold we live" (2 Cor 6:9). Our earthly journey is an unceasing passover, a constant crossing over through death into new life. Between our initial birth and our eventual death, the whole course of our existence is made up of a series of lesser deaths and births.

Every time we fall asleep at night, it is a foretaste of death; every time we wake up again next morning, it is as if we had risen from the dead. There is a Hebrew benediction which says, "Blessed art Thou, O Lord our God, King of the universe, who createst Thy world every morning afresh."[5] So it

3   *Homily* 65(64): tr. Wensinck, 309; tr. Miller, 315.

4   In what follows, I am indebted to a talk by Father John Dalrymple, "Dying Before Death," in Donald Reid (ed.), *The Experience of Death* (Edinburgh: The Fellowship of Saint Andrew, 1985), 1-8.

5   Barbara Green and Victor Gollancz, *God of a Hundred Names* (London: Gollancz, 1962), 19.

is also with ourselves: each morning, as we awake, we are as it were newly created. Perhaps our final death will be in the same way a recreation—a falling asleep followed by an awakening. We are not afraid to drop off to sleep each night, because we expect to wake up once more next morning. Can we not feel the same kind of confidence about our final falling asleep in death? May we not expect to wake up again recreated in eternity?

The death-life pattern is also apparent, in a somewhat different way, in the process of growing up. Repeatedly, something in us has to die so that we may pass on to the next stage of living. The transition from the baby to the child, from the child to adolescent, from the adolescent to the mature adult, involves at each juncture an inner death in order that something new may come alive. And these transitions, particularly in the case of the child becoming a teenager, can often be crisis-ridden and even acutely painful. Yet if at any point we decline to accept the need for a dying, we cannot develop into real persons. As George MacDonald says in his fantasy novel *Lilith*, "You will be dead so long as you refuse to die." It is precisely the death of the old that makes possible the emergence of fresh growth within ourselves, and without the death there would be no new life.

If growing up is a form of death, then so is parting, the separation from a place or person that we have come to love: *partir, c'est mourir un peu*. Yet such separations are a necessary element in our continuing growth into maturity. Unless we have sometimes the courage to leave our familiar surroundings, to part with our existing friends and to forge new links, we shall never realize our true potentiality. By hanging on too long to the old, we are refusing the invitation to discover what is new. In the words of Cecil Day Lewis:

Selfhood begins with a walking away.
And love is proved in the letting go.

Another kind of death that all of us have to face at some point is the experience of being rejected: rejection, perhaps, when we apply for a job—how often does every school-leaver or university graduate today have to live through that particular form of dying!—or else rejection in love. Something does indeed die within us when we find that our love is not returned, and that someone else is preferred in our place. And yet even this death can be a source of new life. For many young people such love is precisely the moment when they really begin to grow up, their initiation into adult life. Bereavement, the loss of a loved one, involves equally a death in the heart of the one who remains alive. We feel that a part of ourselves is no longer there, that a limb has been amputated. Yet bereavement, when faced and inwardly accepted, makes each of us more authentically alive than we were before.

Almost as traumatic as the death of a friend or partner can be, for many believers, the death of faith—the loss of our root certainties (or seeming certainties) about God and the meaning of existence. But this too is a death-life experience through which we have to pass if our faith is to become mature. True faith is a constant dialogue with doubt, for God is incomparably greater than all our preconceptions about Him; our mental concepts are idols that need to be shattered. So as to be fully alive, our faith needs continually to die.

In all these cases, then, death turns out to be not destructive but creative. Out of dying comes resurrection. Something dies—something comes alive. May not the death that ensues at the end of our earthly life fit into this same pattern? It is to be seen as the last and greatest in the long series of deaths and resurrections that we have been experiencing ever since the day that we were born. It is not something totally unrelated to all that has been happening to us previously throughout our life, but it is a larger, more comprehensive expression of what we have been undergoing all the time. If the little deaths through which we have had to pass have each led us beyond death to resurrection, may this not be true of the great moment of death that we await when it is finally time to depart from this world?

Nor is this all. For Christians, the constantly repeated pattern of death-resurrection within our own lives is given fuller meaning by the life, death and Resurrection of our Savior Jesus Christ. Our own story is to be understood in the light of His story—that story which we celebrate annually during Holy Week, and also each Sunday at the Eucharist. Our little deaths and resurrections are joined across history to His definitive death and Resurrection, our little passovers are taken up and reaffirmed in His great passover. Christ's dying, in the words of the Liturgy of St Basil, is a "life-creating death." With His example as our assurance, we believe that our own death can also be "life-creating." He is our forerunner and our first fruits. As we Orthodox affirm at the Paschal midnight service, in words attributed to St John Chrysostom:

Let none fear death, for the death of the Savior has set us free.
He has destroyed death by undergoing death…
Christ is risen, and life reigns in freedom.
Christ is risen, and there is none left dead in the tomb.[6]

Both tragedy and blessing

Death, then, is present with us throughout our life, as a constant, ever-recurring daily experience. Yet, familiar though it may be, at the same time it is deeply unnatural. Death is not part of God's primary purpose for His creation. He created us, not in order that we should die, but in order that we should live. What is more, He created us as an undivided unity. In the Jewish and Christian view, the human person is to be seen in thoroughly holistic terms: we are each of us, not a soul temporarily imprisoned in a body and longing to escape, but an integrated totality that embraces soul and body together. C. G. Jung was right to insist on what he terms the "mysterious truth": "Spirit is the living body seen from within, and the body the outer manifestation of the living spirit—the two being really one."[7] As the separation of body and soul, death is therefore a violent affront against the wholeness of our human nature. Death may be something that awaits us all, but it is at the same time profoundly abnormal. It is monstrous and tragic. Confronted by the death of those close to us and by our own death, despite all our realism we are justified in feeling also a sense of desolation, of horror and even indignation:

Do not go gentle into that good night.
Rage, rage against the dying of the light.[8]

Jesus Himself wept beside the grave of His friend Lazarus (Jn 11:35), and in Gethsemane He was filled with anguish at the prospect of His own coming death (Mt 26:38). St Paul regards death as an "enemy to be destroyed" (1 Cor 15:26), and he links it closely with sinfulness: "The sting of death is sin" (1 Cor 15:56). The fact that we are all going to die is a reflection of the fact that we are all living in a fallen world—in a world that is distorted and out of joint, crazy, écrasé.

Yet, even though death is tragic, it is at the same time a blessing. Al-

6   For the full text, see Lossky, *The Mystical Theology of the Eastern Church*, 247-49.
7   *Modern Man in Search of a Soul*, Ark Paperbacks (London: Routledge & Kegan Paul, 1984), 253.
8   Dylan Thomas, *Collected Poems* (London: Dent, 1952), 116.

though not part of God's original plan, it is nonetheless His gift, an expression of His mercy and compassion. For us humans to live unendingly in this fallen world, caught forever in the vicious circle of boredom and sin, would have been a fate too terrible for us to endure; and so God has supplied us with a way of escape. He dissolves the union of soul and body, so that He may afterwards shape them anew, uniting them again at the bodily resurrection on the Last Day and so recreating them to fullness of life. He is like the potter whom Jeremiah watched: "So I went down to the potter's house, and there he was working at his wheel. The vessel he was making of clay was spoiled in the potter's hand, and he reworked it into another vessel, as seemed good to him" (18:4-5). The Divine Potter lays His hand on the vessel of our humanity, marred by sin, and He breaks it in pieces, so as to mold it again on His wheel and refashion it according to its first glory. Death serves in this way as the means of our restoration. In the words of the Orthodox funeral service:

> Of old Thou hast created me from nothing
> And honored me with Thy divine image.
> But when I disobeyed Thy commandment,
> Thou hast returned me to the earth whence I was taken.
> Lead me back again to Thy likeness.
> Refashioning my ancient beauty.[9]

As Benjamin Franklin stated in the epitaph that he composed for himself, death is the way in which we are "corrected and amended":

> The body of
> Benjamin Franklin, printer,
> (Like the cover of an old book,
> Its contents worn out,
> And stript of its lettering and gilding)
> Lies here; food for worms!
> Yet the work itself will not be lost,
> For it will, as he believed, appear once more
> In a new
> And more beautiful edition,
> Corrected and amended
> By its Author!

9 *The Lenten Triodion*, tr. Mother Mary and Archimandrite Kallistos Ware (London: Faber, 1978), 128.

There is, then, a dialectic in our attitude to death, but the two ways of approach are not in the final analysis contradictory. We see death as unnatural, abnormal, as contrary to the original plan of the Creator, and so we recoil from it with grief and despair. But we see it also as part of the divine will, as a blessing, not a punishment. It is an escape from the *impasse*, a means of grace, the doorway to our recreation. It is our way of return: to quote the Orthodox funeral service once more, "I am the lost sheep: call me back and save me, O Savior."[10] We therefore draw near to death with eagerness and hope, saying with St Francis of Assisi, "Praised be my Lord for our Sister, bodily death," for through this bodily death the Savior is calling home the child of God. We look beyond the separation of body and soul at death to their future reintegration at the final resurrection.

This dialectic is clearly apparent at an Orthodox funeral. No attempt is made to hide the painful and shocking reality of the fact of death. The coffin is left open, and it can often be a harrowing moment when the relatives and friends approach one by one to give the last kiss to the departed. Yet at the same time it is customary in many places to wear not black but white vestments, as in the Resurrection service at Paschal midnight; for Christ, risen from the dead, is summoning the departed Christian to share in His own Resurrection. We are not forbidden to mourn at a funeral; and this is surely wise, for tears can have a healing effect, and when grief is suppressed the wound goes deeper. But we are not to grieve "as others do who have no hope" (1 Thess 4:13). Our grief, however heartrending, is not a hopeless grief; for, as we confess in the Creed, "we are expecting the resurrection of the dead and the life of the age to come."

Continuing communion

Death is, in the third place, a separation that is no separation. This is a point to which Orthodox tradition attaches the utmost importance. The living and the departed belong to a single family. The chasm of death is not impassable, for we can all meet around the altar of God. In the words of the Russian writer Iulia de Beausobre, "The Church...is a meeting-place of persons dead, alive and yet to be born, who, loving one another, come together round the rock of the Altar to proclaim their love of

10 *Ibid.*

God."[11] The point is well developed by another Russian author, the missionary priest Makary Glukharev, in a letter to one recently bereaved:

> In Christ we live and move and have our being. Whether alive or dead, we are
> all in Him. It would be more true to say: We are all alive in Him, for in Him
> there is no death. Our God is not a God of the dead but of the living. He is
> your God, He is the God of her who has died. There is only one God, and in
> that one God you are both united. Only you cannot see each other for the time
> being. But this means that your future meeting will be all the more joyful; and
> then no one will take your joy from you. Yet even now you live together; all
> that has happened is that she has gone into another room and closed the
> door... Spiritual love is not conscious of visible separation.[12]

How is this continuing communion maintained? There is, first, a false
turning which some have found attractive, but which the Orthodox tradition utterly rejects. Communion between the living and the dead is not to
be maintained through spiritualism and necromancy. There can be no
place within true Christianity for any techniques seeking to communicate
with the dead through mediums, ouija boards and the like. Indeed, such
practices are highly dangerous, often exposing those who indulge in them
to invasion by demonic forces. Spiritualism is also the expression of an il-
legitimate curiosity, much in the manner of one trying to look through
the key-hole of a closed door ("What the butler saw..."). As Father Alexander Elchaninov puts it, "We must humbly admit the existence of a
Mystery, and not try to slip round by the backstairs to eavesdrop."[13]

As we learn from the lives of the saints, there are certainly occasions
when the dead communicate directly with the living, either in dreams or
in waking visions. But we on our side are not to attempt to force such
contacts. Any contrivance aimed at manipulating the dead is surely ab-
horrent to the Christian conscience. The fellowship between us and them
is not on the psychic but on the spiritual level, and the place of our meeting is not the séance-parlor but the Eucharistic table. The only legitimate
foundation for our fellowship with the dead is communion in prayer,
above all at the celebration of the Divine Liturgy. We pray for them, and
at the same time we are confident they are praying for us; and it is through

---

11　*Creative Suffering* (Westminster: Dacre, 1940), 44.
12　In S. Tyszkiewicz and T. Belpaire, *Écrits d' Ascètes Russes* (Namur, Belgium: Les Éditions du
　　Soleil Levant, 1957), 104.
13　*The Diary of a Russian Priest* (London: Faber, 1967), 43.

this mutual intercession that we and they are joined, across the boundary of death, in a firm and unbroken bond of unity.

The bond that unites the living and the departed is experienced by Orthodox Christians as being particularly close throughout the forty days immediately after death. There is at such a time but a thin veil between this world and the next, and so during these first few weeks memorial services for the newly departed are celebrated with exceptional frequency. When the forty days are over, public prayers are offered less often, although of course we continue to remember the newly departed daily in our private intercessions. While the bond between living and dead remains unbroken, we the living have as it were gradually to "let go" the one who has died, so that she or he may be free to pursue in peace the appointed journey on the other shore. This does not mean, however, that at the end of the forty days the living cease to mourn for the one who has died; on the contrary, the time of special grieving needs to extend far longer than that—far longer, indeed, than our contemporary western culture usually deems necessary.

Prayer for the dead is not seen by Orthodox Christians as an optional extra, but it is an accepted and unvarying feature in all our daily worship. Here are some of the prayers that we say:

> O Thou who with wisdom profound orderest all things in Thy love for mankind, who bestowest on all, O only Creator, that which is best for each: give rest, O Lord, to the souls of Thy servants, for they have set their hope in Thee, our Maker and Creator and our God.

> With the saints give rest, O Lord, to the souls of Thy servants, where there is no pain, no sorrow, no sighing, but life without end.

> May Christ give you rest in the land of the living, and open for you the gates of paradise; may He receive you as a citizen of the Kingdom, and grant you forgiveness of your sins: for you were His friend.

Yet some of the prayers strike a more somber note, reminding us of the possibility of an eternal separation from God:

> From the ever-burning fire, from the darkness without light, from the gnashing of teeth and the worm that torments without ceasing, from every punishment, deliver, O our Savior, all who have died in faith.[14]

14 For these and other prayers for the departed, see *The Lenten Triodion,* 124-41 (especially 126,

To this intercession for the dead no rigid bounds can be set. For whom do we pray? Strictly interpreted, the Orthodox rules allow prayers by name, in public liturgical worship, only for those who have died in the visible communion of the Church. But there are occasions when our prayers are far more wide-ranging. At Kneeling Vespers on the Sunday of Pentecost, prayers are said even for those in hell:

> On this final and saving festival Thou art pleased to accept intercessory propitiation for those imprisoned in hell, affording us great hopes that Thou wilt send down relaxation and refreshment to all held fast in bondage...[15]

What is the doctrinal basis for this constantly repeated prayer for the dead? How can it be theologically justified? To this the answer is extremely straightforward. The basis is our solidarity in mutual love. We pray for the dead because we love them. The Anglican Archbishop of Canterbury William Temple calls such prayer the "ministry of love," and he states in words that any Orthodox Christian would be happy to make his own: "We do not pray for them because God will otherwise neglect them. We pray for them because we know that He loves and cares for them, and we claim the privilege of uniting our love for them with God's."[16] In the words of another Anglican, Dr. E. B. Pusey, to refuse to pray for the dead is "so cold a thought...so contrary to love" that it must needs, on that ground alone, be false.[17]

No further explanation or defense of prayer for the departed is necessary or, indeed, possible. Such prayer is simply the spontaneous expression of our love for each other. Here on earth we pray for others; should we not continue to pray for them after their death? Have they ceased to exist, that we should cease to make intercession for them? Whether alive or dead, we are all members of the same family; and so, whether alive or dead, we intercede for each other. In the risen Christ there is no separation between the dead and the living; in Father Makary's words, "We are all alive in Him, for in Him there is no death." Physical death cannot sever the bonds of mutual

134); Isabel Florence Hapgood (tr.), *Service Book of the Holy Orthodox-Catholic Apostolic Church*, 2nd edn. (New York: Association Press, 1922), 360-453 (especially 387).

15 *The Pentecostarion* (Boston, MA: Holy Transfiguration Monastery, 1990), 424.

16 Quoted in *Prayer and the Departed: A Report of the Archbishop's Commission on Christian Doctrine* (London: SPCK, 1971), 90.

17 *Op. cit.*, 85.

love and mutual prayer that unite us all to one another in a single Body.

Of course we do not understand exactly *how* such prayer benefits the departed. Yet equally, when we intercede for people still alive, we cannot explain how this intercession assists them. We know from our personal experience that prayer for others is effective, and so we continue to practice it. But, whether offered for the living or for the dead, such prayer works in a way that remains mysterious. We are unable to fathom the precise interaction between the act of prayer, the free will of the other person, and God's grace and foreknowledge. When we pray for the departed, it is enough for us to know that they are still growing in their love for God, and so need our support. Let us leave the rest to God.

If we truly believe that we enjoy an unbroken and continuing communion with the dead, then we shall take care to speak of them so far as possible in the present tense, not the past. We shall not say, "We loved each other," "She was so very dear to me," "We were so happy together." We shall say, "We *still* love each other—now more than before," "She *is* as dear to me as ever," "We *are* so happy together." There is a Russian lady in the Orthodox community at Oxford who strongly objects to being called a widow. Although her husband died many years ago, she insists: "I am his wife, not his widow." She is right.

If we learn to speak of the dead in this way, using the present tense and not the past, this can help with a particular problem that sometimes causes people anguish. All too easily it can happen that we postpone seeking a reconciliation with someone whom we have alienated, and death intervenes before we have forgiven each other. In bitter remorse we are tempted to say to ourselves: "Too late, too late, the chance has gone for ever; there is nothing more to be done." But we are altogether mistaken, for it is not too late. On the contrary, we can go home this very day, and in our evening prayers we can speak directly to the dead friend from whom we were estranged. Using the same words that we would employ if they were still alive and we were meeting them face to face, we can ask their forgiveness and reaffirm our love. And from that very moment our mutual relationship will be changed. Although we do not see their face or hear their response, although we have not the slightest idea how our words reach them, yet we know in our hearts that we and they have together made a fresh start. It is not too late to begin again.

A hundred times finer and more subtle...

There remains a question that in our present state of knowledge is unanswerable, and yet it is often asked. We have said that the human person was originally created by God as an undivided unity of body and soul and that we look, beyond the separation of the two at bodily death, to their ultimate reunification on the Last Day. A holistic anthropology commits us to believing, not merely in the immortality of the soul, but in the resurrection of the body. Since the body is an integral part of the total human person, when we think of our future immortality as persons in the full and true sense, such immortality cannot be simply an immortality of the soul alone, but must also involve the body. What, in that case, is the relationship between our present body and our resurrected body in the Age to come? At the resurrection, shall we have the same body as we do now, or will it be a new body?

Perhaps the best response is to say: it will be the same body, and yet not the same. Let us begin by considering the Resurrection of Christ, already accomplished on the third day; for it is this that forms the model for the future resurrection of all humankind at the Second Coming. Christ is the "first fruits," to use St Paul's imagery, and we are the harvest (1 Cor 15:20-24). Now in Christ's case the Gospel narratives render it abundantly clear that He is raised from the dead not in a new body, but in the same body as He had before. That is why the tomb is found to be empty, and that is why the first action of the risen Christ on meeting the apostles is to show them the wounds of the Crucifixion in His hands and feet and side, so as to assure them that He is once more truly present with them in the selfsame physical body which they had seen hanging on the Cross (Jn 20:20-28; compare Lk 24: 37-40).

Yet, although it is the selfsame physical body, it is also different. It is a body that can pass through closed doors (Jn 20:19), that has "another form" (Mk 16:12), so that it is not at once recognizable to the two disciples on the road to Emmaus (Lk 24:16) or to the apostles at the lake of Tiberias (Jn 21:4). From the Gospel accounts of the forty days between the Resurrection and the Ascension, we gain the impression that Jesus is present with the disciples not continually but intermittently, appearing suddenly and then once more withdrawing His visible presence. His body has not

ceased to be genuinely physical, but it is at the same time released from
the limitations of materiality as now known to us, dwelling as we do in a
fallen world. It has become a *spiritual* body; but by "spiritual" in this context is meant not "dematerialized" but "transformed by the power and
glory of the Spirit."

If such is the condition of the risen Christ, our paradigm and "first
fruits," what does this tell us about our own coming resurrection on the
Last Day? St Paul affirms that in our case, as in that of the risen Christ,
there will be both continuity and change. That there will be continuity is
evident from the Pauline analogy of the seed sown in the earth (1 Cor
15:36-37). The seed is "buried" in the earth and there it undergoes "death"
(compare Jn 12:24); and then out of this "death" there comes new life. The
stalk or plant that shoots up out of the ground is not identical with the
seed that has died, but it is directly derived from it.

Alongside this continuity, however, there will also be change. Describing the relationship between the present and the resurrection body,
St Paul writes: "What is sown is perishable, what is raised is imperishable.
It is sown in dishonor, it is raised in glory. It is sown in weakness, it is
raised in power. It is sown a physical (*or* "natural" [*psychikon*]) body, it is
raised a spiritual [*pnevmatikon*] body" (1 Cor 15: 42-44). By a "spiritual"
body is meant, in our case as in Christ's, not "dematerialized" but "transformed by the Spirit." Christ was not raised as a ghost (Lk 24:39) but in
His integral human nature, soul and body together; and the same will be
true also of us.

Thus our future resurrection body, while transfigured and rendered
"spiritual," will yet be in some significant sense the same physical body as
we have now. But how exactly should this "sameness" be understood? Today, as in the past, many Christians envisage the continuity in a narrowly
literal manner. Typical of this approach is the statement in the *Spiritual
Homilies* attributed to St Macarius of Egypt: "At the resurrection all the
members of the body are raised; not a hair perishes."[18]

St Gregory of Nyssa, however, while still wishing to affirm that our resurrection body is constituted from the same physical elements as comprise
our present body, suggests a slightly less literal approach by introducing the

18   *Spiritual Homilies* 15. 10: ed. Dörries, 132; tr. Maloney, 111-12. Compare Lk 21:18.

notion of a "form" (*eidos*) or configuration imposed upon these physical elements by the soul. Throughout our present life, he points out, the constituent elements making up our material body undergo unceasing change; but the "form" marked by the soul upon these elements remains the same, and thus by virtue of the uninterrupted preservation of this "form" we continue throughout our life to have the same body. At the resurrection, then, the soul will reassemble the scattered fragments of matter which once belonged to our body during this present life, and on which its "form" remains imprinted. In relation to our present body, then, our resurrection body will be indeed the same body, because it will posses the same "form" imposed upon the same physical elements.[19]

In this way Gregory posits a direct material continuity between the present body and the resurrection body. But can we not develop, in a more far-reaching manner than Gregory himself chooses to do, his notion of a distinctive and unique "form" (*eidos*) possessed by the psychosomatic totality of each human person? If the physical elements constituting our body in this present life are always changing, then surely it is not necessary for our body at the final resurrection to be composed of precisely the same material elements as constitute it at the moment of our death. All that we need to assert is that the characteristic "form" imprinted by the soul remains the same.

In considering both the "sameness" of our physical body at the different moments of this earthly life, and likewise the "sameness" of our resurrection body *vis-à-vis* our present body, the crucial point at issue is not the identity of the material constituents but the continuity of the "form." If in each case the "form" remains the same, then the body remains also the same, even though the "form" is imprinted on different matter. We may illustrate the continuity, in both cases, by appealing as C. S. Lewis does to the example of a waterfall: "My form remains one, though the matter in it changes continually. I am, in that respect, like the curve in a waterfall."[20] The drops in a waterfall are never the same from one moment to another, but since the

19 See *On the creation of humanity* 27 (*PG* 44: 225C-228A); *On the soul and the resurrection* (*PG* 46: 73A-80A); tr. Roth, 65-69.

20 *Miracles: A Preliminary Study* (London: Geoffrey Bles, 1947), 180. Gregory uses similar analogies in *On the soul and the resurrection* (*PG* 46: 141AB; tr. Roth, 110: a stream, the flame of a candle).

curve of flowing water preserves the same "form," it is indeed the same waterfall. The resurrection body of each person, then, even though perhaps
formed of different material constituents, will yet be in a truly recognizable
manner the same body as that which the person possesses at present, because it will possess the same "form."

Such an approach saves us from the unhelpful questions which in early
centuries disturbed simpleminded Christians concerning, for example,
the fate of a human being eaten by a wild animal which is then eaten in
turn by other human beings. (Recalling a traditional song, we may style
this the "Ilkley Moor" problematic.) But the approach here suggested in
its turn raises other difficulties. If we suggest that there is no direct material continuity between a person's present body and his or her resurrection
body, are we not in danger of undervaluing the sanctification of our physical body during this earthly life through the Holy Mysteries of Baptism,
Eucharist and Anointing with Oil? If the human body in this life experiences through the sacraments a true inauguration of the bodily glory of
the Age to come, surely there must be some direct physical connection between the present and the resurrection body. What significance, moreover, are we to ascribe to the uncorrupted relics of the saints? I wonder
whether a link between the present and the future can be safeguarded by
emphasizing the *communal* aspect of resurrection and transfiguration in
the Age to come. The sanctification of matter in this life, that is to say,
contributes to the ultimate redemption of humankind and of the cosmos
understood in *corporate* terms.

We have said enough about these puzzling matters, and perhaps too
much. We are reminded, as before, how delicate it is, and indeed how perilous, to attempt any detailed formulations concerning the future life. On
the basis of our existing knowledge we can do no more than conjecture
tentatively about the character of the Age to come. "At present we see only
puzzling reflections in a mirror" (1 Cor 13:12); "what we shall be has not
yet been disclosed" (1 Jn 3:2).

Regarding one point, however, we may certainly be confident. Whatever else can or cannot be said about the resurrection body, it will undoubtedly possess a transparence and vivacity, a lightness and sensitivity,
of which at this moment we can form no more than a dim and totally in-
adequate notion. At this present juncture we experience the material

world and our own material bodies as they are in a fallen state. Despite the precious intimations provided in Scripture and in the lives of the saints, it lies almost entirely beyond the power of our imagination to conceive the qualities that matter and the human body will manifest in a transfigured cosmos from which sin has disappeared.

St Ephraim the Syrian, however, comes closer than most theologians to imagining the unimaginable when he writes:

> Consider the man in whom there dwelt a legion of all kinds of devils (Mk 5:9): they were there though they were not recognized, for their army is of stuff finer and more subtil than the soul itself. That whole army dwelt in a single body.

> A hundred times finer and more subtil is the body of the just when they are risen, at the resurrection: it resembles a thought that is able, if it wills, to stretch out and expand, or, should it wish, to contract and shrink: if it shrinks, it is somewhere; if it expands, it is everywhere.

> The spiritual beings [in paradise]…are so refined in substance that even thoughts cannot touch them![21]

That is perhaps as good a description of the resurrection glory as we can expect to find. Let us leave the rest to silence.

You are the music…

Two weeks before his death, the composer Ralph Vaughan Williams was asked what the future life meant to him. "Music," he said, "music. But in the next world I shan't be doing music, with all the striving and disappointments. I shall be being it."[22]

"You are the music while the music lasts," says T. S. Eliot. And in heaven the music lasts forever.

21 Sebastian Brock, *The Harp of the Spirit: Eighteen Poems of Saint Ephrem*, Studies Supplementary to *Sobornost* 4, 2nd edn. (London: Fellowship of St Alban and St Sergius, 1983), 23-4.
22 D. J. Enright, *The Oxford Book of Death* (Oxford: Oxford University Press, 1983), 332.

3

THE ORTHODOX EXPERIENCE
OF REPENTANCE

This life has been given you for repentance. Do not waste it on other things.

St Isaac the Syrian

Repentance is a great understanding.

The Shepherd of Hermas

The starting point of the Good News

St John the Baptist and our Lord Jesus Christ both begin their preaching with exactly the same words: "Repent, for the Kingdom of heaven is at hand" (Mt 3:2; 4:17). Such is the starting point of the Good News—repentance. Without repentance there can be no new life, no salvation, no entry into the Kingdom.

Turning from Scripture to the Fathers, we find exactly the same truth heavily underlined. Asked what he is doing in the desert, Abba Milesius replies: "I came here to weep for my sins."[1] And this repentance is not just a preliminary stage but lifelong. As Abba Sisoes lies on his deathbed, surrounded by his disciples, he is seen to be talking with someone. "Who are you talking to, father?" the disciples ask. "See," he replies, "the angels have come to take me and I am asking for a little more time—more time to repent." "You have no need to repent," say the disciples. "Truly," the old man replies, "I am not sure whether I have even begun to repent."[2] St Mark the Monk insists:

1 *AP* (*The Sayings of the Desert Fathers*), alphabetical collection, Milesius 2 (*PG* 65:297B); tr. Ward, *Sayings*, 147.
2 *AP*, alphabetical collection, Sisoes 14 (396B); tr. Ward, *Sayings*, 215.

No one is so good and merciful as God, but even He does not forgive the unrepentant… All the wide variety of God's commandments can be reduced to the single principle of repentance… We are not condemned for the multitude of our transgressions, but for our refusal to repent… For great and small alike, repentance remains incomplete until the moment of death.[3]

"Our Lord Jesus Christ," states Abba Isaias of Scetis, "commanded us to go on repenting until our last breath. For if there were no repentance, nobody would be saved."[4] And St Isaac the Syrian teaches: "During every moment of the four and twenty hours of the day we stand in need of repentance."[5]

Spiritual guides in more recent times assign an equally decisive role to repentance. As the nineteenth century drew to a close, St John of Kronstadt wrote his spiritual diary *My Life in Christ,* "Our prayer consists principally in penitence."[6] And Father Seraphim Papakostas, head of the *Zoe* movement in Greece during the years 1927-54, begins the best known of his many works with these words:

In every age, and above all in this present deeply uneasy, tired and restless age, nothing is more essential than repentance. Often there is nothing for which we long more profoundly, but we have no clear idea what we really want.[7]

It is noteworthy that the Jesus Prayer—so much more widely practiced today than was the case fifty years ago—is specifically (although not exclusively) a prayer of repentance, especially when used in its expanded form: "Lord Jesus Christ, Son of God, have mercy on me a sinner."

Bearing in mind this constant insistence on repentance, we would do well to reflect carefully on the way in which we present Orthodoxy in the contemporary West. There is a tendency to draw attention to only one aspect. We speak about the glory of the divine light at Christ's Transfiguration, about the sense of Resurrection triumph at Easter midnight; we talk of the joy of the Kingdom, of the spiritual beauty of icons, of the Divine Liturgy as an inauguration of the Age to come. And we are right to

3   *On those who think they are made righteous by works* 71 (PG 65:940D); *On repentance* 1 (964B), 6 (973C), 11 (980D).
4   *Homily* 16.12: ed. Avgoustinos, 100.
5   *Homily* 70(73): tr. Wensinck, 337; tr. Miller, 340.
6   W. Jardine Grisbrooke (ed.), *Spiritual Counsels of Father John of Kronstadt* (London: James Clarke, 1967), 118.
7   *Repentance* (Athens: Zoe Brotherhood of Theologians, 1995), 9.

emphasize these things. But let us take care not to be one-sided. The Transfiguration and the Resurrection are integrally linked with the Crucifixion. As Christians we are indeed witnesses to the "exceedingly great joy" (Mt 2:10) of the Gospel; but we must not overlook the words "*Through the Cross* joy has come to all the world" (Sunday Matins). Cosmic transfiguration can only be realized through self-denial and ascetic fasting.[8]

"A great understanding"

But what in fact is meant by repentance? It is normally regarded as sorrow for sin, a feeling of guilt, a sense of grief and horror at the wounds we have inflicted on others and on ourselves. Yet such a view is dangerously incomplete. Grief and horror are indeed frequently present in the experience of repentance, but they are not the whole of it, nor even the most important part. We come closer to the heart of the matter if we reflect on the literal sense of the Greek term for repentance, *metanoia*. This means "change of mind": not just regret for the past, but a fundamental transformation of our outlook, a new way of looking at ourselves, at others and at God—in the words of *The Shepherd* of Hermas, "a great understanding."[9] A great understanding—but not necessarily an emotional crisis. Repentance is not a paroxysm of remorse and self-pity, but conversion, the recentering of our life upon the Holy Trinity.

As a "new mind," conversion, recentering, repentance is positive, not negative. In the words of St John Climacus, "Repentance is the daughter of hope and the denial of despair."[10] It is not despondency but eager expectation; it is not to feel that one has reached an *impasse*, but to take the way out. It is not self-hatred but the affirmation of my true self as made in God's image. To repent is to look, not downward at my own shortcomings, but upward at God's love; not backward with self-reproach, but forward with trustfulness. It is to see, not what I have failed to be, but what by the grace of Christ I can yet become.

---

8   This point is well made by Archimandrite Lev Gillet, "Looking unto the Crucified Lord," *Sobornost* 3:13 (1953), 24-33. His words of caution are as timely now as when they were written nearly half a century ago.

9   *Mandate* 4.2.2; cf. Thomas Merton, *Gandhi on Non-Violence* (Boston: Shambhala, 1996), 17.

10 *Ladder* 5 (*PG* 88:764B); tr. Luibheid and Russell, 121.

When interpreted in this positive sense, repentance is seen to be not just a single act but a continuing attitude. In the personal experience of each person there are decisive moments of conversion, but throughout this present life the work of repenting remains always incomplete. The turning or recentering must be constantly renewed; up to the moment of death, as Abba Sisoes realized, the "change of mind" must become always more radical, the "great understanding" always more profound. In the words of St Theophan the Recluse, "Repentance is the starting point and foundation stone of our new life in Christ; and it must be present not only at the beginning but throughout our growth in this life, increasing as we advance."[11]

The positive character of repentance is clearly apparent if we consider what comes just before the words of Christ already quoted, "Repent, for the Kingdom of heaven is at hand." In the preceding verse the Evangelist cites Isaiah 9:2, "The people that walked in darkness have seen a great light; they that dwell in the land of the shadow of death, upon them has the light shone." Such is the immediate context of our Lord's command to repent: it is directly preceded by a reference to "great light" shining on those in darkness, and directly followed by a reference to the imminence of the Kingdom. Repentance, then, is an illumination, a transition from darkness to light; to repent is to open our eyes to the divine radiance—not to sit dolefully in the twilight but to greet the dawn. And repentance is also eschatological, an openness to the Last Things that are not merely in the future but already present; to repent is to recognize that the Kingdom of heaven is in our midst, at work among us, and that if we will only accept the coming of this Kingdom all things will be made new for us.

The connection between repentance and the advent of the great light is particularly significant. Until we have seen the light of Christ, we cannot really see our sins. So long as a room is in darkness, observes St Theophan the Recluse, we do not notice the dirt; but when we bring a powerful light into the room—when, that is, we stand before the Lord in our heart—we can distinguish every speck of dust.[12] So it is with the room

11 Quoted in Igumen Chariton of Valamo (ed.), *The Art of Prayer: An Orthodox Anthology* (London: Faber, 1966), 226.
12 See Igumen Chariton, *The Art of Prayer*, 182.

of our soul. The sequence is not to repent first, and then to become aware of Christ; for it is only when the light of Christ has already in some measure entered our life that we begin truly to understand our sinfulness. To repent, says St John of Kronstadt, is to know that there is a lie in our heart;[13] but how can we detect the presence of a lie unless we have already some sense of the truth? In the words of E. I. Watkin, "Sin…is the shadow cast by the light of God intercepted by any attachment of the will which prevents it illuminating the soul. Thus knowledge of God gives rise to the sense of sin, not vice versa."[14] As the Desert Fathers observe, "The closer we come to God, the more we see that we are sinners."[15] And they cite Isaiah as an example of this: first he sees the Lord on His throne and hears the seraphim crying "Holy, holy, holy;" and it is only after this vision that he exclaims, "Woe is me! For I am lost; for I am a man of unclean lips" (Is 6:1-5).

Such, then, is the beginning of repentance: a vision of beauty, not of ugliness; an awareness of God's glory, not of my own squalor. "Blessed are they that mourn, for they shall be comforted" (Mt 5:4): repentance signifies not merely mourning for our sins, but the "comfort" or "consolation" (*paraklesis*) that comes from the assurance of God's forgiveness. The "great understanding" or "change of mind" signified by repentance consists precisely in this: in recognizing that the light shines in the darkness, and that the darkness does not swallow it up (Jn 1:5). To repent, in other words, is to recognize that there is good as well as evil, love as well as hatred; and it is to affirm that the good is stronger, to believe in the final victory of love. The repentant person is the one who accepts the miracle that God does indeed have power to forgive sins. And, once we accept this miracle, for us the past is then no longer an intolerable burden, for we no longer see the past as irreversible. Divine forgiveness breaks the chain of cause and effect, and unties the knots in our hearts which by ourselves we are not able to unloose.

There are many who feel sorrow for their past acts, but who say in their despair, "I cannot forgive myself for what I have done." Unable to

---

13 See Grisbrooke, *Spiritual Counsels*, 116.

14 "The Mysticism of St. Augustine," in M. C. D'Arcy *et al.*, *A Monument to St. Augustine* (New York: Lincoln MacVeagh, Dial Press, 1930), 108.

15 *AP*, alphabetical collection, Matoes 2 (289C); tr. Ward, *Sayings*, 143.

forgive themselves, they are equally incapable of believing that they are forgiven by God, and likewise by other human beings. Such people, despite the intensity of their anguish, have not yet properly repented. They have not yet attained the "great understanding" whereby a person knows that love is ultimately victorious. They have not yet undergone the "change of mind" that consists in saying: I am accepted by God; and what is asked of me is *to accept the fact that I am accepted*. That is the essence of repentance.

The Lenten springtime

The true nature of repentance will become clearer if we consider three characteristic expressions of repentance in the Church's life: first, and very briefly, the liturgical expression of repentance in the season of Lent; then, in more detail, its sacramental expression in Confession; and finally its personal expression in the gift of tears. In all three cases the positive, light-giving nature of repentance is strongly evident.

First, with regard to Lent, let us note the time of year in which it occurs: not in autumn, amidst the fog and falling leaves; not in winter, when the earth is dead and frozen; but in spring, when the frosts are ending, the days are growing longer, and the whole countryside returns to life. In the words of the *Triodion*:

> The springtime of the Fast has dawned, the flower of repentance has begun to open. O brethren, let us cleanse ourselves from all impurity, and sing to the Giver of Light: Glory be to Thee, who alone lovest mankind.[16]

The Lenten season of repentance is a time of gladness, not of despondency: the Fast is a spiritual springtime, repentance is an opening flower, and Christ is made known to us in Lent as "Giver of light." The sorrow that we feel in Lent is a "joy-creating sorrow," to use the phrase of St John Climacus.[17]

16 *Sticheron* at Vespers, Wednesday in the Week before Lent ("Cheese Week"). For further discussion of the spiritual significance of the Lenten fast, see Kallistos Ware, introduction to *The Lenten Triodion*, 13-28; and also, by the same author, "Lent and the Consumer Society," in Andrew Walker and Costa Carras (eds.), *Living Orthodoxy* (London: SPCK, 1996), 64-84.
17 *Charopoion penthos, charmolype*: *Ladder* 7 (*PG* 88:801C, 804B); tr. Luibheid and Russell, 137.

The sacrament of repentance

The experience of repentance is felt with especial force in the sacrament of Confession. The meaning of this "mystery" may be found summed up in the short exhortation addressed by the priest to the penitent in the Russian rite (the italics are my own):

> Behold, my child, *Christ stands here invisibly and receives your confession*: therefore, do not be ashamed or afraid, and hide nothing from me; but tell me without hesitation all the things that you have done, *and so you will have pardon from our Lord Jesus Christ*. See, His holy icon is before us; and *I am only a witness*, bearing testimony before Him of all the things you have to say to me. But if you hide anything from me, you will have greater sin. Take care, then, lest *having come to the physician's* you depart unhealed.[18]

Paraphrasing this exhortation, St Tikhon of Zadonsk writes (once more, my own italics):

> When giving instruction on the sacrament of Repentance, the priest should speak to the penitent in this manner: My child, you are confessing to God, who is displeased at any sin; and I, His servant, am the unworthy witness of your repentance. Do not conceal anything, do not be ashamed or afraid, *for there are only three of us here, you and I and God*. It is before God that you have sinned, and He knows all your sins and how they were committed. God is everywhere, and wherever you said, thought, or did anything evil, He was there and knew all about it; and He is here with us now, and is waiting for your words of repentance and confession. You too know all your sins: do not be ashamed to speak of all that you have committed. And *I who am here, am a sinner just like you*; so then, do not be ashamed to confess your sins in my presence.[19]

"Having come to the physician's," says the priest; alternatively, we might use the translation, "having come to the house of the Physician." In Confession, that is to say, we are to see Christ the Judge lifting from us the

18 For the Orthodox order of Confession, both Greek and Russian, see *A Manual of Eastern Orthodox Prayers*, published for the Fellowship of St Alban and St Sergius (London: SPCK, 1945), 51-60; the passage cited occurs on 58-59. Compare *The Great Book of Needs*, vol. I (South Canaan, PA: St Tikhon's Seminary Press, 1998), 127; Paul N. Harrilchak, *Confession with Examination of Conscience and Common Prayers* (Reston, VA: Holy Trinity Church, 1996), 163. For a helpful introductory discussion of the sacrament of Confession, see John Chryssavgis, *Repentance and Confession in the Orthodox Church* (Brookline, MA: Holy Cross Orthodox Press, 1990).
19 Cited in Nadejda Gorodetzky, *Saint Tikhon Zadonsky* (London: SPCK, 1951), 126-27.

sentence of condemnation; but also, and more fundamentally, we are to see Christ the Physician, restoring what is broken and renewing life. The sacrament is to be envisaged not primarily in juridical but in therapeutic terms. Above all it is a *sacrament of healing*. It is significant that in some of the Byzantine liturgical commentaries Confession and the Anointing of the Sick are treated not as two distinct sacraments but as complementary aspects of a single "mystery" of healing. What we seek in Confession is much more than an external, forensic absolution; above all we desire noetic medicine for our chronic spiritual wounds. Indeed, what we bring before Christ is not just specific sins but also the fact of deep sinfulness within us—the profound corruption that cannot be fully expressed in words, that seems to elude our conscious brain and will. It is of this, above all else, that we ask to be cured. And as a sacrament of healing, Confession is not simply a painful necessity, a discipline imposed on us by church authority, but an action full of joy and saving grace. Through Confession we learn that God is in full reality "the hope of the hopeless" (The Liturgy of St Basil).

"There are only three of us here"—priest, penitent and Christ the Physician. What does each of these three do, and whose action is the most important? Many people tend to put the greatest emphasis on what the *priest* does, on his words of counsel and encouragement; and if the priest fails to say anything eloquent or unexpected, they tend to assume that little or nothing has been achieved. Or else they overstress the second aspect, what *they themselves* are doing. They imagine that they must be deeply stirred on an emotional level—even though, as we have said, repentance is not primarily a matter of the emotions. And because they put the main emphasis on their own efforts, they are in danger of regarding Confession in bleak and discouraging terms, as something to be got over and done with, necessary yet disagreeable, like a cold bath. But in reality the most important action is not that of penitent or priest, but that of *God*. While the penitent is required to prepare himself by self-examination and to conduct a searching scrutiny of his conscience, in the last resort he comes to Confession empty-handed, helpless, not claiming to be able to heal himself, but asking for healing from another. And this other whose help he invokes is not the priest but God. The priest is simply a witness, bearing testimony before God of what we have to say. To vary the analogy, he is no more than "God's usher," introducing us into the divine Presence; he is merely the receptionist in the hospital waiting room or the attendant in the operating theatre, whereas the surgeon is Christ Himself. It is to Christ, not to the priest, that the confession is made ("Christ stands here invisibly and receives your confession"); and it is from Christ, not from the priest, that the forgiveness comes ("so you will have pardon from our Lord Jesus Christ").

Once we regard Confession as fundamentally Christ's action rather than our own, then we shall begin to understand the sacrament of repentance in a far more positive way. It is an experience of God's healing love and pardon, not merely of our own disintegration and weakness. We are to see, not just the prodigal son, plodding slowly and painfully upon the long road home, but also the father, catching sight of him when he is still a long way off and running out to meet him (Lk 15:20).[20] As Tito Colliander puts it, "If we take one step toward the Lord, He takes ten toward us."[21] That is precisely what we experience in Confession. In common with all the sacraments, Confession involves a joint divine-human action, in which there is found a convergence and "cooperation" (*synergeia*) between God's grace and our free will. Both are necessary; but what God does is incomparably the more important.

Repentance and confession, then, are not just something that we do by ourselves or with the help of the priest, but above all something that God is doing with and in both of us. In the words of St John Chrysostom, "Let us apply to ourselves the saving remedy (*pharmakon*) of repentance; let us accept from God the repentance that heals us. For it is not we who offer it to Him, but He who bestows it upon us."[22] It should be remembered that in Greek the same word *exomologesis* means both confession of sins and thanksgiving for gifts received.

What, more specifically, is the part of the priest in this shared action? From one point of view his power is very wide-ranging. All who have experienced the blessing of having as their confessor one imbued with the

20 See also Lk 15:28, where the father once more goes out, this time to speak to the elder brother who will not come into the feast. This double going out of the father is one of the most important points in the parable.
21 *The Way of the Ascetics* (London: Hodder and Stoughton, 1960), 74.
22 *On repentance* 7.3 (*PG* 49:327).

grace of true spiritual fatherhood (*starchestvo*) will testify to the importance of the priest's role. Nor is his function simply to give advice. There is nothing automatic about the absolution which he pronounces. He can bind as well as loose. He can withhold absolution—although this is very rare—or he can impose a penance (*epitimion*), forbidding the penitent to receive Communion for a time or requiring the fulfillment of some task. This, again, is not very common in contemporary Orthodox practice, but it is important to remember that the priest possesses this right.

In the ancient Church penances were often severe. For fornication (*porneia*, i.e., sexual intercourse between unmarried persons) St Basil the Great enjoins seven years of exclusion from Holy Communion, and St Gregory of Nyssa nine years; in the later canonical legislation attributed to St John the Faster, this is reduced to two years, with rigorous fasting. For adultery (*moicheia*) the penances are more severe. For involuntary manslaughter—for instance (to give a contemporary example), killing someone in a car accident—Basil prescribes ten or eleven years' deprivation of Communion, Gregory of Nyssa nine years; if the penitent fasts strictly, John the Faster allows this to be reduced to three years. Parents who allow their child to die unbaptized are deprived of Communion for three years.

Even in early times there existed, of course, the possibility for the bishop or confessor-priest to modify these penances, applying "economy" (*oikonomia*) or pastoral flexibility according to the particular situation of each person. Today it would be altogether exceptional for the canons to be enforced in their full rigor; a broad measure of "economy" is normal. But in principle the confessor-priest still retains the power to decide how he should act; he is responsible before God for the manner in which he administers the sacrament, and he can at his own discretion impose a penance, involving if need be a lengthy period of exclusion from Holy Communion.

Not that the penance should be regarded as a punishment; still less should it be viewed as a way of expiating an offence. Salvation is a free gift of grace. By our own efforts we can never wipe out our guilt; Christ the one mediator is our only atonement, and either we are freely forgiven by Him, or else we are not forgiven at all. We do not acquire "merit" by fulfilling a penance, for in our relation to God we can never claim any merit of our own. Here, as always, we should think primarily in therapeutic rather than juridical terms. A penance is not a punishment, nor yet a form of expiation, but a means of healing. It is a *pharmakon* or medicine. If the actual Confession is like an operation, the penance is the tonic that restores the patient to health during his convalescence. The penance, therefore, in common with the whole act of Confession, is essentially positive in its purpose; it does not set up a barrier between the sinner and God, but serves as a bridge between the two. "Behold the goodness and the severity of God" (Rom 11:22): the penance is an expression not of divine severity alone but equally of divine love.

Entrusted with authority to bind and to loose, to withhold or to confer absolution, enjoying wide discretion as to the advice that he gives and the healing penance that he chooses, the confessor-priest has laid upon him a heavy responsibility. And yet his role is also limited. The confession, as we have already insisted, is made to God, not to the priest; and it is God who grants forgiveness. "I am only a witness," says the priest; and, still more explicitly in St Tikhon's paraphrase, "I am a sinner just like you." If at the moment of absolution, when laying his hand on the penitent's head, the priest stands to a certain degree in God's place, yet during the earlier part of the sacramental action he stands at the penitent's side, as himself a fellow-penitent, "a sinner just like you," who also needs divine forgiveness. There is, indeed, a two-way relationship between the priest and the one who is making the confession; the spiritual father is helped by his children, as well as they by him. The confessor-priest has also to go in his turn to Confession; and, when he does so, it is usual for him to remove the priestly cross from round his neck.

The priest's role as witness and fellow-penitent is clearly indicated in the outward setting of the sacrament. In some parts of the Orthodox Church, as in the Roman Catholic and Anglican practice, the priest sits while the penitent kneels. But most Orthodox confessor-priests prefer to avoid such an arrangement, for it might seem to suggest that the priest is judge rather than witness. More commonly in the Orthodox Church, during the opening prayers at the start of Confession, the penitent stands facing the icon of Christ or the Book of the Gospels, while the priest stands to one side. Then, for the actual confession of sins, they may both sit (Greek practice) or both remain standing (Russian practice): in either case, both do the same and are placed as it were on an equal footing. If, as occasionally happens, the penitent kneels and the priest remains standing, the priest will need to bow down in order to hear what is said; and this gesture also has its own significance. During the concluding absolution the penitent bows his head, or else kneels—not, however, in the direction of the priest but before the icon or the Book of the Gospels, symbolizing the invisible presence of Christ, who alone has power to remit sins. The prayer of absolution makes it clear beyond all doubt that it is Christ, not the priest, who confers forgiveness. In the more ancient form, still employed by the Greeks,[23] the priest does not say "I forgive you" but "May God forgive you." In the seventeenth century, under Roman Catholic influence, this was changed in the Slavonic books to the first person, "I, an unworthy priest, through the power given to me by Him, forgive you…"; however, this should be seen as an unfortunate distortion, for in no other sacrament of the Orthodox Church does the celebrant use the personal pronoun "I" in the act of administration. The older tradition is reflected in the custom of mutual forgiveness still observed by the Russians and by other Orthodox before receiving Communion. One member of the laity—or the clergy—says to another, "Forgive me," and the other replies, "God will forgive."

The healing that we experience through the sacrament of Confession takes the more specific form of *reconciliation*. This is stressed in several of the prayers of absolution: "Do not separate him [her] from Thy Holy, Catholic and Apostolic Church, but unite him [her] to the pure flock of Thy sheep" (Greek use); "Reconcile and unite him [her] to Thy Holy Church" (Russian use). Sin, as we learn from the parable of the prodigal son, is exile, alienation, exclusion from the family—more exactly, self-exclusion; in the words of Alexis Khomiakov, "When any one of us falls, he falls alone."[24] Repentance is to come back home, to return from isolation to fellowship, to be reintegrated in the family, to share once more in the life of the community.

---

23 There is in fact a variety of absolution prayers in the Greek *Euchologion*, the priest being left free to use one or more at his discretion.

24 "The Church is One," in Birkbeck (ed.), *Russia and the English Church*, 216. But, from a different viewpoint, there are of course no private sins; when we fall we always drag others down with us.

The gift of tears

The gift of tears, prominent in the contemporary charismatic movement, has also an important place in the spiritual tradition of the Christian East.[25] The "theology of tears" plays a particularly significant role in the teaching of St John Climacus, St Isaac the Syrian, and St Symeon the New Theologian. For Climacus, tears represent a renewal of the grace of Baptism:

> The fountain of tears after Baptism is greater than Baptism itself, although this may seem a bold thing to say... Our first Baptism we received as babies, but we have all polluted it; through tears we regain the purity of our first Baptism.[26]

St Isaac regards tears as the crucial boundary between the "bodily" and the "spiritual state," as the point of transition between the present age and the Age to come, which may be entered by anticipation even in this life. The newborn child weeps as it is born into the world; similarly, the Christian weeps as he is reborn into the age to come.[27] St Symeon insists that we should never receive Communion without shedding tears.[28] And according to Symeon's disciple, Nicetas Stethatos, tears can even restore lost virginity.[29]

What has this gift of tears to teach us about the meaning of repentance? There are many kinds of tears, and it is important to discriminate between them. The crucial distinction lies between sensual or natural tears and spiritual tears (there is also a third possibility: tears may be demonic). Sensual tears are emotional; spiritual tears are ascetic. In the case of sensual tears the face is often contorted and flushed, and the whole body may shake with uncontrollable sobbing; but in the case of spiritual weeping the tears flow

25 The basic modern study on the subject is still Irénée Hausherr, *Penthos. La doctrine de la componction dans l'Orient chrétien,* Orientalia Christiana Analecta 132 (Rome: Pont. Institutum Studiorum Orientalium, 1944); English translation, *Penthos. The Doctrine of Compunction in the Christian East,* Cistercian Studies Series 53 (Kalamazoo, MI: Cistercian Publications, 1982). See also M. Lot-Borodine, "Le mystère du don des larmes dans l'Orient chrétien," *La Vie Spirituelle* (supplement for September 1936), reprinted in Olivier Clément and others, *La douloureuse joie,* Spiritualité orientale 14 (Bégrolles: Abbaye de Bellefontaine, 1974), 131-95; Lev Gillet, "The Gift of Tears," *Sobornost* n.s. 12 (1937), 5-10; G. A. Maloney, *The Mystic of Fire and Light: St. Symeon the New Theologian* (Denville, NJ: Dimension Books, 1975), 129-37.

26 *Ladder* 7 (PG 88:804AB); tr. Luibheid and Russell, 137.

27 *Homilies* 14 and 35(37): tr. Wensinck, 85-86, 164-65; Miller, 82-83, 174-75. Quoted in Kallistos Ware, *The Orthodox Way* (revised edition, Crestwood, NY: St Vladimir's Seminary Press, 1995), 101.

28 *Discourse* 4: ed. Krivochéine, 1:314; tr. deCatanzaro, 70.

29 *Century* 2.50 (PG 120:924B); tr. *Philokalia,* 4:120-1.

gently and peacefully, without facial contortion or bodily shuddering. Sensual tears are usually bound up with the passions; they are often the result of anger, frustration, envy, self-pity, or simply nervous excitement. Spiritual tears, as their name indicates, are a gift of grace from God the Holy Spirit, not just the result of our own efforts, and they are closely linked to our prayer. Sensual tears express our earthly sadness, living as we do in a fallen world of corruption that is moving relentlessly towards death; spiritual tears lead us to the new life of the Resurrection.

It would be misleading, however, to make a radical and clear-cut division between these two types of tears. Natural or sensual tears may sometimes have a positive and purifying effect, as when we weep out of loving compassion for the suffering of others, or when we mourn for the dead.[30] Grace cooperates with nature and builds upon it; and so natural tears, when purged of sinful self-centeredness and of disordered emotionalism, can lead us to the threshold of spiritual weeping. Moreover, because grace often works within us in a secret and unnoticed manner, we ourselves may not always be aware whether our tears are natural or spiritual. To keep us in simplicity God may hide our spiritual progress from us, and it is not for us to measure ourselves. Nonetheless there is in principle an important distinction to be made between the levels of sensual and of grace-given weeping, even if in practice the two may sometimes overlap.

Spiritual tears, so the Fathers teach, are of two main types. On the lower level they are bitter; on the higher level, sweet. On the lower level they are a form of purification; on the higher level, of illumination. On the lower level they express contrition, sorrow for sin, grief at our separation from God—Adam lamenting outside the gates of Paradise;[31] on the higher level they express joy at God's love, thanksgiving at our undeserved restoration to sonship. The lower level is exemplified by the prodigal, still in exile, weeping for his lost homeland; the higher level, by the prodigal weeping for joy at the feast in the father's house. On the lower level tears are like "blood from the wounds in our soul," to use a phrase of St Greg-

30 On the value of tears shed for the departed and the danger of repressing our grief, see above, 32.

31 See the *kontakion* and *ikos* for the Sunday of Forgiveness (the Sunday before Lent), in *The Lenten Triodion*, 175; also the moving prose-poem by St Silouan, in Archimandrite Sophrony (Sakharov), *Saint Silouan the Athonite* (Tolleshunt Knights, Essex: Monastery of St John the Baptist, 1991), 448-56.

ory of Nyssa;[32] on the higher level, they signify the spiritualizing of the senses, and form an aspect of the total transfiguration of the human person by deifying grace.

Yet, as with the distinction between natural and spiritual weeping, so here with the two levels of spiritual tears, we must be on our guard against making too emphatic a contrast. The one level of spiritual tears leads gradually into the other. What begin as tears of sorrow for sin are changed by degrees into tears of gratitude and gladness. And so, in this gift of tears, we see illustrated yet again the point on which we have constantly insisted: that repentance is not negative but positive, not destructive but life-giving, not despondent but full of hope.

Sorrowful, yet always rejoicing

Such, then, is our experience of the "great understanding" or "change of mind" designated by the word repentance. Filled with grief yet at the same time filled with joy, repentance expresses the creative tension found at all times in the Christian life on this earth, and described with such vividness by St Paul: "...always carrying in our body the death of Jesus, so that the life of Jesus may also be manifested in our body...dying, and behold we live...sorrowful, yet always rejoicing" (2 Cor 4:10; 6:9-10). As a life of continual repentance, our Christian discipleship is a sharing at one and the same time in Gethsemane and the Transfiguration, in the Cross and the Resurrection. St John Climacus sums the matter up by saying: "If you put on blessed and grace-filled mourning as a wedding robe, you will know the spiritual laughter of the soul."[33]

---

32 *Funeral Oration on the Empress Flacilla:* ed. Spira, 477.
33 *Ladder* 7 (*PG* 88:809A); tr. Luibheid and Russell, 140.

4

THE THEOLOGY
OF WORSHIP

"The principal thing," states St Theophan the Recluse, "is to stand before God with the mind in the heart, and to go on standing before Him unceasingly day and night, until the end of life."[1]

In this concise yet far-seeing definition of worship, St Theophan underlines three things:

—first, the basic essence of worship: it is to *stand before God*;

—second, the faculties with which the human person offers worship: *with the mind in the heart*;

—third, the time when worship is appropriate: *unceasingly day and night, until the end of life*.

Stand before God

First, then, to worship or to pray is to stand before God. Note immediately the wideness of St Theophan's definition. To pray is not necessarily to ask God for something; it need not even be to employ words, for often the deepest and most powerful of all prayers is simply to wait upon God in silence. But whether we are worshiping with words, through symbolic and sacramental actions, or in silence, always our underlying attitude is the same: we are standing before God.

To stand before God: this implies that worship is an encounter, a meeting between persons. The purpose of worship is not just to arouse emotions and to produce appropriate moral attitudes, but to enter into a direct and personal relationship with God the Holy Trinity. "As a friend

---

1   Quoted in Igumen Chariton, *The Art of Prayer*, 63.

talking with his friend," writes St Symeon the New Theologian, "we speak with God, and with boldness we stand before the face of Him who dwells in light unapproachable."[2] Here St Symeon briefly indicates the two poles of Christian worship, the two contrasting aspects of this personal relationship: God "dwells in light unapproachable," yet we human beings are able to draw near "with boldness" and to speak with Him "as a friend talking with his friend." God is beyond all being, infinitely remote, unknowable, "the Wholly Other," the *mysterium tremendum et fascinans*. But this transcendent God is at the same time a God of personal love, uniquely close, around us and within us, "everywhere present and filling all things" (Orthodox prayer to the Holy Spirit).

In worship, then, the Christian stands before God with a double attitude, conscious of "the nearness yet otherness of the Eternal," to use the phrase of an Anglican writer who had a deep love for Orthodoxy, Evelyn Underhill.[3] As he or she prays, the worshiper feels both the mercy and the judgment of God, both His goodness and His severity (Ps 100 [101]:1; Rom 11:22). To the end of our earthly life we stand always between assurance and awe: in the words of St Amvrosy, Starets of Optino, "between hope and fear." This double attitude is strikingly apparent in the liturgical services of the Orthodox Church, which at their best succeed in combining the two qualities of mystery and informality: to quote Evelyn Underhill once more, "...so deeply sensible of the mystery of the Transcendent, yet so childlike in its confident approach."[4]

Again and again in the liturgical texts of the Christian East these contrasted feelings of hope and fear, of confidence and awe, are set side by side. The Holy Gifts are "the life-giving and terrible mysteries." Inviting the people to approach the chalice, the priest says: "With fear of God, with faith and love draw near"—fear and loving trust go hand in hand. In a precommunion prayer attributed to St Symeon the New Theologian, we use the words:

> Rejoicing at once and trembling,
> I who am straw receive the Fire
> And, strange wonder!

2   *Theological, Gnostic and Practical Chapters,* 2.9: ed. Darrouzès, 73-74; tr. McGuckin, 65.
3   *Worship* (London: Nisbet, 1936), 263.
4   *Worship,* 263.

I am ineffably refreshed
As the bush of old
Which burned yet was not consumed.

"Rejoicing at once and trembling": such precisely should be our attitude as we stand before God. Our worship should be marked by a vivid sense of reverence and compunction, for it is a dreadful thing to fall into the hands of the living God (Heb 10:31); and equally by a feeling of homeliness and affectionate simplicity, for this living God is our brother and our friend. As we worship, we are both slaves before the throne of the King of heaven, and children who are happy to be in their Father's house. The tears that we shed as we approach for communion are at once tears of penitence, as we consider our own unworthiness—"I who am straw"—and tears of joy, as we contemplate the merciful compassion of God. "Those who have tasted the gift of the Spirit," so the *Homilies* of Macarius insist, "are conscious of two things at the same time: on the one hand, of joy and consolation; on the other, of trembling and fear and mourning."[5] Both these feelings simultaneously should characterize our worship if we are to stand aright in the Divine presence.

With the mind in the heart

In the second place, to pray and worship is to stand before God with the mind in the heart. Here, however, care is necessary; for when St Theophan—and the Orthodox tradition in general—use these two words "mind" and "heart," they are employing them in a sense significantly different from that which is commonly attached to them in the contemporary West. By "mind" or "intellect" (in Greek, *nous*) is meant not only or primarily the reasoning brain, with its power of discursive argumentation, but also and much more fundamentally the power of apprehending religious truth through direct insight and contemplative vision. The reason is not to be repudiated or repressed, for it is a faculty conferred upon us by God; but it is not the chief or the highest faculty we possess, and there are many occasions in our worship when it is transcended.

Equal care is needed when interpreting the word "heart" (*kardia*). When St Theophan—and the Orthodox spiritual tradition in general—

5   *Homilies* (Collection B) 33.2.1: ed. Berthold, 2:29.

speak about the heart, they understand the word in its Semitic and Biblical sense, as signifying not just the emotions and affections but the primary center of our human personhood. The heart signifies the deep self;
it is the seat of wisdom and understanding, the place where our moral decisions are made, the inner shrine in which we experience divine grace
and the indwelling presence of the Holy Trinity. It indicates the human
person as a "spiritual subject," created in God's image and likeness.[6]

To speak, then, as St Theophan does, of standing before God "with
the mind in the heart," means that we are to worship Him with the totality of our human personhood. The rational faculties are in no way rejected, for we are rational creatures—what St Clement of Alexandria
termed "logical sheep"[7]—and therefore our worship should be *logike
latreia*, "reasonable worship" (Rom 12:1). Likewise, our emotions and
affections are not to be excluded from our worship, for they too are part of
our personhood. Our prayer should be animated by *eros*, intense and fer-
vent longing for the Divine, so that our worship becomes truly an expression of "erotic ecstasy," to use a phrase of St Maximus the Confessor.[8] But
logos and *eros*, reason, emotions and affections, are to be combined with
the other layers of our personality, and all of them are to be integrated
into a living unity, on the level of the deep self or the heart. Our experience of God, to cite Evelyn Underhill again, "spreads from the field of
consciousness to transform and bring into the total act of worship the
deep instinctive levels of the mind."[9] Our worship is to be all-embracing.

"With the mind in the heart." In this "total act of worship," then, we
are to stand before God with the entire person: with the conscious mind,

6   On the meaning of the terms "intellect" (*nous*) and "heart" (*kardia*), see the glossary in
    Philokalia, 1:361; also Kallistos Ware, "Prayer in Evagrius of Pontus and the Macarian
    Homilies," in Ralph Waller and Benedicta Ward (eds.), *An Introduction to Christian
    Spirituality* (London: SPCK, 1999), 14-30.

7   *Pedagogue*, Book 3, "Hymn to Christ the Savior," line 29. But the term *logikos*, when applied
    to the human person, should not be understood as referring exclusively to our rational
    faculties. It signifies all the spiritual powers within us that reflect the divine Logos, and, among
    other things, it includes the body; for when St Paul speaks of *logike latreia*, he is in fact
    referring directly to the body.

8   *First Century on Theology* 39; tr. *Philokalia*, 2:122. But our *eros* has also to be crucified: St
    Ignatius of Antioch, *To the Romans* 7 (a text that can be interpreted in several different ways:
    see Charles Williams, *The Descent of the Dove* [London: Faber, 1950], 46).

9   *Worship*, 249.

certainly, but also with the aspects of our inner self that reach out into the unconscious; with our instinctive feelings, with our aesthetic sense, and likewise with that faculty of intuitive understanding and of direct spiritual awareness which, as we have noted, far surpasses the discursive reason. All these have their part to play in our prayer; and so also has our physical and material constitution, our body. "The flesh is also transformed," writes St Gregory Palamas; "it is exalted with the soul, communes together with the soul in the Divine, and itself likewise becomes the possession and dwelling-place of God."[10]

How is this "total act" to be accomplished? In our worship we make use, in the first place, of words, and these words bear a literal meaning, grasped by the reasoning brain. But far more than the literal meaning of words is involved in the act of worship. Beyond and beneath their literal sense, particular syllables and phrases are rich in associations and undertones, and possess a hidden power and poetry of their own. Thus in our prayer we use words not just literally but beautifully; through poetic imagery—even if the texts are in rhythmic prose rather than rhymed stanzas—we endow the words with a new dimension of meaning. We worship, moreover, not through words only but in a wide variety of other ways: through music, through the splendor of the priestly vestments, through the color and lines of the holy icons, through the articulation of sacred space in the design of the church building, through symbolic gestures such as the sign of the cross, the offering of incense, or the lighting of a candle, and through the employment of all the great "archetypes," of all the basic constituents of human life, such as water, wine and bread, fire and oil.

In our literal use of words we reach the reasoning brain; by means of poetry and music, of art, symbol and ritual act, we reach the other layers of the human personality. The one aspect of worship is as essential as the other. If our words possess no literal meaning—or if we recite or sing them in such a way as to render the meaning unintelligible—then our worship will degenerate into magic and mumbo jumbo, and will be no longer worthy of logical sheep. If, on the other hand, our worship is exclusively through words, interpreted literally and rationally, it may be true

10 *Triads in Defense of the Holy Hesychasts*, 1.2.9: ed. Meyendorff 1:93; *Philokalia*, 4:339.

worship of the mind, but it will not yet be worship of the mind *in the heart*. It may be admirably clear, logical, and systematic, but it will fall short of being the prayer of the whole person. This is a point which liturgical reformers in the West during the 1960s and 1970s often failed keep in view. They undervalued the sense of mystery; for without the sense of mystery we are not truly human. Worship is more than a form of proclamation through the spoken word, and the liturgical assembly is more than a public meeting with speeches and announcements.

It is often claimed that the symbols and objects used in traditional Christian worship, and the style of beauty which it displays, have become outdated and irrelevant in the contemporary world. These symbols, so it is argued, are drawn from an agricultural way of life, and are in many instances no longer appropriate to an urban and industrial environment. Why should we worship God with a candle or a censer in our hand, and not with a stethoscope or a pneumatic drill? Are we not restricting our worship to one particular type of person, and excluding the rest? To this an Orthodox would reply that the acts and symbols which we employ in worship possess a universal significance. Although the Divine Liturgy has been influenced externally by the social and artistic conventions of particular eras—for example, by the ceremonial of the Byzantine court—yet in its inner essence it transcends these limitations and speaks to the fundamental condition of humankind, whether ancient or modern, eastern or western. The Orthodox Church in her prayer makes use of the primary realities of human existence, such as bread and water, light and fire. If people in an urban and technological environment no longer find these primary realities meaningful, then is this not a disturbing indictment of the artificiality and unreality of contemporary "civilization"? Perhaps what is needed is not a change in the symbols but a change in us, a cleansing of the doors of our perception.

In this connection, Orthodox may feel somewhat encouraged by the current western enthusiasm for icons. Surprising numbers of "modern" men and women, although they stand altogether outside any church membership and seem not at all interested in contemporary liturgical reforms, are yet intensely attracted by Orthodox icons. Let us not be too quick to dismiss this attraction as sentimental and superficial. Is it not a curious paradox that, in an age of technology and secularism, people should feel drawn to a form of art that is *par excellence* spiritual and theological? Would they feel drawn in the same way if the art of the icon was brought "up to date"?

To an Orthodox Christian it is of the utmost importance that the act of worship should express the joy and beauty of the Kingdom of heaven. Without the dimension of the beautiful our worship will never succeed in being prayer in the fullest sense, prayer of the heart as well as the reasoning brain. This joy and beauty of the Kingdom cannot be properly expounded in abstract arguments and logical explanations; it has to be *experienced*, not discussed. And it is above all through symbolic and ritual actions—through the burning of incense, through the lighting of a lamp or candle before an icon—that this living experience is rendered possible. These simple gestures express, far better than any words, our whole attitude towards God, all our love and adoration; and without such actions our worship would be grievously impoverished.

Why offer incense or burn candles? Why make prostrations or the sign of the Cross? If we attempt a verbal explanation, we know perfectly well that it embodies only a small part of the truth. And that, surely, is precisely the reason for the symbolic action. If the poet could express in plain prose what he has said in his poetry, if the artist or musician could express in words what she has said in paint or sound, then there would be no need for the poem or picture or symphony. Each exists because it expresses something which cannot be expressed in any other way. So it is in worship. If it were possible to say in words why we burn candles and incense, then we could rest content with the verbal explanation and forego the symbolic act altogether. The whole value of the symbol in worship is that it expresses something which cannot be said through the spoken word alone, that it reaches a part of our being which cannot be touched by rational arguments. The symbol is on the one hand simpler and more immediately accessible than a verbal explanation, and on the other hand it penetrates more deeply into the heart of reality.

On the purely pragmatic level all the beauty and symbolism in our worship is unnecessary and useless. We can use odor-destroying sprays instead of incense, neon lighting instead of candles. But the human being is not simply a pragmatic and utilitarian animal, and those who look more deeply into human nature will quickly appreciate how much we need this "useless" beauty. As Archpriest Alexander Schmemann has rightly said:

> The liturgy is, before everything else, the joyous gathering of those who are to meet the risen Lord and to enter with Him into the bridal chamber. And it is this joy of expectation and this expectation of joy that are expressed in singing and ritual, in vestments and in censing, in that whole "beauty" of the liturgy, which has so often been denounced as unnecessary and even sinful.

> Unnecessary it is indeed, for we are beyond the categories of the "necessary." Beauty is never "necessary," "functional" or "useful." And when, expecting someone whom we love, we put a beautiful tablecloth on the table and decorate it with candles and flowers, we do all this not out of necessity, but out of love. And the Church is love, expectation and joy. It is heaven on earth, according to our Orthodox tradition; it is the joy of recovered childhood, that free, unconditioned and disinterested joy which alone is capable of transforming the world. In our adult, serious piety we ask for definitions and justifications, and they are rooted in fear. Fear of corruption, deviation, "pagan influences," whatnot. But "he that feareth is not made perfect in love" (1 Jn 4:18). As long as Christians will love the Kingdom of God, and not only discuss it, they will "represent" it and signify it, in art and beauty. And the celebrant of the sacrament of joy will appear in a beautiful chasuble, because he is vested in the glory of the Kingdom, because even in the form of man God appears in glory. In the Eucharist we are standing in the presence of Christ, and like Moses before God, we are to be covered with His glory.[11]

"Beauty will save the world," said Dostoevsky. It is a primary function of worship to render manifest the saving power of this divine beauty. When the envoys of Prince Vladimir of Kiev were won over to the Orthodox faith, what converted them was not words, not logical arguments, but the beauty of the Holy Liturgy which they attended in Constantinople : "we cannot forget that beauty," they said when they returned home.[12] "Wherein does your prayer consist?" St John of the Cross asked one of his penitents; and she replied, "In considering the Beauty of God, and in rejoicing that He has such beauty."[13] Such is the nature of worship. To pray and to worship is to perceive the spiritual beauty of the heavenly Kingdom; to express that beauty alike through words, through poetry and mu-

---

11   A. Schmemann, *For the Life of the World: Sacraments and Orthodoxy* (Crestwood, NY: St Vladimir's Seminary Press, 1988), 29-30.

12   *The Russian Primary Chronicle*, tr. Cross and Sherbowitz-Wetzor, 111.

13   E. Underhill, *Worship*, 5.

sic, through art and symbolic acts, and through our whole lives; and in this way to extend the divine beauty in the world around us, transforming and transfiguring the fallen creation.

Unceasingly day and night

There remains the third point in St Theophan's definition: to worship is to stand before God unceasingly day and night, until the end of life. "Pray without ceasing," St Paul insisted (1 Thess 5:17). Prayer and worship should not be merely one activity among others, but *the* activity of our entire existence. Everything we do is done in God's sight: the attitude of standing before God, then, should not be restricted to specific times and places, to the occasions when we "say our prayers" at home or when we "go to church," but it should be an all-inclusive attitude, embracing every object and every moment. We should seek to make our whole being into a continuing act of worship, an uninterrupted doxology.

Nothing should be dismissed as irredeemably secular, as incapable of being turned into worship. "A Christian," Father Alexander Schmemann justly observes, "is the one who, wherever he looks, finds Christ, and rejoices in Him."[14] In the words of an ancient "Saying of Jesus," "Lift up the stone, and there you will find Me; cleave the wood, and I am there."[15] "Can you take too much Joy in your fathers Works?" asks Thomas Traherne. "He is Himself in evry Thing. som Things are little on the outside, and Rough and Common. but I remember the Time, when the Dust of the Streets were as precious as Gold to my Infant Eys, and now they are more precious to the Ey of Reason."[16] To worship is to see God in everything, to encompass the whole world and to offer it all back to God in joy.

Prayer and worship, then, continue "unceasingly day and night" in the sense that they are a part of our being, not something that we do or say or think, but something that we are. "Remember God more often than you breathe," says St Gregory of Nazianzus.[17] Prayer is more essential to us,

14 *For the Life of the World*, 113.

15 From the *Gospel of Thomas* (P. Oxy. 1), in J. K. Elliott, *The Apocryphal New Testament* (Oxford: Clarendon Press, 1993), 139-40.

16 *The Centuries* 1.25: ed. H. M. Margoliouth, *Thomas Traherne: Centuries, Poems, and Thanksgivings* (Oxford: Clarendon Press, 1958), 1:13-14.

17 *Oration* 27.4 (*Theological Oration* 1.4) (PG 36:16B).

more an integral part of ourselves, than the rhythm of our breathing or the beating of our heart. We were created to pray. Prayer is our true nature, and everything is to be turned into prayer. "In the immense cathedral which is the universe of God," writes Paul Evdokimov, "every person, whether scholar or manual laborer, is called to act as the priest of his or her whole life—to take all that is human, and to turn it into an offering and a hymn of glory."[18] And elsewhere the same author remarks: "In the catacombs, the most frequent image is the figure of a woman in prayer, the *Orans*; she represents the one true attitude of the human soul. It is not enough to *say* prayers: we must become, *be* prayer, prayer incarnate. It is not enough to have moments of praise. All of life, each act, every gesture, even the smile of the human face, must become a hymn of adoration, an offering, a prayer. One should offer not what one has but what one is."[19]

18 "Le sacerdoce universel des laïcs dans la tradition orientale," in L. A. Elchinger (ed.), *L'Église en dialogue* (Paris, 1962), 39-40.
19 *The Sacrament of Love. The Nuptial Mystery in the Light of the Orthodox Tradition* (Crestwood, NY: St Vladimir's Seminary Press, 1985), 62.

5

A SENSE OF WONDER[1]

O Lord, how manifold are Thy works!
In wisdom hast Thou made them all;
the earth is full of Thy riches.

Psalm 103 [104]:24

The beginning of philosophy is to feel a sense of wonder.

Plato, *Theaetetus*

There is a service, striking in its symbolism, that members of the Orthodox Church perform at the start or conclusion of any major task or period; on the first day of the month, for example, or at the blessing of a foundation stone, and equally at the commencement or ending of the academic year. It is the ceremony known as the Great Blessing of the Waters. Water is placed in a large bowl, prayers are said over it, the grace and power of the Holy Spirit is called down upon it, and finally the cross is plunged into the water.

This service of blessing is performed above all on January 6, the Feast of Theophany or Epiphany. On this day the Orthodox Church is commemorating, not the three wise men—whose coming has already been remembered on December 25—but the Baptism of Christ in the Jordan. The blessing is often held in the open air, by a river or spring or on the seashore. I can vividly recall the occasions when I have taken part in the Epiphany Blessing of the Waters on the island of Patmos. The abbot of the Monastery of St John the Theologian—the monastery to which I myself belong—comes down with the monks and parish clergy to the harbor and the service is performed at the quayside, with the fishing boats, some

---

1   This text was originally given as a sermon at commemoration services in All Souls College, Oxford (November 6, 1988), and in Malvern College (July 1, 1989). In its original form it dealt with the meaning of education from a Christian viewpoint. But, since the "sense of wonder" to which it refers is equally a central element in our prayer and worship, I have ventured to include it here in a slightly modified version.

thirty or forty of them, drawn up in a great semicircle. At the culminating moment, when the abbot throws a wooden cross into the water, all the surrounding boats sound their sirens simultaneously, and the young men and boys dive from the boats, racing each other to see who will be the first to retrieve the cross and return it to the abbot.[2]

In an unexpected way this ceremony of the Great Blessing of the Waters helps us to understand the purpose, from a Christian standpoint, of a college or university, and also more broadly the true meaning of Christian worship. Christ's Baptism is seen in the Orthodox tradition as possessing a cosmic significance, as embracing the whole created order. His Baptism is in a sense the reverse of our own. In our case, Baptism is a purification from sin. But Christ is sinless; why, then, should He be baptized? Such precisely is the query posed by St John the Baptist: "I need to be baptized by You, and do *You* come to me?" (Mt 3:14). The Orthodox answer to this question can best be put in simple picture language. We are dirty; at Baptism we go down into clean water and we come out cleansed. At our Baptism, then, we are sanctified by the waters. But Christ is clean; at His Baptism He goes down into the dirty water and Himself cleanses the waters, making them pure. As we affirm in the liturgical texts for the feast of Epiphany, "Today the Master has come to sanctify the nature of the waters."[3] At His Baptism it is not the waters that sanctify Christ, but Christ who imparts holiness to the waters, and so by extension to the entire material creation.

If we speak of the waters as "dirty," by this we mean that the world around us, while filled with meaning and beauty, is yet a fallen world, broken and shattered, marred by suffering and sinfulness. Into this fallen world God Himself enters, accepting a total solidarity with it, assuming into Himself the entirety of our human nature, body, soul and spirit. Through this act of assumption at His Incarnation and through all that follows after it—through His Baptism in the streams of Jordan, His Transfiguration, Crucifixion and Resurrection—Christ cleanses and heals the marred and fallen world, effecting the renewal not of humankind alone but of the whole creation.

2   For the full text of the Great Blessing at Theophany, see Mother Mary and Archimandrite Kallistos Ware, *The Festal Menaion* (London: Faber, 1969), 348-59.

3   *op. cit.*, 381.

What we are doing, then, at each celebration of Epiphany, at every Blessing of the Waters, is to reaffirm our sense of wonder before the essential goodness and beauty of the world, as originally created by God and as now recreated in Christ. Nothing is intrinsically ugly or despicable; it is solely our distorted vision that makes it seem so. Through the power of God incarnate shown in His Baptism in the Jordan, all persons and all things can be made holy, can be transfigured and rendered Spirit-bearing. All things are capable of acting as sacraments of God's presence. As we express it in one of our Epiphany hymns:

> At Thine appearing in the body,
> The earth was sanctified,
> The water blessed,
> The heaven illumined,
> And humankind delivered
> From the bitter tyranny of the enemy.[4]

Water, earth, sky, the human body and the whole human person with its emotions and affections—through Christ's Incarnation and Baptism these are all reborn, transformed, hallowed. The Great Blessing of the Waters is in this way a proclamation that the universe around us is not a chaos but a cosmos. There is glory in everything; this is a world full of wonder.

Now this is vitally important if we are to understand the full dimensions of Christian worship; it also helps us more specifically to understand the purpose of Christian education. The word "education" comes from the Latin *educere*, "to evoke;" and so a school or university is precisely a place in which with rigor and discipline we evoke and cultivate a sense of wonder. As teachers and students we are here in order to pursue truth and knowledge; but truth and knowledge, as Plato recognized, are impossible without a sense of wonder: "The beginning of philosophy is to feel a sense of wonder."[5] A university, then, is a structured environment in which we are to develop our sense of wonder before the universe that God has made, before the human person whose vocation it is to serve as microcosm and mediator at the center of that universe, before all that is con-

---

4   *op. cit.*, 298.
5   Plato, *Theaetetus* 155D; cf. Aristotle, *Metaphysics* 1.2.15 (982b12). Plato's statement is quoted by Clement of Alexandria, *Miscellanies* 2.9: ed. Stählin, 137.1-2.

ceived by the human mind or fashioned by human hands. It is a place where we are to discover how varied and unexpected is the world in which we live. It is a place where we "lift up our eyes to the hills" (cf. Ps. 120 [121]:1), acknowledging with astonishment the broadness and generosity of our surroundings. It is a place where we are saying explicitly or implicitly, "O Lord, how manifold are Thy works! In wisdom hast Thou made them all." All this is equally applicable to each of our acts of worship.

Plato's insistence upon the link between wonder and truth is confirmed by the seventeenth-century poet Sidney Godolphin:

> Lord when the wise men came from farr,
> Led to thy Cradle by a Starr,
> Then did the shepheards too rejoyce,
> Instructed by thy Angells voyce:
> Blest were the wisemen in their skill,
> And shepheards in their harmlesse will...
>
> There is no merrit in the wise
> But love, (the shepheards sacrifice).
> Wisemen all wayes of knowledge past,
> To th' shepheards wonder come at last:
> To know, can only wonder breede,
> And not to know, is wonders seede.[6]

"To know, can only wonder breede": the "wisemen" at our modern universities cannot afford to dispense with the wonder of the shepherds. For knowledge and wonder go hand in hand.

Some months ago I had a dream. I was back at the boarding school where I studied over half a century ago. A friend took me first through rooms already familiar to me in my waking life. But then in my dream we entered other rooms that I had never seen before—spacious, elegant, filled with light. Finally we entered a small, dark chapel, with mosaics gleaming in candlelight. "How strange," I said to my companion, "that I have lived here for years, and yet I never knew about the existence of all these rooms." And he replied, "But it is always so."

Such exactly is the aim of all authentic worship, and it is the aim equally of every school or college. A college is a place where we constantly discover new rooms in the universe and in the human heart, in both mac-

6   Helen Gardner (ed.), *The Metaphysical Poets* (Harmondsworth: Penguin Books, 1957), 182.

rocosm and microcosm; a place where we open the door to each other and invite one another to explore these rooms together.

There is also a second, connected aspect to the Christian meaning of a college or school. As a place for the cultivation of wonder and the pursuit of truth, it is equally a place for the cultivation of freedom. Wonder and freedom, truth and freedom—these things are essentially linked. Wonder can be evoked but not compelled; and truth, as Christ observed, makes us free (Jn 8:32). In any university it is our task to bear witness to the value of freedom, and to resist all that erodes or diminishes our liberty. If I am asked by my students at Oxford, "What are you trying to teach us here?" then perhaps my best answer is to say no more than this: "We want you to learn to be free."

"Learn to be free": freedom cannot simply be assumed; it has to be *learnt*. Suppose that you ask me, "Can you play the violin?" and I reply, "I don't know, I've never tried." You might feel that there was something odd about my answer. Unless I have learnt to play the violin through the exacting discipline of a musical training, I am not free to play Beethoven's violin sonatas. And so it is with every form of freedom. Freedom has to be learnt through the *ascesis*, the ascetic discipline, of precise observation and imaginative thinking; and then it needs to be defended with courage and self-sacrifice. As Nicolas Berdyaev observed, "Freedom gives birth to suffering, while the refusal to be free diminishes suffering. Freedom is not easy, as its enemies and slanderers allege: freedom is hard; it is a heavy burden. Men, as Dostoevsky has shown with such amazing power, often renounce freedom to ease their lot."[7] Yet if we renounce freedom, we become less than truly human; and if we deny others their freedom, we dehumanize them.

Freedom is not easy, and this means that in a university we are not offering either to ourselves or to others an easy path. We are never to forget that culminating moment in the Great Blessing at Epiphany. The cross has to be plunged into the waters. There is no other way of transfiguration. It can come about only through repentance, *metanoia*, a radical change of mind; and that means through the creative suffering of the Cross.

---

7   *Dream and Reality: An Essay in Autobiography* (London: Geoffrey Bles, 1950), 47. Compare the Tale of the Grand Inquisitor in Dostoevsky's *The Brothers Karamazov*.

Such, in part, is the Christian meaning of a college or school. As a place for the cultivation of wonder, its vocation is summed up in words attributed to Christ in the Gospel according to Thomas: "Let him who seeks not cease seeking until he finds and, when he finds, he will become troubled. When he is troubled, he will marvel and he will reign over the All."[8] As a place for learning freedom, its role is well expressed in a Jewish saying recorded by Martin Buber in his *Tales of the Hasidim*. Rabbi Shelomo asked: "What is the worst thing the evil urge can achieve?" And he answered: "To make us forget that we are each the child of a king."[9]

---

8   From the Gospel of Thomas, in Elliott, *The Apocryphal New Testament*, 135-36.
9   *Tales of the Hasidim: The Early Masters* (New York: Schocken Books, 1968), 282.

6

PRAY WITHOUT CEASING:
THE IDEAL OF CONTINUAL PRAYER IN
EASTERN MONASTICISM

The literal interpretation

"Pray without ceasing" (1 Thess 5:17): the short but emphatic command of St Paul to the Thessalonians has exercised a decisive influence upon the spirit of Eastern Orthodox monasticism.[1] From the fourth century onwards, the idea has been firmly established in the monastic tradition of the East that prayer is not merely an activity restricted to certain moments of the day, but something that should continue uninterrupted throughout the entire life of a monk or nun. The point is briefly expressed in one of the *Sayings of the Desert Fathers*: "A monk who prays only when he stands up for prayer is not really praying at all."[2] With the same idea in mind a Palestinian monk of the seventh century, Antiochus of the Monastery of St Sabas, alludes to the words of Ecclesiastes 3:1-7: "To every thing there is a season, and a time to every purpose under the heaven: a time to be born, and a time to die...a time to weep, and a time to laugh...a time to keep silence, and a time to speak." And Antiochus comments, "There is a proper time for everything except prayer: as for prayer, its proper time is always."[3]

---

1   The best discussion of the subject, to which I am much indebted, is still Irénée Hausherr, *Noms du Christ et voies d'oraison*, Orientalia Christiana Analecta 157 (Rome: Pont. Institutum Orientalium Studiorum, 1960), especially 123-75; English translation, *The Name of Jesus*, Cistercian Studies Series 44 (Kalamazoo, MI: Cistercian Publications, 1978), especially 119-89. For a briefer treatment, see Igumen Chariton, *The Art of Prayer*, especially 80-88.

2   *AP*, anonymous collection 104: ed. Nau, *ROC* 12 (1907), 402.

3   *Pandect*, Homily 91 (*PG* 89:1712B).

"Pray without ceasing": but how in practice is such a command to be carried out? One type of answer was proposed by the Messalians, an ascetic movement widespread in Syria and elsewhere in the Near East during the late fourth and the fifth centuries. The title "Messalian"—in Greek, "Euchite"—means precisely "one who prays"; and the Messalians (so at any rate their critics alleged) interpreted St Paul's injunction with uncompromising literalness. For them, prayer seems to have meant essentially vocal prayer. They envisaged "praying" as a conscious and deliberate activity which excludes all other activities: "to pray" is "to say prayers." On Messalian principles, if people are to pray without ceasing it is impossible for them to undertake work of any kind, whether manual or intellectual. They will not garden, cook, wash up, clean their room, or answer letters. They will simply pray, and do nothing else. The Messalian movement therefore contained a spiritual elite, "praying ones," men and women whose sole activity was prayer, and whose material needs were provided by the ordinary believers.[4]

Such an understanding, or rather misunderstanding, of continual prayer was quickly and vigorously condemned by the Church at large, for easily intelligible reasons. The Messalian answer, or what others have taken to be the Messalian answer, is objectionable both socially and spiritually. From the social point of view, it makes the monastic life entirely parasitic, dependent on the charity of others. Against this the mainstream monastic tradition has always insisted that the monk, whether solitary or in community, should under normal circumstances be self-supporting; and not only self-supporting, but a support to others. Admittedly, monastic life in the Christian East has on the whole been less concerned than in the West with organized "active" works—with maintaining schools, hos-

4   What is said in the above paragraph reflects the view of the Messalians adopted by their opponents, but it may be doubted whether the Messalians themselves would have expressed their standpoint in such an extreme fashion. It is in fact difficult to determine exactly what the Messalians believed, and recent studies suggest that they were by no means as "heretical" as they have usually been depicted. For the purposes of the present discussion, I have adoped the conventional view of Messalianism, using it as a "limiting case," so as to identify and then set aside one particular way of understanding continual prayer (whether or not the Messalians themselves actually adopted this view). For a full discussion of the ancient evidence, together with an assessment of the relationship between Messalianism and the *Spiritual Homilies* attributed to Macarius, see Columba Stewart, *"Working the Earth of the Heart": The Messalian Controversy in History, Texts, and Language to* AD 431 (Oxford: Clarendon Press, 1991).

pitals, and orphanages;[5] but on a less organized and more personal level Eastern monks have been sharply conscious of an obligation to their "neighbor" in the world, an obligation not merely in spiritual but in material things. Again and again, and not least in early texts from the Desert Fathers, it is insisted that the monk must work with his hands, so as to provide both for himself and for those in need: for the poor and the sick, for the widows and orphans. "Blessed are the merciful: for they shall obtain mercy" (Mt 5:7). These are words that apply to all Christians.

If the Messalian approach is objectionable socially, it is also objectionable from the viewpoint of a monk's own spiritual life. There are few, if any, who are capable of doing nothing but say prayers, without any kind of variety in their outward activities. The very first story in the *Sayings of the Desert Fathers* insists clearly upon this need for balance and diversity in the program of a monk's daily life, for an ordered succession of different tasks:

> The holy Abba Antony, as he once sat in the desert, fell into discouragement [*acedia*] and a great darkening of thoughts, and he said to God: "Lord, I wish to be saved, but my thoughts do not allow me: what shall I do in my distress? How shall I be saved?" And rising up and going a little way outside his cell, Antony saw someone who looked exactly like himself, sitting down and working, and then standing up from the work and praying, and then sitting down again and plaiting a length of rope, then standing up once more for prayer. It was the angel of the Lord, sent to correct Antony and to keep him safe. And he heard the angel saying: "Do thus and you will be saved." When he heard this, he was filled with great joy and confidence; and he did as the angel had told him and he was saved.[6]

Another story told of Antony develops the same idea. No one can remain without interruption on the heights of spiritual experience; the tension must sometimes be relaxed:

> A hunter, wandering through the desert, came upon Abba Antony while he was making jokes with the brethren; and he was shocked. Wishing to teach the hunter that it is necessary sometimes to relax with the brethren, the old man

5 There are, however, some notable exceptions here. In the fourth century, for example, St Basil the Great founded an ambitious center for charitable work, the *Basileiados*, so vast that it was termed "the new city," and this was administered largely by monastics, both male and female. See Philip Rousseau, *Basil of Caesarea* (Berkeley/Los Angeles/Oxford: University of California Press, 1994), 139-44, 203-9; Peter Brown, *The Body and Society: Men, Women and Sexual Renunciation in Early Christianity* (New York: Columbia University Press, 1989), 289-91.

6 *AP*, alphabetical collection, Antony 1 (*PG* 65:76A); tr. Ward, *Sayings*, 1-2.

said to him: "Put an arrow in your bow and bend it." The hunter did so. "Bend it a little more," said Antony. The hunter obeyed. "And still more," Antony told him. "But if I draw the string too tight," said the hunter, "the bow will snap." And the old man said to him: "It is the same in the work of God. If in the case of the brethren we draw the string too tight, they will snap under the strain. So it is necessary sometimes to relax with them." When the hunter heard this, he was filled with compunction, and profiting much from what the old man had said, he went his way. And the brethren, greatly strengthened, departed to their own place.[7]

Lacking St Antony's discretion, the Messalians drew the string too tight. Their ideal of prayer, to the exclusion of all else, was more likely to lead to insanity than to sanctity.

The answer of Abba Lucius

A third objection to the Messalian interpretation of 1 Thess 5:17 is that it renders St Paul's command impossible to fulfil. Assuming that "to pray" means "to say prayers," then even if someone says prayers at every moment of his waking life, there soon comes a time when he must sleep, however briefly: and then what becomes of his attempt to "pray without ceasing"? This is precisely the objection made to the Messalians by Abba Lucius, who at the same time suggests another and far more promising approach to the question of continual prayer. Notice how Lucius, like so many of the Desert Fathers, is mindful of the poor:

> There came to Abba Lucius in Ennaton certain monks of the kind called Euchites; and the old man asked them, "What kind of handiwork do you do?" They replied, "We touch no kind of handiwork, but following the Apostle's words, we pray without ceasing." And the old man said to them, "So you do not eat?" They said, "Yes, we eat." And he said, "Now while you are eating, who prays for you?" Then he asked them again, "You do not sleep?" And they said, "Yes, we do sleep." The old man said, "And while you sleep, who prays for you?" And they could find no answer to this. And he said to them, "Forgive me, but see, you fail to do as you say. But I will show you how I work with my hands and at the same time pray without ceasing. For with God's aid I sit steeping my few palm leaves, and from them I weave a rope; and all the time I say, 'Have mercy upon me, O God, according to Thy great mercy, and according to the multitude of Thy mercies, blot out my transgression'" (Ps 50 [51]:1). And he said to them: "Is not this a prayer?" And they said, "Yes, it is."

7   *AP*, alphabetical collection, Antony 13 (77D); tr. Ward, *Sayings*, 3-4.

And he said, "So I continue all day working and praying, and in this way I earn more or less sixteen pence; and out of them I leave two at the door, and I spend the rest on food. Whoever finds the two pennies prays for me while I am eating and sleeping; and thus by the grace of God there is fulfilled in me the command, 'Pray without ceasing.'"[8]

Such is Lucius' solution: continual prayer offered by collaboration. The same solution was adopted, in a more highly developed form, by the celebrated monastery of the *Akoimetai* or "sleepless ones" at Constantinople. Here the monks performed the office on a "shift" system: as soon as one group finished, the worship was taken up by the next, so that unceasingly throughout the twenty-four hours prayer was offered by at any rate part of the community.

Lucius' notion of prayer by collaboration, for all its apparent naiveté, underlines a point of crucial significance. Prayer is not an individual but essentially a corporate activity: we pray always as members one of another in the Body of Christ. Even the hermit in the most remote corner of the desert never stands before God alone, but always as one of a great family. All the rest of the Church prays in and with him, and when he cannot pray, the prayer of others still continues. "The monk," said Evagrius of Pontus, "is one who is separated from all *and united with all*."[9]

There is also another and yet more interesting point that emerges from Abba Lucius' response to the Messalians. For him, prayer does not exclude manual labor. Unlike the Messalians, he prays as he works, using a very short formula of prayer that is constantly repeated. In this way his time of prayer is not restricted simply to the moments when "he stands up to pray," but he is enabled to "retain" his prayer while he is fulfilling his rule of work.

Lucius' prayer from Psalm 50 is but one among many possible formulae for constant repetition. St John Cassian, who received his monastic training in Egypt, recommended another verse from the Psalms, "O God, make speed to save me; O Lord, make haste to help me" (Ps 69 [70]:1).[10]

---

8 *AP*, alphabetical collection, Lucius 1 (253B); tr. Ward, *Sayings*, 120-21.

9 *On prayer* 124 (*PG* 79:1193C); tr. *Philokalia*, 1:69. The word used here for " monk," *monachos*, carries more specifically the sense of "solitary." For the way in which the hermit prays always with the total Church, see Peter Damian, *The Book which is called "The Lord be with you"* (*PL* 145:231-52).

10 *Conferences* 10.10.

Abba Apollo, guilty in earlier life of a particularly appalling sin, used like Lucius a penitential phrase, "As a man I have sinned; as God, be merciful."[11] On occasion the formula could be even simpler. St Macarius of Egypt teaches:

> There is no need for much speaking; but stretch out your hands and say, "Lord, as You wish and as You know best, have mercy upon me." And if the warfare grows fierce, say "Lord, help." And He knows what is best for us and is merciful to us.[12]

But among all the short formulae designed for constant repetition, the one richest in meaning and most commonly employed over the centuries is undoubtedly the Jesus Prayer, "Lord Jesus Christ, Son of God, have mercy on me." In modern Orthodox practice the words "a sinner" are often added.[13]

Here, then, is a way to fulfil the command "Pray without ceasing" while avoiding the extremes of Messalianism. Prayer can be combined with work. The monk chooses a short phrase—the Jesus Prayer or some other, according to his own wish and the guidance of his spiritual father—and this he attempts to recite wherever he goes and whatever he does. (Or perhaps, if his spiritual father so directs, he recites it only for specified periods.) In this way he seeks to carry his prayer with him throughout his daily tasks, dwelling in two realms at once, the outer and the inner. As St Theophan the Recluse puts it, "The hands at work, the mind and heart with God."[14]

The monk has therefore two kinds of "activity": his visible work, manual or intellectual, which of course he must perform as well as he possibly can to the glory of God; and beyond this, his "inner activity." "A person," said the Desert Fathers, "should always have activity within him."[15] This "inner activity" is also termed "hidden meditation," or quite simply "the

---

11 *AP*, alphabetical collection, Apollo 2 (136A); tr. Ward, *Sayings*, 36. But Apollo seems to approach dangerously close to the Messalian standpoint, for the account in the *apophthegmata* adds: "He did no handiwork, but prayed always."

12 *AP*, alphabetical collection, Macarius the Great 19 (269C); tr. Ward, *Sayings*, 131.

13 For a short history of the Jesus Prayer, with further bibliography, see A Monk of the Eastern Church (Archimandrite Lev Gillet), *The Jesus Prayer*, new edition revised by Kallistos Ware (Crestwood, NY: St Vladimir's Seminary Press, 1987).

14 Igumen Chariton, *The Art of Prayer*, 92.

15 *AP*, anonymous collection 241: ed. Nau, *ROC* 14 (1909), 363; tr. Ward, *Wisdom*, §108 (33).

remembrance of God" (*mnene Theou*). In the words of the Macarian Homilies:

> Christians ought at all times to preserve the remembrance of God...in order that they may show love to the Lord not only when they go into the place of prayer, but that also when they are walking, talking, or eating, they may preserve the remembrance of God, and a sense of love and yearning towards Him.[16]

Such ideas as these obviously are in no sense exclusive to the Christian East. A western example that springs readily to mind is Brother Lawrence with his "Practice of the Presence of God" in the midst of his duties in the kitchen.

Continual prayer as an implicit state

Our answer to the Messalians, however, is not yet entirely complete. Abba Lucius rightly perceives that it is possible to work and to pray at the same time; what is more, he suggests a practical method whereby this double activity may be maintained—the constant repetition of a very short and simple prayer. But his understanding of the nature of prayer as such is unduly restricted. He still thinks essentially in terms of vocal prayer: for him, as for the Messalians, "to pray" means "to say prayers." Against this it may be urged—and we come here to the true solution of the problem of continual prayer—that prayer, properly understood, is in the deepest sense not so much an activity as a state. To be in a state of continual prayer, it is not necessary to recite an unending series of prayers; for there is such a thing as implicit continual prayer. Certainly, the constant repetition of a short formula, such as Lucius recommends, is an excellent way of seeking to attain this implicit state. But there may come a point when the state of prayer continues even though the repetition does not; when the formula, instead of being something that we have continually to say, has somehow passed into the very fiber of our being, so that even when it is not said it is still always there. In this sense, then, there are people who pray even when they are asleep; for they pray, not primarily by virtue of anything they say or think, but rather by virtue of what they

---

16 *Homily* 43:3: ed. Dörries, 286; tr. Maloney, 220. How far the Macarian *Homilies* are Messalian in inspiration remains a much debated question. Here, at any rate, the *Homilies* clearly dissociate themselves from what is supposed to be the extreme Messalian view.

are. And in so far as they "are" this thing continually, they may be said to have attained, in the fullest possible sense, continual prayer.

St Basil the Great suggests ideas such as these in his *Homily on the Martyr Julitta*:

> Prayer is a request for what is good, offered by the devout to God. But we do not restrict this "request" simply to what is stated in words... We should not express our prayer merely in syllables, but the power of prayer should be expressed in the moral attitude of our soul and in the virtuous actions that extend throughout our life... This is how you pray continually—not by offering prayer in words, but by joining yourself to God through your whole way of life, so that your life becomes one continuous and uninterrupted prayer.[17]

"We should not express our prayer merely in syllables...": but manifestly it is with prayer in syllables that we must all begin. In the standard spiritual teaching of the Orthodox Church, prayer is usually divided into three broad stages:

of the lips
of the mind or intellect (*nous*)
of the heart (or, more exactly, of the mind in the heart)

Our prayer, constantly repeated—let us suppose it is the first verse of Psalm 50, as with Abba Lucius, or alternatively the Jesus Prayer—begins as a prayer of the lips, recited with conscious effort. At such a stage, again and again our attention wanders away; and again and again, firmly but without violence, it has to be brought back to the meaning of what we recite. Then by degrees the prayer grows increasingly inward: it becomes something offered by the mind as well as the lips—perhaps by the mind alone, without any physical framing of words by the mouth. Then there comes a further stage—the prayer descends from the mind into the heart; mind and heart are united in the act of prayer.

By the "heart," in this context, as we have already seen,[18] is meant not simply the seat of the emotions and affections but, as in the Bible, the primary organ of our human personhood, the center of our whole being. When our prayer becomes, in the fullest sense, "prayer of the heart," we have already approached the threshold of unceasing prayer, of that "im-

17 *Homily on the Martyr Julitta* 3-4 (*PG* 31:244A, 244D).
18 See above, 61-62.

plicit" continual prayer mentioned earlier. True prayer of the heart is no longer just something that we recite, but it is part of ourselves, just as the drawing of breath or the beating of our heart is part of ourselves. And so by God's grace the prayer comes to be, no longer something that a person has to say, but something that says itself within him: in St Theophan the Recluse's terminology, it ceases to be "strenuous" and becomes "self-impelled." The prayer that began as an occasional activity is now an unceasing state—what Thomas of Celano meant when he said of St Francis of Assisi, *totus non tam orans quam oratio factus:* "in his whole being he was not so much a person who said prayers, as himself transformed into prayer."[19]

For St Isaac the Syrian, this unceasing prayer of the heart is not so much "our" prayer as the prayer of the Holy Spirit within us:

> *The disciple.* What is the culmination of all the labors of asceticism, which a person, on reaching, recognizes as the summit of his course?
>
> *The teacher.* This happens when he is counted worthy of continual prayer. When he has reached this point, he has attained the end at which all the virtues aim, and henceforth he possesses a dwelling-place in the Spirit. If a person has not received in all certainty the gift of the Comforter, it is not possible for him to accomplish unceasing prayer in quiet. When the Spirit makes Its dwelling-place in someone, he does not cease to pray, because the Spirit will constantly pray in him. Then, neither when he sleeps nor when he is awake, will prayer be cut off from his soul; but when he eats and when he drinks, when he lies down or when he does any work, even when he is immersed in sleep, the perfumes of prayer will breathe in his heart spontaneously. From this point onwards he will not possess prayer at limited times, but always; and when he has outward rest, even then prayer is ministered to him secretly. For as a man clad in Christ has said, the silence of the serene is prayer, for their very thoughts are divine impulses. The motions of the pure mind are quiet voices, secretly chanting psalms to Him who is invisible.[20]

The silence of the serene is prayer: even the silence of the saints, their repose and inactivity, is in itself a prayer to God, for their prayer has become an essential part of themselves.

Such is the meaning which the spiritual tradition of Orthodoxy has come to attach to St Paul's words, "Pray without ceasing." It must not for

19 *Legend* 2.61.
20 *Homily* 35(37): tr. Wensinck, 174; tr. Miller, 182.

one moment be imagined that the state here described by St Isaac is easily or frequently attained. Indeed, as his words make abundantly plain, it is not something acquired by our own efforts, but it is a gift from God: and as such He confers it when He will and on whom He will, without regard to any rules or principles that we may choose to frame.

Sometimes, it is true, this continual prayer—prayer of the mind in the heart—may be granted comparatively quickly. St Silouan of Mount Athos had only been practicing the Jesus Prayer for three weeks when it descended into his heart and became unceasing:[21] but this is altogether exceptional. Father Agapy, one of the *startsi* (spiritual elders) of Valamo, also conveys the impression that prayer of the mind in the heart may be gained with relative rapidity:

> Of three people known to me, it entered into one as soon as he was told about it, in that same hour; to another it came in six months' time; to a third after ten months, while in the case of one great *starets* it came only after two years. Why this happens so, God alone knows.[22]

The Way of a Pilgrim likewise suggests that such prayer is acquired in a comparatively short time, almost mechanically and automatically.

Now certainly this may happen in some instances. But it needs to be said with great emphasis that this is not invariably or even normally the case. On the contrary, there are men and women of deeply spiritual life who have prayed the Jesus Prayer humbly and faithfully for many years, and yet have never been granted the grace of continual prayer. I recall a conversation in January 1963 with a Russian monk now dead, Father Antony, at the Monastery of St Sabas near Jerusalem. He told me that he was acquainted personally with a number of monks in the Judaean wilderness who had prayed earnestly to receive this gift; and he assured me that to not one of them had it been granted. Perhaps, he added, it was not God's will for our present generation that this particular gift should be conferred. Although he did not refer directly to himself, I imagine that he was one of those who had so prayed. And he was a true monk, of deep understanding, endowed with the powers of a *starets*.

In this connection St Isaac sounds a salutary note of warning:

21 Archimandrite Sofrony (Sakharov), *Saint Silouan the Athonite*, 23.
22 Quoted in Igumen Chariton, *The Art of Prayer*, 277.

As among ten thousand there is scarcely to be found a single one who has fulfilled the commandments and the Law to any great extent and who has been counted worthy of serenity of soul, so there is rarely to be found one among many who, on account of his strenuous vigilance, has been counted worthy to attain pure prayer... Not many are counted worthy of pure prayer, only a very few. But as for the mystery that lies beyond pure prayer, there is scarcely to be found a single person in each generation who has drawn near to this knowledge of God's grace.[23]

Yet such words should not wholly discourage us. It may be true that during this present life only a very few reach the upper slopes of the mountain—one in ten thousand, one in a generation—but the path of ascent lies open to all, and everyone may advance at any rate some distance along it. There is no privileged elite which alone is called. No one whatsoever is necessarily excluded.

No one is necessarily excluded. While we have been speaking so far primarily in terms of the monastic tradition, the way of prayer here described is in no sense limited exclusively to monks and nuns. In the words of St Nicodemus of the Holy Mountain:

Let no one think, my fellow Christians, that only priests and monks need to pray without ceasing, and not laypeople. No, no: every Christian without exception ought to dwell always in prayer. Gregory the Theologian teaches all Christians that the Name of God must be remembered in prayer as often as one draws breath...

When the Apostle commanded us, "Pray without ceasing," he meant that we must pray inwardly with our intellect: and this is something that we can always do. For when we are engaged in manual labor and when we walk or sit down, when we eat and when we drink, we can always pray with our intellect and practice inner prayer, true prayer, pleasing to God. Let us work with our body and pray with our soul. Let our outer self perform physical work, and let the inner self be consecrated wholly and completely to the service of God and never flag in the spiritual work of inner prayer.[24]

---

23 *Homily*, 22(23): tr. Wensinck, 113; tr. Miller, 117. St Isaac speaks here of "pure" rather than "continual" prayer, but his remarks surely apply to "continual" prayer as well.

24 This is from a text included in the *Philokalia ton Hieron Neptikon*, 5 vols. (Athens: Aster/ Papademetriou, 1957-63), 5:107-12. The text in question bears the title, "From the Life of St. Gregory, Archbishop of Thessalonica" (Gregory Palamas), but it is only loosely based on the *Vita* by Patriarch Philotheos Kokkinos; it seems to be mainly by the editor of the *Philokalia*, St Nicodemus (or possibly by St Macarius of Corinth). In the *Vita* of Philotheos, compare in particular the debate with the monk Job (*PG* 151: 573B-574B). The citation from St Gregory

Certainly it is in principle easier for a hermit, dwelling in the silence of the desert and performing, like Abba Lucius, a very simple form of manual labor, to succeed in "retaining" his prayer amongst his daily occupations. For a monk or nun devoted to "active" service in the world—teaching in a school, for example, or nursing the sick in hospital—the task of "retention" is inevitably harder: harder, but not impossible. And for the lay person lacking the ordered framework of a religious community, it may seem harder still. Yet it is the firm conviction of the Orthodox spiritual tradition that all of these can, through God's mercy, come to share in the grace of inner prayer. Even if only a few, either in the desert or in the city, enjoy unceasing prayer in the full sense, everyone can succeed, through the Jesus Prayer or some other, in praying at the same time as he or she works. Indeed, the Jesus Prayer, because of its very shortness and simplicity, is eminently well suited for those living under tension and outward pressure, for whom more complicated forms of prayer would be inappropriate.

No external condition, however distracting, is in itself incompatible with inner prayer of the heart. "It may happen," state the *Homilies* of Macarius, "that the saints of God sit in the theater and look at the deception of the world: but with their inner self they are talking with God."[25] There can be few forms of life more exacting, requiring a greater concentration upon the cares of this world, than the work of a doctor. Yet in the *Sayings of the Desert Fathers* it is recorded that a doctor in Alexandria—we are not even told his name—was spiritually the equal of St Antony, the greatest of Christian solitaries:

> It was revealed to Abba Antony in the desert: "In the city there is one like you, a doctor by profession, who gives to those in need whatever he can spare; and throughout the whole day he sings the Thrice-Holy Hymn with the angels."[26]

Any one of us, with the help of the Holy Spirit, can come to do the same as this doctor. The Kingdom of heaven is within each of us. To pray is, quite simply, to enter into this inner Kingdom of our heart, and there

the Theologian (Gregory of Nazianzus) occurs in *Oration* 27.4 (*PG* 36:16B) (see above, 67). Compare Igumen Chariton, *The Art of Prayer*, 87.

25 *Homily* 15.8: ed. Dörries, 131-32; tr. Maloney, 111.

26 *AP*, alphabetical collection, Antony 24 (84B); tr. Ward, *Sayings*, 6. On the significance of this *apophthegma*, see Kallistos Ware, "The Monk and the Married Christian: Some Comparisons in Early Monastic Sources," *Eastern Churches Review* 6:1 (1974), 72-81.

to stand before God, conscious of His indwelling presence; to "pray without ceasing" is to do this constantly. Although the full glory of this Kingdom is revealed to but few in this present age, we can all discover at any rate some part of its riches. The door is before us and the key is in our hands.

7

SILENCE IN PRAYER:
THE MEANING OF HESYCHIA

Divine truth consists not in talk but in silence,
in remaining within the heart by long suffering.

The Book of the Poor in Spirit

...Jesus Christ, the Word that came out of silence.

St Ignatius of Antioch

Different levels of hesychia

One of the stories in the *Sayings of the Desert Fathers* describes a visit by Theophilus, Archbishop of Alexandria, to the monks of Scetis. Anxious to impress their distinguished guest, the assembled brethren appealed to Abba Pambo: "Say something to the Archbishop that he may be edified." And the old man replied, "If he isn't edified by my silence, then he won't be edified by my words."[1] It is a story that indicates the extreme importance attached by the Desert tradition to *hesychia*, the quality of stillness or silence. "God has chosen *hesychia* above all other virtues," it is affirmed elsewhere in the *Sayings of the Desert Fathers*.[2] As St Nilus of Ancyra insists, "It is impossible for muddy water to grow clear if it is constantly stirred up; and it is impossible to become a monk without *hesychia*."[3]

Hesychia means, however, far more than merely refraining from outward speech. It is a term that can be interpreted at many different levels. Let us try to distinguish the main senses, working from the more external to the more inward.

1   *AP*, alphabetical collection, Theophilus 2 (*PG* 65:197D); tr. Ward, *Sayings*, 81.
2   *AP, Concerning thoughts*: ed. J.-C. Guy, "Un dialogue monastique inédit," *Revue d'Ascétique et de Mystique* 33 (1957), 180; tr. Guy, *Les Apophtegmes*, 413.
3   *Exhortation to monks* (*PG* 79:1236B).

(1) *Hesychia and solitude.* In the earliest sources, the term "hesychast" (*hesychastes*) and its related verb *hesychazo* usually denote a monk living in solitude, a hermit as opposed to the member of a cenobitic community. This sense is found already in Evagrius of Pontus (fourth century)[4] and in Nilus and Palladius (early fifth century).[5] The word also occurs with this meaning in the *Sayings of the Desert Fathers*,[6] Cyril of Scythopolis,[7] John Moschus,[8] Barsanuphius,[9] and the legislation of Justinian.[10] *Hesychia* continues to be used in this sense in later authors such as St Gregory of Sinai († 1346).[11] On this level, the term refers primarily to a person's relationship in space with other human beings. This is the most external of the various senses.

(2) *Hesychia and the spirituality of the cell.* "*Hesychia,*" says Abba Rufus in the *Sayings of the Desert Fathers*, "is to sit in your cell with fear and in the knowledge of God, abstaining entirely from rancour and vainglory. Such *hesychia* is the mother of all the virtues and guards the monk from the fiery arrows of the enemy." Rufus goes on to connect *hesychia* with the remembrance of death, and he concludes by saying: "Be vigilant (*nephe*) over your own soul."[12] *Hesychia* is thus associated with another key term in the Desert tradition, *nepsis*, spiritual sobriety or vigilance.

When *hesychia* is linked in this way with the cell, the term still refers to the external situation of the hesychast in space, but its meaning is at the

---

4   *On Prayer* 107, 111 (79:1192A,C); tr. *Philokalia*, 1:67, 68.

5   Nilus, *Letters* 4.1 and 17 (*PG* 79:541C and 557D); *On the superiority of desert hesychasts* 1 (*PG* 79:1061A); Palladius, *Life of St. John Chrysostom* 8: ed. Coleman-Norton, 50, 6.

6   *AP*, alphabetical collection, Antony 34 (*PG* 65:85D); Elias 8 (185A: this is relatively late, probably from the sixth century, since it refers to a monk in the community of St Sabas in Palestine); Poemen 90 (344A); tr. Ward, *Sayings*, 8, 72, 179.

7   *Life of St. Sabas* 21: ed. Schwartz, 105, 19.

8   *Meadow* 52 (*PG* 87:2908A); tr. Wortley, 42 .

9   *Questions and Answers*, ed. Schoinas, §164; ed. Regnault and Lemaire, §68. Here we find the doublet "those who live in enclosure (*enkleistoi*) and hesychasts." A critical edition of the Greek text of Barsanuphius and John, *Questions and Answers*, edited by François Neyt and Paula de Angelis-Noah (following the enumeration of Regnault and Lemaire), has commenced publication: *Sources Chrétiennes* 426-427 (Paris: Cerf, 1997-98). See also the uncompleted critical edition of Derwas J. Chitty, in *PO* 31:3 (1966).

10 *Novella* 5.3 (AD 535): ed. von Lingenthal, 63, 17; this speaks of "anchorites and hesychasts." For the same usage of *hesychia* compare the Council *in Trullo* (AD 692), canon 41.

11 *On Prayer: Seven Texts* 5 (*PG* 150:1333D); tr. *Philokalia*, 4:278.

12 *AP*, alphabetical collection, Rufus 1 (389BC); tr. Ward, *Sayings*, 210.

same time more interiorized and spiritual. The hesychast, in the sense of one who remains with watchful vigilance in his cell, need not always be a solitary but can be equally a monk living in community.

The hesychast, then, is one who obeys the injunction of Abba Moses, "Go and sit in your cell and your cell will teach you everything."[13] He bears in mind the advice which Arsenius gave to a monk who wished to perform works of mercy. "Someone said to Arsenius, 'My thoughts trouble me, saying, You cannot fast or labor; at least go and visit the sick, for this also is a form of love.' The old man, recognizing the seeds sown by the demons, said to him: 'Go—eat and drink and sleep without doing any work; only do not leave your cell.' For he knew that to remain patiently in the cell brings a monk to the true fulfillment of his calling."[14]

The link between *hesychia* and the cell is clearly stated in a famous saying of St Antony of Egypt: "Fishes die if they tarry on dry land; and in the same way monks, if they linger outside their cell or pass their time with people of the world, lose the pitch of their *hesychia*."[15] The monk who remains within his cell is like the string of a well-tuned instrument. *Hesychia* keeps him in a state of alertness; if he lingers outside the cell, his soul grows limp and flabby.

The cell, understood in this way as the outward framework of *hesychia*, is envisaged above all as a workshop of unceasing prayer. The monk's chief activity, while remaining still and silent within his cell, is the constant remembrance of God (*mneme Theou*), accompanied by a sense of compunction and mourning (*penthos*). "Sit in your cell," says Abba Ammonas to an old man who proposes to adopt some ostentatious form of asceticism. "Eat a little every day and have the words of the publican ever in your heart. Then you can be saved."[16] The words of the publican, "God, be merciful to me a sinner" (Lk 18:13), are closely parallel to the formula of the Jesus Prayer, as found from the sixth century onwards in Barsanuphius, the *Life of Abba Philemon* and other sources. We shall return in

13 *AP*, alphabetical collection, Moses 6 (284C); tr. Ward, *Sayings*, 139.

14 *AP*, alphabetical collection, Arsenius 11 (89C); compare Hierax 1 (232D); tr. Ward, *Sayings,* 10, 104.

15 *AP*, alphabetical collection, Antony 10 (77B); tr. Ward, *Sayings*, 3. For the connection between *hesychia* and the cell, see also Evagrius, *The foundations of the monastic life* 8 (*PG* 40:1260C).

16 *AP*, alphabetical collection, Ammonas 4 (120C); tr. Ward, *Sayings*, 26.

due course to the subject of *hesychia* and the Invocation of the Name. The enclosure of the monastic cell and the Name of Jesus are explicitly linked in a statement by John of Gaza about his fellow hermit Barsanuphius: "The cell in which he is enclosed alive as in a tomb, for the sake of the Name of Jesus, is his place of repose; no demon enters there, not even the prince of demons, the devil. It is a sanctuary, for it contains the dwelling-place of God."[17]

For the hesychast, then, the cell is a house of prayer, a sanctuary and place of meeting between the human person and God. All this is strikingly expressed in the saying, "The monk's cell is the furnace of Babylon, in which the three children found the Son of God; it is the pillar of cloud, from which God spoke to Moses."[18] This notion of the cell as a focus of the *shekinah* is reflected in the words of a contemporary Coptic hermit, Abûna Mattâ al-Maskîn. When asked if he ever thought of going on pilgrimage to the Holy Places, he replied: "Jerusalem the Holy is right here, in and around these caves; for what else is my cave, but the place where my Savior Christ was born; what else is my cave, but the place where my Savior Christ was taken to rest; what else is my cave, but the place from where He most gloriously rose again from the dead. Jerusalem is here, right here, and all the spiritual riches of the Holy City are found in this *wadi*."[19]

In all this we are moving steadily from the external to the inner sense of *hesychia*. Interpreted in terms of the spirituality of the cell, the word signifies not only an outward and physical condition but a state of soul. It denotes the attitude of one who seeks, in the words of St Theophan the Recluse, "to stand before God with the mind in the heart, and to go on standing before Him unceasingly day and night, until the end of life."[20] That is precisely what the stillness and silence of his cell signify to the hesychast.

(3) *Hesychia and the "return into oneself."* This more interiorized understanding of *hesychia* is plainly emphasized in the classic designation of the

---

17 *Questions and Answers*, ed. Schoinas, §73; ed. Regnault and Lemaire, §142.
18 *AP*, anonymous collection, 206: ed. Nau, *ROC* 13 (1908), 279; Ward, *Wisdom*, §74(24).
19 Otto Meinardus, "The Hermits of Wadî Rayân," *Studia Orientalia Christiana, Collectanea* 11 (Cairo, 1966), 308.
20 Cited in Igumen Chariton, *The Art of Prayer*, 63; see above, 59.

hesychast supplied by St John Climacus: "The hesychast is one who strives to confine his incorporeal being within his bodily house, paradoxical though this may sound."[21] The hesychast, in the true sense of the word, is not someone who has journeyed outwardly into the desert, but someone who has embarked upon the journey inwards into his own heart; not someone who cuts himself off physically from others, shutting the door of his cell, but someone who "returns into himself," shutting the door of his mind. "He came to himself," it is said of the prodigal son (Lk 15:17); and this is what the hesychast also does. As St Basil puts it, he returns to himself; and having so returned inwards, he ascends to God.[22] The hesychast is in this way one who responds to Christ's words, "The Kingdom of God is within you" (Lk 17:21), and who also seeks to "guard the heart with all watchfulness" (Prov 4:23). In the words of St Isaac the Syrian, he "dives into himself," discovering within himself the ladder that leads to the Kingdom.[23] Reinterpreting our original definition of the hesychast as a solitary living in the desert, we may say that solitude is a state of soul, not a matter of geographical location, and that the real desert lies within the heart.

At this point in our exploration it will be helpful to pause briefly and to distinguish with greater precision between the external and inner senses of the word *hesychia*.[24] Three levels are indicated in a famous *apophthegma* of Abba Arsenius. While still tutor to the imperial children in the palace, Arsenius prayed to God, "Show me how to be saved." And a voice came to him, "Arsenius, flee from other people and you will be saved." He withdrew into the desert and became a solitary; and then he prayed again in the same words. This time the voice said: "Arsenius, flee, keep silent (*siopa*), be still (*hesychaze*), for these are the roots of sinlessness."[25]

---

21 *Ladder* 27 (*PG* 88:1097B); tr. Luibheid and Russell, 262.

22 *Letter* 2 (*PG* 32:228A).

23 *Homily* 2: tr. Wensinck, 8; tr. Miller, 11; compare above, xi.

24 In what follows, I have drawn upon the fundamental study of Irénée Hausherr, "L'hésychasme. Étude de spiritualité," *Orientalia Christiana Periodica* 22 (1956), 5-40, 247-85, especially 18ff. This essay is reprinted in the collected volume of Father Hausherr's writings, *Hésychasme et Prière*, Orientalia Christiana Analecta 176 (Rome: Pont. Institutum Studiorum Orientalium, 1966), 163-237.

25 *AP*, alphabetical collection, Arsenius 1, 2 (88BC); tr. Ward, *Sayings*, 9 (the translation needs correcting).

Flee from other people, keep silent, be still: such are the three degrees of *hesychia*. The first is spatial, to "flee from others" externally and physically. The second is still external, to "keep silent," to desist from outward speech. Neither of these things can by itself make us into a real hesychast; for we may be living in outward solitude and may keep our mouth closed, and yet inwardly we may be full of restlessness and agitation. To achieve true stillness it is necessary to pass from the second level to the third, from external to interior *hesychia*, from the mere absence of speech to what St Ambrose of Milan terms *negotiosum silentium*,[26] active and creative silence. The same three levels are distinguished by St John Climacus: "Close the door of your cell physically, the door of your tongue to speech, and the inner door to the evil spirits."[27]

This distinction between the levels of *hesychia* has important implications for the relationship of the hesychast to society. One person may accomplish the visible and geographic flight into the desert, and yet in his heart may still remain in the midst of the city; conversely, another person may continue physically in the city and yet be a true hesychast in his heart. What matters is not our spatial position but our spiritual state.

It is true that some writers in the Christian East, most notably St Isaac the Syrian, have come close to maintaining that inner *hesychia* cannot exist without external solitude. But such is far from being the universal view. There are stories in the *Sayings of the Desert Fathers* where laypeople, fully committed to a life of active service in the world, are compared with hermits and solitaries; a doctor in Alexandria, for instance, is regarded as the spiritual equal of St Antony the Great himself.[28] St Gregory of Sinai refused to tonsure one of his disciples named Isidore, but sent him back from Mount Athos to Thessalonica, to act as exemplar and guide to a circle of lay people, thereby implying that the vocation of an urban hesychast is by no means an impossibility.[29] St Gregory Palamas, the Sinaite's contemporary, insisted in the most unambiguous fashion that

---

26 *On the Clerical Office* 1.3(9) (*PL* 16:26B).

27 *Ladder* 27 (*PG* 88:1100A); tr. Luibheid and Russell, 263.

28 *AP*, alphabetical collection, Antony 24 (84B), tr. Ward, *Sayings*, 6; see above, 86.

29 Patriarch Philotheos, *Life of St Isidore* 22: ed. A. Papadopoulos-Kerameus, *Zapiski Istoriko— Filologicheskago Fakul'teta Imperatorskago S.-Peterburgskago Universiteta* 76 (St Petersburg: Tip. V. Kirshbauma, 1905), 77, 21-26.

the command of St Paul, "Pray without ceasing" (1 Thess 5:17), applies to all Christians without exception.[30]

In this connection it should be remembered that, when Greek ascetic writers such as Evagrius or St Maximus the Confessor use the terms *praxis* (or *praktike*) and *theoria*, usually translated as "active life" and "contemplative life," the "active life" signifies for them not the life of direct service to the world—preaching, teaching, social work and the like—but the inner struggle to subdue the passions and acquire the virtues. Using the phrase in this sense, it may be said that many hermits and monastics living in strict enclosure are still predominantly concerned with the "active life." By the same token, there are men and women fully devoted to a life of service in the world who yet possess prayer of the heart; and of them it may justly be said that they are living the "contemplative life." St Symeon the New Theologian insists that the fullness of the vision of God is possible "in the middle of cities" as well as "in mountains and cells." Married people, so he believed, with secular jobs and children, burdened with the anxieties of running a large household, may yet ascend to the heights of contemplation; St Peter had a mother-in-law, yet the Lord called him to climb Tabor and behold the glory of the Transfiguration.[31] The criterion is not the external situation but the inner reality.

Just as it is possible to live in the city and yet to be a hesychast, so there are some whose duty it is to be constantly talking and who yet are silent inwardly. In the words of Abba Poemen, "One person appears to be keeping silent and yet condemns others in his heart; such a person is speaking all the time. Another person talks from morning till evening and yet keeps silent; that is, he says nothing except what is helpful to others."[32] This applies exactly to the position of *startsi* such as St Seraphim of Sarov and the spiritual fathers of Optino in nineteenth-century Russia; compelled by their vocation to receive an unending stream of visitors—dozens and even hundreds in a single day—they did not thereby forfeit their inner *hesychia*. Indeed, it was precisely because of this inner *hesychia* that they were enabled to act as guides to others. The words that they spoke to each

---

30 Patriarch Philotheos, *Life of St Gregory of Thessalonica* (*PG* 151:573B-574B); see above, 85, n. 24.
31 *Discourses* 5, 122-141; 6, 153-61: ed. Krivochéine, 1:386-88, 2:26-28; tr. deCatanzaro, 93, 123.
32 *AP*, alphabetical collection, Poemen 27 (329A); tr. Ward, *Sayings*, 171.

visitor were words of power because they were words that came out of silence.

In one of his answers, John of Gaza made a clear distinction between inner and outer silence. A brother living in community, who found his duties as monastic carpenter a cause of disturbance and distraction, asked whether he should become a hermit and "practice the silence of which the Fathers speak." John did not agree to this. "Like most people," he replied, "you do not understand what is meant by the silence of which the Fathers speak. Silence does not consist in keeping your mouth shut. One person may speak ten thousand useful words, and it is counted as silence; another speaks a single unnecessary word, and it is counted as a breach of the Lord's commandment, 'You shall give account in the day of judgment for every idle word that comes out of your mouth' (Mt 12:32)."[33]

(4) *Hesychia and spiritual poverty.* Inner stillness, when interpreted as a guarding of the heart and a return into oneself, implies a passage from multiplicity to unity, from diversity to simplicity and spiritual poverty. To use the terminology of Evagrius, the mind must become "naked." This aspect of *hesychia* is made explicit in another definition provided by St John Climacus: "*Hesychia* is a laying aside of thoughts."[34] Here he is adapting an Evagrian phrase, "Prayer is a laying aside of thoughts."[35] *Hesychia*, that is to say, involves a progressive self-emptying, in which the mind is stripped of visual images and of humanly devised concepts, and so contemplates in purity the realm of God. The hesychast, from this point of view, is precisely the one who has advanced from *praxis* to *theoria*, from the active to the contemplative life. St Gregory of Sinai contrasts the hesychast with the *praktikos*, and goes on to speak of "...the hesychasts who are content to pray to God alone within their heart and to abstain from thoughts."[36] The hesychast, then, is not so much one who refrains from meeting and speaking with others, as one who in his life of prayer re-

---

33 Barsanuphius and John, *Questions and Answers*, §554 (in the numbering both of Schoinas and of Regnault and Lemaire).

34 *Ladder* 27 (PG 88:1112A); tr. Luibheid and Russell, 269. The phrase is repeated by St Gregory of Sinai, *On Prayer: Seven Texts* 5 (PG 150:1333B); tr. *Philokalia*, 4:278.

35 *On Prayer* 70(71) (PG 79:1181C); tr. *Philokalia*, 1:64.

36 *On Prayer: Seven Texts* 5 (PG 150:1333B); tr. *Philokalia*, 4:278.

nounces all images, words and discursive reasoning, who is "lifted above the senses into pure silence."[37]

This "pure silence," although it is termed "spiritual poverty," is far from being a mere absence or privation. If the hesychast strips his mind of all humanly devised concepts, so far as this is possible, his aim in this "self-noughting" is altogether constructive—that he may be filled with an all-embracing sense of the divine indwelling. The point is well made by St Gregory of Sinai: "Why speak at length? Prayer is God, who accomplishes everything in everyone."[38] Prayer is God; it is not primarily something which I do but something which God is doing in me—"...not I, but Christ in me" (Gal 2:20). The hesychast program is exactly delineated in the words of the Baptist concerning the Messiah, "He must increase, but I must decrease" (Jn 3:30). The hesychast ceases from his own activity, not in order to be idle, but in order to enter into the activity of God. His silence is not vacant and negative—a blank pause between words, a short rest before resuming speech—but intensely positive: an attitude of alert attentiveness, of vigilance, and above all of *listening*.

The hesychast is *par excellence* the one who listens, who is open to the presence of Another: "Be still and know that I am God" (Psalm 45 [46]:11). In the words of St John Climacus, "The hesychast is one who cries out plainly, 'O God, my heart is ready' (Ps 56 [57]:8); the hesychast is one who says, 'I sleep, but my heart keeps vigil' (Song 5:2)."[39] Returning into himself, the hesychast enters the secret chamber of his own heart in order that, standing there before God, he may listen to the wordless speech of his Creator. "When you pray," observes a contemporary Orthodox writer in Finland, "you yourself must be silent; let the prayer speak"[40]—more exactly, let God speak. "Man...should always remain silent and let God alone speak."[41] That is what the hesychast is aiming to achieve.

Hesychia therefore denotes the transition from "my" prayer to the prayer of God working in me—to use the terminology of St Theophan, from "strenuous" or "laborious" prayer to the prayer that is "self-acting"

---

37 *The Book of the Poor in Spirit*, 2.3.2: ed. Kelley, 151.
38 *On Commandments and Doctrines* 113 (*PG* 150:1280A); tr. *Philokalia* 4:238.
39 *Ladder* 27 (*PG* 88:1100A); tr. Luibheid and Russell, 263.
40 Tito Colliander, *The Way of the Ascetics*, 79.
41 *The Book of the Poor in Spirit*, 2.3.2: ed. Kelley, 151.

or "self-impelled." True inner silence or *hesychia*, in the deepest sense, is identical with the unceasing prayer of the Holy Spirit within us. As St Isaac the Syrian expresses it, "When the Spirit makes Its dwelling-place in someone, he does not cease to pray, because the Spirit will constantly pray in him."[42] Elsewhere St Isaac likens this entry into self-acting prayer to a person passing through a door after the key has been turned in the lock, and to the silence of servants when the master arrives in their midst.[43] Understood in these terms, as an entering into the life and the activity of God, *hesychia* is something which during this present age we can achieve only to a limited and imperfect degree. It is an eschatological reality, reserved in its fullness for the future life in heaven. In the words of St Isaac, "Silence is a mystery of the Age to come."[44]

Hesychia and the Jesus Prayer

In principle, therefore, *hesychia* is a general term for inner prayer, and so it embraces a wide variety of more specific ways of praying.[45] In practice, however, the majority of Orthodox writers in recent centuries use the word to designate one spiritual path in particular: the invocation of the Name of Jesus. Occasionally, although with less justification, the term "hesychasm" is employed in a yet more restricted sense to indicate the physical technique, involving especially control of the breathing, which is sometimes used in conjunction with the Jesus Prayer.[46] The association of *hesychia* with the Name of Jesus—and, so it would seem, with the breath-

---

42 *Homily* 35(37): tr. Wensinck, 174; tr. Miller, 182. The passage is quoted at greater length above, 83.

43 *Homily* 22(23): tr. Wensinck, 112; tr. Miller, 116 (quoted above, 14).

44 *Homily* 66(65): tr. Wensinck, 315; tr. Miller, 321.

45 Compare the comprehensive definition given by Pierre Adnès in his article "Hésychasme," *DS* 7:384: "Hesychasm may be defined as a spiritual system, essentially contemplative in orientation, which regards human perfection as consisting in union with God by means of prayer or perpetual prayerfulness."

46 St Gregory Palamas and the other Hesychast masters regard the physical technique (control of the breathing, inner "exploration," etc.) as no more than an accessory, helpful to some but by no means obligatory or indispensable. Modern teachers add that the technique should be used only under the personal guidance of an experienced spiritual father. The Jesus Prayer can be practiced in its fullness without any bodily exercises at all, and it is thus a misnomer to call these exercises (as some writers do) "*the* hesychast method of prayer." See my article, "Praying with the body: the hesychast method and non-Christian parallels," *Sobornost* 14:2 (1992), 6-35.

ing—is found already in St John Climacus: "*Hesychia* is to stand before God in unceasing worship. Let the remembrance of Jesus be united to your breathing, and then you will know the value of *hesychia*."[47]

What is the relationship between the Jesus Prayer and *hesychia*? How does the invocation of the Name help in establishing the kind of inner silence that has just been described?

Prayer, it was said, is a "laying aside of thoughts," a return from multiplicity to unity. Now when we first make a serious effort to pray inwardly, standing before God with the mind in the heart, immediately we become conscious of our inward disintegration—of our powerlessness to concentrate ourselves in the present moment, in the *kairos*. Thoughts move restlessly through our head, like the buzzing of flies (St Theophan) or the capricious leaping of monkeys from branch to branch (Ramakrishna).[48] This lack of concentration, this inability to be *here* and *now* with the whole of our being, is one of the most tragic consequences of the Fall.

What is to be done? The Orthodox ascetic tradition distinguishes two main methods of overcoming "thoughts." The first is direct, to "contradict" our *logismoi*, to meet them face to face, attempting to expel them by an effort of will. Such a method, however, may well prove counter-productive. When violently suppressed, our fantasies tend to return with increased force. Unless we are extremely sure of ourselves, it is safer to employ the second method, which is oblique. Instead of fighting our thoughts directly and attempting to drive them out by an effort of will, we can seek to direct our attention away from them and to look elsewhere. Our spiritual strategy in this way becomes positive instead of negative; our immediate objective is not to empty our mind of what is evil but rather to fill it with what is good. It is this second method that is recommended by Barsanuphius and John of Gaza. "Do not contradict the thoughts suggested by your enemies," they advise, "for that is exactly what they want and they will not desist. But turn to the Lord for help against them, laying before Him your own helpless-

---

47 *Ladder* 27 (*PG* 88:1112C); tr. Luibheid and Russell, 269-70.
48 I take these two similes from the article of Dr André Bloom (now Metrop   Anthony of
   Sourozh), "Contemplation et ascèse: contribution orthodoxe," in André !
   nique et contemplation, Études Carmélitaines 28 (Paris: Desclée de Brouwer
   is an important discussion of the various physical centers in the human pe
   cations for the spiritual life.

ness; for He is able to expel them and to reduce them to nothing."[49] Now the Jesus Prayer is precisely a way—the supreme way—whereby we "turn to the Lord for help." The Jesus Prayer combats our temptations specifically by enabling us to look elsewhere.

It is surely evident to each one of us that we cannot halt the inward flow of our images and thoughts by a crude exertion of will-power. It is of little or no value to say to ourselves, "Stop thinking"; we might as well say, "Stop breathing." "The rational intellect cannot rest idle," insists St Mark the Monk.[50] How then are we to achieve spiritual poverty and inner silence? Although we cannot make the never-idle mind desist altogether from its restlessness, what we can do is to simplify and unify its activity by continually repeating a short formula of prayer. The flow of images and thoughts will persist, but we shall be enabled gradually to detach ourselves from it. The repeated invocation will help us to "let go" the thoughts presented to us by our conscious or unconscious self. This "letting go" seems to correspond to what Evagrius has in view when he speaks of prayer as a "laying aside" or "shedding" of thoughts— not a savage conflict, not a ruthless campaign of furious aggression, but a gentle yet persistent act of detachment.

This, then, is the ascetic strategy presupposed in the use of the Jesus Prayer. It assists us in applying the second or oblique method of combating thoughts: instead of trying to obliterate our corrupt or trivial imaginings by a direct confrontation, we turn aside and look at the Lord Jesus; instead of relying on our own power, we take refuge in the power and grace that act through the Divine Name. The repeated invocation helps us to detach ourselves from the ceaseless chattering of our *logismoi*.

At the same time the Jesus Prayer, by progressively detaching us from a multiplicity of disconnected or conflicting thoughts, helps us to focus our disintegrated personhood upon a single point. "Through the remembrance of Jesus Christ," writes St Philotheus of Sinai, "gather together your scattered intellect."[51] We concentrate and unify our ever-active mind by feeding it with a single thought, by nourishing it on a spiritual diet that is at

49 *Questions and Answers*, ed. Schoinas, §91; ed. Regnault and Lemaire, §166.
50 *On Repentance* 11 (*PG* 65:981B). I have emended the Greek text, which is given inaccurately in Migne.
51 *Forty Texts on Watchfulness*, 27; tr. *Philokalia*, 3:27.

once rich yet exceedingly simple. "To stop the continual jostling of your thoughts," says St Theophan, "you must bind the mind with one thought, or the thought of One only"[52]—the thought of the Lord Jesus. In the words of St Diadochus of Photice, "When we have blocked all its outlets by means of the remembrance of God, the intellect requires of us imperatively some task which will satisfy its need for activity. For the complete fulfillment of its purpose we should give it nothing but the prayer 'Lord Jesus...'"[53]

Such in outline is the manner whereby the Jesus Prayer can be used to establish *hesychia* within the heart. Two important consequences follow. First, to achieve its purpose the invocation should be rhythmical and regular, and in the case of an experienced hesychast—although not of the beginner, who needs to proceed with caution, if possible under the guidance of a spiritual father—it should be uninterrupted and continuous during long periods of the day. External aids, such as the use of a prayer-rope (*komvoschoinion, tchotki*) and the control of the breathing, have as their main purpose precisely the establishment of a regular rhythm.

In the second place, during the recitation of the Jesus Prayer the mind should be so far as possible empty of mental pictures. For this reason, it is best to practice the Prayer in a place where there are few if any outward sounds; it should be recited in darkness or with the eyes closed, rather than gazing at an icon illuminated by candles or a votive lamp. St Silouan of Mount Athos, when saying the Prayer, used to stow his clock away in the cupboard in order not to hear its ticking, and then pulled his thick woolen monastic cap over his eyes and ears.[54] While visual images will inevitably arise within us as we pray, they are not to be deliberately encouraged. The Jesus Prayer is not a form of discursive meditation on different incidents in the life of Christ. Those who invoke the Lord Jesus should have in their hearts an intense and burning conviction that they stand in the immediate presence of the Savior, that He is before them and within them, that He is listening to their invocation and replying in His turn. This consciousness of God's presence should not, however, be accompa-

52 Quoted in Igumen Chariton, *The Art of Prayer*, 97.

53 *On Spiritual Knowledge* 59: ed. des Places, 119, 1-5; tr. *Philokalia*, 1:270.

54 Archimandrite Sophrony (Sakharov), *The Undistorted Image: Staretz Silouan* (London: Faith Press, 1958), 40-41.

nied by any visual concept, but should be confined to a simple conviction or feeling. As St Gregory of Nyssa puts it, "The Bridegroom is present but He is not seen."[55]

What practical use is the hesychast to others?

Hesychia, then, involves a separation from the world—a separation either external or internal, and sometimes both at once: external through flight into the desert; internal through the "return into oneself" and the "laying aside of thoughts." To quote the *Sayings of the Desert Fathers*, "Unless someone says in his heart, I alone and God are in the world, he will have no rest."[56] "Alone to the Alone":[57] but is this not selfish, a rejection of the spiritual value of the material creation and an evasion of our responsibility towards our fellow humans? When the hesychast shuts his eyes and ears to the outside world, as St Silouan did in his cell on Mount Athos, what positive and practical service is he rendering to his neighbor?

Let us consider this problem under two main aspects. In the first place, is hesychasm guilty of the same distortions as those for which the Quietists were condemned in the seventeenth-century West? Hitherto we have deliberately refrained from translating *hesychia* as "quiet," because of the suspect sense attached to the term "Quietist." Is the hesychast in fact upholding the same standpoint as the Quietist? In the second place, what is the attitude of the hesychast to his environment, whether human or physical? What practical use is he or she to others?

Let us take the description of Quietism in a standard work of reference, *The Oxford Dictionary of the Christian Church*, without attempting to judge how far this is a just summary of the viewpoints of Miguel de Molinos or Madame Guyon. "The fundamental principle of Quietism," states *The Oxford Dictionary*, "is its condemnation of all human effort... Man, in order to be perfect, must attain complete passivity and annihilation of will, abandoning himself to God to such an extent that he cares neither for Heaven nor Hell, nor for his own salvation... The soul con-

---

55 *Commentary on the Song of Songs* 11 (*PG* 44:1001B); ed. Langerbeck, 324, 8-9.

56 *AP*, alphabetical collection, Alonius 1 (133A); tr. Ward, *Sayings*, 35. Compare the famous words of John Henry Newman in the early part of his *Apologia pro Vita Sua*: "...two and two only supreme and luminously self-evident beings, myself and my Creator..."

57 Cf. Plotinus, *Enneads* 6.9.11: ed. Henry and Schwyzer, 3:328, §51.

sciously refuses not only all discursive meditation but any distinct act such as desire for virtue, love of Christ or adoration of the Divine Persons, and simply rests in the presence of God in pure faith... As this passive prayer expresses the height of perfection, it makes any outward acts of mortification, almsgiving, going to confession, etc., superfluous. Once a man has attained to it, sin is impossible."[58]

If this is Quietism, then the hesychast tradition is definitely not quietist. *Hesychia* signifies not passivity but vigilance (*nepsis*), "not the absence of struggle but the absence of uncertainty and confusion."[59] Even though a hesychast may have advanced to the level of *theoria* or contemplation, he or she is still required to struggle at the level of *praxis* or action, striving with positive effort to acquire virtue and to reject vice. *Praxis* and *theoria*, the active and the contemplative life in the sense defined earlier, should be envisaged not as alternatives, nor yet as two stages that are chronologically successive—the one ceasing when the other begins—but rather as two interpenetrating levels of spiritual experience, present simultaneously in the life of prayer. Everyone is required to fight on the level of *praxis* to the end of his life. This is the clear teaching of St Antony of Egypt: "A person's chief task is to be mindful of his sins in God's sight, and to expect temptation until his last breath... He who sits in the desert and preserves stillness (*hesychazon*) has escaped from three wars: hearing, speaking, seeing; but against one thing he must continually struggle—the warfare in his own heart."[60]

It is true that the hesychast, like the Quietist, does not use discursive meditation in his prayer. But, although *hesychia* involves a "letting go" or "laying aside" of thoughts and images, this does not imply on the hesychasts's part an attitude of "complete passivity" or an absence of "any distinct act such as...love of Christ." The "letting go" of evil or trivial *logismoi* during the saying of the Jesus Prayer, and their replacement with the one thought of the Name, is not passivity but an affirmative and powerful way of controlling our thoughts with the help of God's grace. The invo-

---

58 F. L. Cross and E. A. Livingstone (ed.), *The Oxford Dictionary of the Christian Church*, 3rd edn. (Oxford: Oxford University Press, 1997), 1357.

59 A. Bloom, "Contemplation et ascèse," *art. cit.*, 54.

60 *AP*, alphabetical collection, Antony 4 and 11 (77A,C), tr. Ward, *Sayings*, 2, 3 (in Saying 11, Ward follows the text as given in *PG*; I follow the alternative reading in the footnote).

cation of the Name is certainly a form of "resting in the presence of God in pure faith," but it is at the same time marked by an active love for the Savior and an acute longing to share ever more fully in the divine life. Readers of the *Philokalia* cannot but be struck by the warmth of devotion displayed by hesychast authors, by the sense of immediate and personal friendship for "my Jesus." This note of personal vividness is especially apparent in the Sinaite author Hesychios of Vatos.[61]

Unlike the Quietist, the true hesychast makes no claim to be sinless or impervious to temptation. The *apatheia* or "dispassion" of which Greek ascetic texts speak is not a state of passive indifference and insensibility, still less a condition in which sinning is impossible. "*Apatheia*," states St Isaac the Syrian, "does not mean that someone feels no passions, but that he does not accept any of them."[62] As St Antony insists, a person must "expect temptation until his last breath," and with the temptation there goes always the genuine possibility of falling into sin. "The passions remain alive," states Abba Abraham, "but they are bound by the saints."[63] When an old man claims, "I have died to the world," his neighbor gently rejoins, "Do not be so confident, brother, until you depart from the body. You may say, 'I have died,' but Satan has not died."[64]

In Greek writers from Evagrius onwards, *apatheia* is closely linked with love, and this clearly indicates the positive and dynamic content of the term "dispassion." In its basic essence, it is a state of spiritual freedom, in which we are able to reach out toward God with ardent longing. It is "no mere mortification of the physical passions of the body but its new and better energy;"[65] "it is a state of soul in which a burning love for God and men leaves no room for selfish and animal passions."[66] To denote its dynamic character, St Diadochus even uses the expressive phrase "the fire

61 See *Philokalia* 1:162-98.

62 *Homily* 74(71): tr. Wensinck, 345; tr. Miller, 347.

63 *AP*, alphabetical collection, Abraham 1 (132B); tr. Ward, *Sayings*, 34.

64 *AP*, anonymous collection, 266: ed. Nau, *ROC* 14 (1909), 369-70; tr. Ward, *Wisdom*, §134 (39).

65 Father (later Archbishop) Basil Krivocheine, *The Ascetic and Theological Teaching of Gregory Palamas*, reprint from *The Eastern Churches Quarterly* (London: Geo. E. J. Coldwell, 1954), 5.

66 Archimandrite Lazarus Moore, in St John Climacus, *The Ladder of Divine Ascent* (London: Faber, 1959), 51, note 3.

of *apatheia*."[67] All this convincingly indicates the gulf between hesychasm and Quietism.

To come now to the second question: accepting that the hesychast way of prayer is not "quietist" in any suspect or heretical sense, how far is it negative in its view of the material world and antisocial in its attitude toward other human beings? The difficulty may be illustrated from a story in the *Sayings of the Desert Fathers* about three friends who become monks. As his ascetic labor the first adopts the task of peacemaker, seeking to reconcile those who go to law against one another. The second cares for the sick, and the third goes into the desert to become a solitary. After a time the first two grow utterly weary and discouraged. However hard they struggle, they are physically and spiritually incapable of meeting all the demands placed upon them. Close to despair, they go to the third monk, the hermit, and tell him about their troubles. At first he is silent. After a while he pours water into a bowl and says to the others, "Look." The water is murky and turbulent. They wait for some minutes. The hermit says, "Look again." The sediment has now sunk to the bottom and the water is entirely clear; they see their own faces as in a mirror. "That is what happens," says the hermit, "to someone who lives among others: because of the turbulence he does not see his own sins. But when he has learnt to be still, above all in the desert, he recognizes his own faults."[68]

So the story ends. We are not told how the first two monks applied the hermit's parable. Perhaps they both returned to the world, resuming their previous work; for, after all, society urgently needs mediators and nurses. But perhaps they also tried to take back with them something of the *hesychia* of the desert. In that case, they interpreted the words of the third monk to mean that social action, however urgent and necessary, is insufficient on its own. Unless we maintain contact with our inner depths, unless there is a still center in the middle of the storm, unless in the midst of all our activism we preserve a secret room in our heart where we stand alone before God, we will lose all sense of direction and be torn in pieces. Doubtless this is the moral which most readers in the twentieth century would be inclined to draw: that all of us must be in some measure hermits of the heart. But was this the original intention of the story?

67 *On Spiritual Knowledge* 17: ed. des Places, 94, 3; tr. *Philokalia*, 1:258.
68 *AP*, anonymous collection 134: ed. Nau, *ROC* 13 (1908), 47; tr. Ward, *Wisdom*, §2 (1).

Probably not. It is far more likely that it was meant as propaganda for the eremitic life in the literal and geographical sense. And this raises at once the whole question of the apparent selfishness and negativity of this type of contemplative prayer. What, then, is the true relationship of the hesychast to society?

It must be admitted at once that, alike in the hesychast movement of the fourteenth century, in the hesychast *renaissance* of the eighteenth century, and in contemporary Orthodoxy, the chief centers of hesychast prayer have been the lesser *sketes*, the hermitages housing only a handful of brothers or sisters, living as a small and closely integrated monastic family hidden from the world. Many hesychast authors express a definite preference for the *skete* over the fully organized *cenobium;* life in a large community is considered too distracting for the intense practice of inward prayer. Life in the middle of society is obviously still more distracting.

Yet, if the outward setting of the *skete* is considered ideal, few would go so far as to claim that it enjoys an exclusive monopoly. Always the criterion is not our exterior condition but our inner state. Certain external settings may prove more favorable than others for interior silence; but there is no situation whatever which renders interior silence altogether impossible. St Gregory of Sinai, as we have seen, sent his disciple Isidore back into the world; many of his closest companions on Mount Athos and in the desert of Paroria became patriarchs and bishops, leaders and administrators of the Church. St Gregory Palamas, who taught that continual prayer is possible for every Christian, himself concluded his life as archbishop of the second largest city in the Byzantine Empire.[69]

The fourteenth-century layman St Nicolas Cabasilas, a civil servant and courtier who was the friend of many leading hesychasts, maintains with great emphasis: "And everyone should keep their art or profession. The general should continue to command; the farmer to till the land; the artisan to practice his craft. And I will tell you why. It is not necessary to

69 Compare Dimitri Obolensky, *The Byzantine Commonwealth: Eastern Europe, 500-1453* (London: Weidenfeld and Nicolson, 1971), 301-8, 336-43, Kallistos Ware, *'Act out of Stillness': The Influence of Fourteenth-Century Hesychasm on Byzantine and Slav Civilization,* The "Byzantine Heritage" Annual Lecture May 28, 1995, ed. Daniel J. Sahas (Toronto: The Hellenic Canadian Society of Constantinople and The Thessalonikean Society of Metro Toronto).

retire into the desert, to take unpalatable food, to alter one's dress, to compromise one's health, or to do anything unwise, because it is quite possible to remain in one's own home without giving up all one's possessions, and yet to practice continual meditation."[70] In the same spirit, St Symeon the New Theologian insists that there is no "highest life" in an abstract and absolute sense, because the "highest life" for each of us is the particular state to which God calls each one personally: "Many have called the eremitic life blessed, others, the communal or cenobitic life. Others again have described in this way leadership of the faithful, or the counseling, teaching and administration of the churches... But for my part, I would not judge any one of them to be better than the others, nor would I say that one merits praise and another censure. But in every case, whatever our work or activity, it is the life led for God and according to God that is most blessed."[71]

The way of *hesychia*, then, lies open to all: the one thing needful is inner silence, not outer. And though this inner silence presupposes the "laying aside" of images in prayer, the final effect of this negation is to assert with fresh vividness the ultimate value of all persons and created things in God. The way of negation is at the same time the way of super-affirmation. This point emerges very plainly from *The Way of a Pilgrim*. The hero of this tale, the anonymous Russian peasant-wanderer, finds that the constant repetition of the Jesus Prayer transfigures his relationship with the material world around him, changing all things into a sacrament of God's presence and rendering them transparent. "When I began to pray with my heart," he writes, "everything surrounding me took on a delightful form: the trees, the grass, the birds, the earth, the air, and the light. All things seemed to be saying to me that they existed for humanity's sake, that they were testifying to God's love for humankind, that they were all praying and singing the glory of God. And I understood from this

---

70 *The Life in Christ* 6:42 (*PG* 150:657D-660A); ed. M. H. Congourdeau, *Sources Chrétiennes* 361 (Paris: Cerf, 1990), 76-78; quoted in J. M. Hussey, "Symeon the New Theologian and Nicolas Cabasilas: Similarities and Contrasts in Orthodox Spirituality," *Eastern Churches Review* 4:2 (1972), 139. Some have thought that, by "meditation," Nicolas means specifically the Jesus Prayer; Professor Hussey wisely prefers to give the phrase a wider application.

71 *Chapters* 3.65: ed. Darrouzès, 100, 9-16; tr. McGuckin, 91. Probably Symeon has in view here the various possibilities open to a monk or celibate priest, but the final sentence quoted above has much broader implications.

what the *Philokalia* calls 'the knowledge of the speech of all creatures.' …I felt love for Jesus Christ and all God's creation." Equally, the invocation of the Name transforms the Pilgrim's relationship with his fellow humans: "Again I went wandering from one place to the next, but I no longer walked with difficulties as before. The invocation of the Name of Jesus Christ cheered me on my way, and all people treated me rather well; it seemed as if they all loved me… If someone insults or injures me, I only recall how sweet is the Jesus Prayer, and then and there both insult and anger pass and I forget everything."[72]

Further evidence of the world-affirming nature of *hesychia* is to be found in the central position assigned by the hesychasts to the mystery of the Transfiguration. Metropolitan Anthony (Bloom) gives a striking description of two icons of the Transfiguration which he saw in Moscow, the one by Andrei Rublev and the other by Theophan the Greek. "The Rublev icon shows Christ in the brilliancy of His dazzling white robes which cast light on everything around. This light falls on the disciples, on the mountains and the stones, on every blade of grass. Within this light, which is… the divine glory, the divine light itself inseparable from God, all things acquire an intensity of being which they could not have otherwise; in it they attain to a fullness of reality which they can have only in God." In the other icon "the robes of Christ are silvery with blue shades, and the rays of light falling around are also white, silvery and blue. Everything gives an impression of much less intensity. Then we discover that all these rays of light falling from the Divine Presence… do not give relief but give transparency to things. One has the impression that these rays of divine light touch things and sink into them, penetrate them, touch something within them so that from the core of these things, of all things created, the same light reflects and shines back as though the divine life quickens the capabilities, the potentialities, of all things and makes all reach out towards itself. At that moment the eschatological situation is realized and, in the words of St Paul, 'God is all and in all.'"[73]

---

72 *The Pilgrim's Tale*, tr. T. Allan Smith, The Classics of Western Spirituality (New York/Mahwah: Paulist Press, 1999), 77, 83, 66, 67.

73 "Body and Matter in Spiritual Life," in A. M. Allchin (ed.), *Sacrament and image: Essays in the Christian Understanding of Man* (London: Fellowship of St Alban and St Sergius, 1967), 40-41.

Such is the double effect of the Transfiguration glory: to make each person and each thing stand out in full distinctiveness, in their unique and unrepeatable essence; and at the same time to make each person and each thing transparent, to reveal the divine presence beyond and within them.[74] The same double effect is produced by *hesychia*. The prayer of inner silence is not world-denying but world-embracing. It enables the hesychast to look beyond the world toward the invisible Creator; and so it enables him to return back to the world and see it with new eyes. To travel, it has been often said, is to return to our point of departure and to see our home afresh as though for the first time. This is true of the journey of prayer, as of other journeys. The hesychast, far more than the sensualist or the materialist, can appreciate the value of each thing, because he sees each in God and God in each. It is no coincidence that, in the Palamite controversy of the fourteenth century, St Gregory and his hesychast supporters were concerned to defend precisely the spiritual potentialities of the material creation and, in particular, of the physical body of each human person.

Such, in brief, is the answer to those who see hesychasm as negative and dualist in its attitude to the world. The hesychast denies in order to reaffirm; he withdraws in order to return. In a phrase which sums up the relationship between the hesychast and society, between inner prayer and outward action, Evagrius of Pontus remarks: "The monk is one who is separated from all and united with all."[75] The hesychasts make an act of separation—externally, by retiring into solitude; inwardly, by the "laying aside of thoughts"—yet the effect of this flight is to join them to others more closely than ever before, to make them more deeply sensitive to the needs of others, more sharply conscious of their hidden possibilities. This is seen most strikingly in the case of the great spiritual fathers and mothers. People such as St Antony of Egypt or St Seraphim of Sarov lived for whole decades in all but total silence and physical isolation. Yet the ultimate effect of this silence and isolation was to confer on them clarity of vision and exceptional compassion. Precisely because they had learnt to be alone, they could spontaneously make their own the joys and sorrows of

---

74 Compare the remarks on "double vision" in my lecture *Through the Creation to the Creator* (London: Friends of the Centre, 1997), 13-15.

75 *On Prayer* 124 (*PG* 79:1193C); tr. *Philokalia*, 1:69.

all who came to seek their aid. They were able to discern immediately the deep characteristics of each person, perhaps speaking to them only two or three sentences; but those few words were the one thing that at that particular juncture each person needed to be told.

St Isaac the Syrian says that it is better to acquire purity of heart than to convert whole nations of heathen from error.[76] Not that he despises the work of the apostolate; he means merely that unless and until we have gained some measure of inner silence, it is improbable that we will succeed in converting anybody to anything. The point is made less paradoxically by Ammonas, the disciple of St Antony of Egypt: "Because they had first practiced profound *hesychia*, they possessed the power of God dwelling within them; and then God sent them into the midst of human society."[77] And even if many solitaries are never in fact sent back into the world as apostles or spiritual guides but continue the practice of inner silence throughout their life, totally unknown to others, that does not mean that their hidden contemplation is useless or their life wasted. They are serving society not by active works but by prayer, not by what they do but by what they are, not externally but existentially. They can say, in the words of St Macarius of Alexandria, "I am guarding the walls."[78]

76 *Homily* 4: tr. Wensinck, 32; tr. Miller, 32.
77 *Ep.* 1: ed. F. Nau, *PO* 11 (1915), 433, 4-5.
78 Palladius, *Lausiac History* 18; ed. Butler, 58, 11.

8

THE SEED OF THE CHURCH:
MARTYRDOM AS A UNIVERSAL
VOCATION

Times of peace are favorable to Satan, for they rob Christ of His
martyrs and the Church of its glory.

Paul Evdokimov

The Triumph of Orthodoxy

In the calendar of the Orthodox Church, there are two occasions in particular at which the central importance of martyrdom is underlined. The
first is the observance of the "Triumph of Orthodoxy" on the first Sunday
in Lent. This commemorates the ending of the Iconoclast Controversy in
842-43. The holy icons are carried in procession, the heretics are anathematized, and "Eternal memory" is sung in honor of those who defended the
faith. It is a festal and exultant celebration, in striking contrast to the penitential spirit of the Lenten services during the preceding week. At this "Triumph of Orthodoxy," however, special reference is made to the sufferings
and struggles undergone by the saints, to the persecutions, torture and exile
that they faced for Christ's sake:

> Remember, O Lord, the reproaches and insults inflicted on Thy servants...
> Our God has indeed been mindful of the tribulations and abasement that all
> the saints have endured with Christ.

So the "Triumph of Orthodoxy" turns out to be a feast in honor of the
martyrs and confessors. The only triumph that the Church on earth can
or should expect is that of martyrdom.

The same truth is emphasized on the Sunday of All Saints, which in
Orthodox practice occurs one week after Pentecost. The two feasts are

seen as closely connected, All Saints being devoted to the consequences that the descent of the Holy Spirit has had in the life of the Church. It is significant that the special hymns appointed for All Saints Day, the *apolytikion* and *kontakion*, both refer explicitly to martyrdom:

> With the blood of Thy martyrs, O Christ our God,
> Thy Church is adorned throughout the world,
> As with purple and fine linen…

> As the first fruits of nature to the Gardener of the creation
> The inhabited earth offers to Thee, O Lord,
> The God-bearing martyrs…

The feast of All Saints thus proves to be in fact the feast of All Martyrs. The saint *par excellence* is the martyr.

Present-day Christians surely have particular reason to reflect on the centrality of martyrdom, for the century that has just come to a close has been preeminently an age of martyrs. In the twenty years between the two world wars incomparably more Christians died for their faith than in the whole of the three hundred years following the Crucifixion. The ordeal undergone by twentieth-century believers—in the Soviet Union during 1917-1988, in Ethiopia during 1974-1991, to mention but two examples—makes the persecution of the early Church in the Roman Empire, even under Diocletian, appear relatively mild and humane.

The experience of Iulia de Beausobre

What is a martyr? What is it that changes suffering from a destructive into a creative force, that transforms a violent death into an act of martyrdom, a miscarriage of justice into an atoning sacrifice?

The answer is provided by a Russian Christian, Iulia de Beausobre. One day in Moscow during the late 1920s, with her husband interned by the GPU but not yet herself arrested, she was preparing his weekly food parcel to deliver at the prison. She felt engulfed by a sense of hopelessness; her husband's suffering, her own and that of all those round her seemed so meaningless and futile. "To what end?" she asked herself. Suddenly, as she was moving from one room to another, she felt a blow on the back of her neck, and heard what she describes as "the unspoken words of Another." They were words that marked a new dawn in her life:

Of course it's no earthly use to any one of you. It can only cripple your bodies and twist your souls. But I will share in every last one of your burdens as they cripple and twist you. In the blending heat of compassion I will know the full horror of your deliberate destruction by men of your own race. I will know the weight of your load through carrying it alongside of you, but with an understanding greater than yours can be. I want to carry it. I need to know it. Because of My Incarnation and your Baptism there is no other way—*if you agree.*[1]

There are two things here that are particularly significant: the value attached to voluntary acceptance, and the insistence upon participation and solidarity.

"*If you agree,*" says our Lord to Iulia. Christ the protomartyr went voluntarily to His death, and the martyr as *alter Christus*, a "second Christ," is called to do the same. Innocent suffering does not by itself make someone into a martyr. It is also required that we on our side should voluntarily *accept* that suffering, even though we may not have originally chosen it. Self-dedication is needed; and it is this that changes the martyr from someone who suffers and dies into someone who *bears witness*. We are to *take up* our cross; it is not simply imposed upon us by exterior coercion. Suffering is made creative and death becomes sacrificial, if and only if they are willingly accepted by the one who has to suffer or die.

Christ also says, "I will share." Suffering is made creative and death becomes sacrificial as soon as we become aware that Christ our God is Himself suffering with us, and that through this divine co-suffering we in turn are enabled to suffer with, in and for others. "Because of My Incarnation…": at His birth in Bethlehem, Christ enters into all the fullness of human life, sharing in it totally and unreservedly. Then at Gethsemane and Calvary He goes still further, participating in all the fullness of human death—once more, totally and unreservedly. Bearing our griefs, carrying our sorrows, He associates Himself entirely with us in our alienation and takes our burden upon Himself. "Because of your Baptism…": baptized into Christ's death—and so into His Resurrection (Rom 6:3-5)—the

---

1   Constance Babington Smith, *Iulia de Beausobre: A Russian Christian in the West* (London: Darton, Longman & Todd, 1983), 26-27. Iulia de Beausobre—Iulia Mikhailovna, Lady Namier—will be known to many through her books *The Woman Who Could Not Die* (London: Chatto & Windus, 1938), *Creative Suffering* (Westminster: Dacre, 1940), *Macarius, Starets of Optino: Russian Letters of Direction 1834-1860* (Westminster: Dacre, 1944), and *Flame in the Snow* (London: Constable, 1945).

Christian is likewise called to carry the griefs and burdens of others in union with the Savior. "Bear one another's burdens and so fulfil the law of
Christ" (Gal 6:2).

Let us look more closely at these two points.

Voluntary acceptance

The first thing, then, that distinguishes a martyrdom from a murder or a
miscarriage of justice is the element of voluntary acceptance: "if you
agree." An exercise of free will is required. Martyrdom signifies not just
suffering but self-offering. The martyr *offers* himself or herself, thereby
changing a death into a sacrifice; for the verb "to sacrifice" bears precisely
the meaning "to sanctify something by offering it to God," whether
through a death or in some other way. The martyr is the one who chooses
to say at the moment of crisis, "Here am I" (Is 6:8), "Lo, I come to do Thy
will, O God" (Heb 10:7). True martyrs do not draw punishment upon
themselves by any gesture of willful and aggressive provocation, but
equally they do not tell lies or run away.

All this is plainly apparent from the example of Christ Himself. "I lay
down My life for the sheep," He says. "No one takes it from Me, but I lay
it down of My own accord" (Jn 10:15, 18). He is "obedient unto death"
(Phil 2:8)—He is not compelled. In the words of Thomas Aquinas,
"When He had done as much as He deemed sufficient, then came His
hour, not of necessity but of will, not of condition but of power."[2] The
voluntary character of Christ's martyrdom is evident above all in the garden of Gethsemane. As Pascal puts it, "Jesus suffers in His passion the torments inflicted on Him by others; but in His agony He suffers the
torments He inflicts on Himself."[3] If Christ is at that moment in agony,
"sorrowful even to death," with His sweat falling to the ground "like great
drops of blood," this is because He is free, because He is at that moment
confronted by a choice. Humanly speaking He does not have to die; it is
still possible for Him to withdraw and make His escape. Freely, deliberately and at incalculable cost, He brings His human will into conformity
with the divine will: "Not as I will but as Thou wilt"(Mt 26:39). So, by

2   Quoted in Charles Williams, *The Passion of Christ* (London: Oxford University Press, 1939), 1.
3   *Pensées* 919 (553).

virtue of this deliberate choice made alone in the garden, His ensuing death and passion are constituted into an act of self-offering and redemptive sacrifice.

The same element of free choice recurs again and again in the stories of the martyrs. In T. S. Eliot's *Murder in the Cathedral*, when the four knights arrive, there is still time for Thomas Becket to run away. "My Lord, they are coming," the priests warn him. "...Make haste, my Lord." But the Archbishop refuses: "Unbar the doors," he insists, "throw open the doors!... I *give* my life... I am here...*ready* to suffer with my blood" (my italics). The scriptural echo is surely intentional: "I am now ready to be offered" (2 Tim 4:6). So many parallel examples spring to mind: St Polycarp at Smyrna around 155, who "could have escaped to another place but refused, saying *May the will of God be done*,"[4] the New Martyr Elias the Barber at Kalamata, in 1686, who might have remained hidden on Mount Athos, but chose to return to the place where he was known, so as to atone for the sin of apostasy by a voluntary death;[5] Vivian Redlich in New Guinea in the second world war, who was given the chance to leave before the arrival of the Japanese but chose to remain at his post; Mother Maria (Skobtsova) at Ravensbrück on Easter Eve 1945, voluntarily taking the place of another prisoner and going instead of her to die in the gas chamber.[6] Each of these, in his or her way, can affirm with Jesus Christ, "No one takes my life from me, but I lay it down of my own accord."

A similar act of voluntary choice is required in monasticism, which serves as a substitute for martyrdom in times of peace when there is no exterior persecution; St Peter of Damascus speaks in this connection of the "deliberate death" of the monk.[7] At the tonsuring—the decisive moment in the monastic profession service—the abbot places the scissors on the Gospel Book, saying to the candidate, "Take the scissors, and give them

---

4   *Martyrdom of Polycarp* 7.1.
5   St Nicodemus of the Holy Mountain (ed.), *Neon Martyrologion* (Athens: Aster/ Papademetriou, 1961), 105-6; L. J. Papadopoulos and G. Lizardos (tr.), *The New Martyrs of the Turkish Yoke* (Seattle: St Nectarios Press, 1985), 40. On the New Martyrs, see Norman Russell, "Neomartyrs of the Greek Calendar," *Sobornost* 5:1 (1983), 36-62.
6   Sergei Hackel, *Pearl of Great Price*, 2nd edn. (London: Darton, Longman & Todd, 1981), 148.
7   *A Treasury of Divine Knowledge*, tr. *Philokalia*, 3:87, 161, 183, 281. Compare David Balfour, "Extended notions of martyrdom in the Byzantine ascetical tradition," *Sobornost* 5:1 (1983), 20-35.

to me." When the candidate does so, the abbot replaces them on the Gospel Book, repeating the same words. This happens yet a third time; and only after that does the abbot proceed to cut the novice's hair. Underscoring the significance of this threefold ceremony, the abbot says: "See, no one compels you to be clothed in the habit. See, you have freely chosen to receive it."[8] No one has taken away the new monk's freedom, but he has himself offered it to Christ. Once more it is clear beyond all doubt that the vocation of martyrdom is not imposed but accepted.

What has just been said about Christ, about the martyr and the monk, is also true in a certain measure of every Christian without exception. Each of us is called at some point in life to face disappointment, the loss of those we love, and pain either physical or mental. In a fallen world such suffering is unavoidable. The crucial question is how we face this suffering. For only by confronting it affirmatively, with willing acceptance, can we make the suffering creative. In itself suffering is an evil. It is not part of God's original plan for His creation: He made us not for sorrow but for joy—as St John Climacus puts it, not for mourning but for laughter.[9] Upon some people the effects of suffering are utterly destructive, leading to nothing but bitterness and despair. We are not to say that suffering as such is a blessing from God. And yet, by the divine mercy, what is in itself evil can be turned to good. As Iulia de Beausobre insists in *Creative Suffering*—probably her most profound work—suffering can be used. Something can be made of it.

It all depends upon the inward attitude of the sufferer, and of those close to him or her. We can meet suffering with resentment and rebellious defiance, in which case it may well annihilate us spiritually. Alternatively we can meet it with passive resignation, in which case it may act like an acid, corroding our character, making us unpersons, moral zombies. Or we may meet it actively, in a spirit of love; in which case the suffering can be accepted, offered, and through this offering transfigured. It is certainly not easy, but it is the way of Christ. As He said to Iulia, "if you agree." It is the presence or absence of this agreement that makes all the difference.

---

8   N. F. Robinson, *Monasticism in the Orthodox Churches* (London: Cope & Fenwick, 1916), 83.
9   *Ladder* 7 (*PG* 88:809c); tr. Lubheid and Russell, 141.

Solidarity

The second characteristic mark of a martyrdom, as contrasted with a mere act of violence, is the presence of sharing and participation, of what Charles Williams calls "substituted love," "coinherence," or "the way of exchange."[10] "I will share in every last one of your burdens," Christ assures Iulia, and goes on to speak of the "blending heat of compassion." We become fellow-martyrs with Christ the protomartyr, the "man for others," when in love we unite our sufferings with His and so with those of all humankind. In the words of *The Book of the Poor in Spirit*, "Love makes others' sufferings its own, not one, but all."[11] Suffering becomes creative and death becomes martyrdom when they are vicarious.

This notion of exchange, of solidarity in suffering, forms one of the master-themes of Martin Buber's *Tales of the Hasidim*. It is said of one of the most attractive of the Hasidic teachers, Rabbi Zusya, "He felt the sins of the people he met as his own, and blamed himself for them." So powerful was his sense of identification that he could say of a certain man who was a sinner, "I climbed down all the rungs until I was with him, and bound the root of my soul to the root of his." It is recorded of Rabbi Moshe Leib, who was ill for two-and-a-half years, racked with pain: "He grew more and more certain that he was suffering for the sake of Israel, and his pain did not grow less, but it was transfigured."[12]

To make others' sufferings His own, to climb down all the rungs until He is with the lowest sinner, to bind the root of the sinner's soul to the root of His own, to suffer for the sake of Israel, both the Old and the New—that is exactly what Christ has done; and the martyrs are enabled to do the same precisely because they are convinced that Christ is suffering in and with them. Applying Father Alexander Elchaninov's test of catholicity, we may define the martyr as the quintessential churchperson: "'And when one member suffers, all the members suffer with it' (1 Cor 12:26) is said of the Church. If we do not feel this, we are not within the Church."[13]

---

10 See *The Image of the City and Other Essays*, ed. Anne Ridler (London: Oxford University Press, 1958), 147-54.

11 4.4.2: ed. Kelley, 233.

12 *Tales of the Hasidim: The Early Masters* (New York: Schocken Books, 1968), 237, 242; *Tales of the Hasidim: The Later Masters* (New York: Schocken Books, 1966), 93.

13 *The Diary of a Russian Priest*, 124.

This solidarity is expressed in particular through the martyr's prayer of intercession. "Father, forgive them," Christ intercedes as He is crucified (Luke 23:34). When the soldiers come to arrest Polycarp, he stands in prayer for two hours without interruption, "remembering by name all whom he had ever met, old and young, celebrated and unknown, and the whole Catholic Church throughout the world."[14] The New Martyr Jordan of Trebizond, beheaded in 1650, as he is taken to the place of execution, "asked forgiveness from all those whom he met on the way, young and old";[15] another New Martyr, Iakovos of Arta, hanged in 1520, immediately before his death tells his two companions to kneel down, saying, "Let us pray to Christ for the whole world and for the Church."[16] Once the martyr is dead, this intercession continues, at the same time acquiring within the communion of saints a wider scope and a more dynamic power.

Sometimes the solidarity takes the form of an actual exchange, as in the case of Mother Maria at Ravensbrück. A similar exchange took place in the case of the third-century martyr Nicephorus, whose story particularly appealed to Mother Maria. His lifelong friendship with the priest Sapricius had been disrupted by a petty quarrel, and despite all Nicephorus' efforts at a reconciliation Sapricius had refused to make it up. When the persecution came, Sapricius apostasized; but Nicephorus, the friend whom he had rejected and humiliated, accepted a martyr's execution in his place and for his sake.[17] A somewhat different kind of exchange is that made by the nun Helen (Manturov), instructed by St Seraphim of Sarov to die in place of her sick brother Michael, whose work was not yet done; Michael recovered, while Helen fell ill and died.[18]

Solidarity, mutual sharing, is also a dominant feature in the voluntary martyrdom of the monastic life. Not only does the monk living in community share with others his daily work and daily prayer, together with all his possessions, but he may also be called to express this solidarity on a far deeper level as well. St Symeon the New Theologian prayed to God, so he

14   *Martyrdom of Polycarp* 8.1.
15   *Neon Martyrologion*, 72; tr. Papadopoulos and Lizardos, 46.
16   *Neon Martyrologion*, 42; tr. Papadopoulos and Lizardos, 330.
17   Hackel, *Pearl of Great Price*, 15.
18   Archimandrite Lazarus Moore, *St. Seraphim of Sarov: A Spiritual Biography* (Blanco, TX: New Sarov Press, 1994), 382-87.

tells us, "with scalding tears and with all his soul," that his brethren might enter heaven with him, or else that he might be condemned to hell with them: "Spiritually bound to them by a holy love in the Holy Spirit, he did not want to enter into the Kingdom of heaven itself if it meant that he would be separated from them."[19]

Bound as he is in this way to his brethren, the monk—like Zusya—takes their guilt upon himself and joins with them in their repentance. In the *Sayings of the Desert Fathers* there are a number of stories such as the following:

> Two brethren journeyed to the market to sell their handiwork. In the city they went different ways, and one of them fell into fornication. After a while the other monk met him and said, "Let's go back to our cell, brother." But the first answered, "I'm not coming." And the other questioned him, saying, "Why not, my brother?" And he said, "When we parted, I fell into fornication." Then the other, wishing to win him back, began to say to him: "When I left you, the same thing happened to me. But let us go and do heavy penance, and God will forgive us." So they returned and told the old men what had happened to them; and the old men enjoined on them the rules of penance that they were to perform. So the one offered repentance on behalf of the other, just as if he himself had sinned. God, seeing his labor of love, after a few days revealed to one of the old men that, because of the great love of the brother who had not sinned, He had forgiven the brother who had. That is what it means to lay down one's life for one's brother.[20]

The last sentence is particularly significant, making explicit as it does the connection with martyrdom.

The ninth-century hermit St Ioannikios the Great goes yet further, accepting not merely the penance but the temptations of another. Meeting a young nun troubled by "lustful impulses," he called the girl to him and told her to lay her hand on his neck. When she had done as he ordered, he prayed that she might be set free from the evil that was troubling her, and that the scourge might fall on himself. So she was released from the carnal warfare that had afflicted her, and returned to live with the nuns as before;

---

19 *Discourse* 8:62-64: ed. Krivochéine, 2:90; tr. deCatanzaro, 145. Compare the prayer made by St Barsanuphius (note 22).

20 *AP*, anonymous collection 179: ed. Nau, *ROC* 13 (1908), 269-70; similar stories in §§180, 346, 354, 389; tr. Ward, *Wisdom*, §§47, 48, 215, 223 (15, 58-59, 61).

but fearful temptations now assailed the saint. This was also a story that particularly appealed to Mother Maria.[21]

The idea that one Christian may, in a realistic and liberating sense, bear the burden of another's fear and temptation forms the central theme in the novel of Charles Williams, *Descent into Hell*. Pauline Anstruther is set free when she allows Peter Stanhope to assume the weight of her secret anxiety; in contrast, Lawrence Wentworth refuses the "way of exchange" and descends in ever-increasing isolation into hell.

Burden-bearing is an essential aspect of the ministry of the spiritual father or mother, as this is understood in Orthodox monasticism. For St John Climacus or St Symeon the New Theologian, as for the nineteenth-century Russian *startsi*, the spiritual guide is not merely a counselor proffering detached advice from a safe distance, or one who pronounces absolution in a narrowly juridical fashion, but also, and more fundamentally, a sponsor or *anadochos*, who stands surety for his children, taking their load of anxiety and guilt upon his own shoulders, answering for them at the Last Judgement, uniting himself with them in love.[22] As St Barsanuphius of Gaza assured his disciples: "I care for you more than you care for yourself... Lord, either bring my children with me into Your kingdom, or blot me too out of Your book... I have spread out my wings over you, and I am bearing your burdens and your offences... You are like someone sitting under a shady tree... I would gladly lay down my life for you."[23] As an icon of Christ the Good Shepherd, the spiritual father lays down his life for the sheep (Jn 10:11):[24] spiritual fatherhood is a form of martyrdom.

21 Symeon Metaphrastes, *Life of St Ioannikios* 14 (*PG* 116:48D); cf. Hackel, *Pearl of Great Price*, 15; also, more fully, in the first edition, *One, of Great Price* (London: Darton, Longman & Todd, 1965), 15-16. For a parallel story, with the same gesture of laying the hand on the neck of the other, see Climacus, *Ladder* 23 (*PG* 88:980AB); tr. Luibheid and Russell, 213.

22 See my introduction to Climacus, *The Ladder of Divine Ascent,* tr. Luibheid and Russell, 41-43; also my foreword to Irénée Hausherr, *Spiritual Direction in the Early Christian East*, Cistercian Studies Series 116 (Kalamazoo, MI: Cistercian Publications, 1990), xxii-xxvii. Compare *AP*, alphabetical collection, Lot 2 (*PG* 65:256B).

23 *Questions and Answers*, ed. Schoinas, §§39, 110, 239, 353; tr. Regnault and Lemaire, §§39, 187, 239, 353.

24 Climacus, *To the Shepherd* 5 (*PG* 88:1177B); tr. Archimandrite Lazarus (Boston: Holy Transfiguration Monastery, 1978), 234.

A *universal vocation*

In our consideration of martyrdom, we have been led to speak not only of martyrs in the outward and literal sense—of those who have died for Christ's sake in persecutions—but also of others, such as the monk and the spiritual father or mother, whose martyrdom is inner and hidden. This is inevitable, for martyrdom is an all-inclusive category, a universal vocation. If martyrdom means taking up the cross with Christ—taking it up by an act of voluntary acceptance and, as we carry it, uniting our suffering with Christ's and that of all the world—then this is something that every Christian is called to undertake. All are cross-bearers, all are in some sense martyrs. Whether we are called to die outwardly for Christ, in the arena, the gas chamber or the prison camp, depends largely on factors outside our control, on the political situation under which we live. What does depend directly on us, however, is whether we take up the cross inwardly.

The importance of inner martyrdom was quickly appreciated by the Christian community. "I die every day," said St Paul (1 Cor 15:31): martyrdom, death for Christ, is not merely an ultimate possibility but an immediate fact of daily experience. Writing in the early third century, St Clement of Alexandria affirms of the "true gnostic" that he will be a constant and incessant martyr: "He will be a martyr by night, a martyr by day, a martyr in his speech, his daily life, his character."[25] Origen develops the point in his *Exhortation to Martyrdom*. As a young man he saw his own father die in the persecution at Alexandria in 202, and it had been his ardent desire to share the same fate. Disappointed in this, he turned to a life of asceticism, which he regarded both as a preparation for the future call to martyrdom, and at the same time as a substitute if that future call should not in fact come. He makes a distinction between "outward martyrdom" and "secret martyrdom" or martyrdom of the conscience.[26] The first is for some only, the second is for all.

St Cyprian of Carthage, in the middle of the same century, renders the distinction more vivid by speaking of "red" and "white" martyrdom—the red martyrdom of blood in times of persecution, the white martyrdom of

---

25 *Miscellanies* 2.20: ed. Stählin, 170. 10f.
26 *Exhortation to Martyrdom* 21; tr. Greer, 55. On Origen's ascetic life, see Eusebius of Caesarea, *Ecclesiastical History* 6.3.

self-sacrificing compassion and acts of charity in times of peace.[27] The Irish elaborated the idea still further by speaking of a threefold martyrdom, red, white and green: red martyrdom is to shed one's blood for Christ; white martyrdom is "to abandon everything one loves for God's sake," that is, to accept the vocation of wandering, pilgrimage, voluntary exile for Christ; green martyrdom is "to free oneself from evil desires by means of fasting and labor," pursuing the ascetic way in one's homeland.[28]

Origen's notion of secret martyrdom is taken up and applied in fourth-century monasticism. Around the year 311 the "father of monks," St Antony of Egypt, goes up from the desert to Alexandria during the persecution of Maximinus Daia to support and encourage the martyrs in their trials, ready himself to suffer if so called. The call does not come; so, the persecution ended, he returns to the desert and intensifies his life of asceticism, "suffering as a martyr every day in his conscience," in the words of his biographer St Athanasius.[29] There was a saying that circulated among the early monks, "Give your blood and receive the Spirit"[30]: the gift of the Paraclete is won through the martyrdom of conscience, through the "daily death" of ascesis. St Barsanuphius states, "To abandon your self-will is to shed your blood."[31] All sanctity, so it is affirmed by Evagrius of Pontus, involves an inner martyrdom: "Do not think that you have acquired virtue, unless you have struggled for it to the point of shedding your blood."[32] The monks are the martyrs within an "established" Christendom, no longer subject to outward persecution from the state.

Yet the ascetic path of secret martyrdom is not restricted only to monks and nuns. Those who follow the married life are also called to be

27 *On works and almsgiving*, 26.
28 See J. Ryan, *Irish Monasticism* (Dublin: Talbot, 1931), 197-98, citing the so-called Cambray Homily (late seventh or early eighth century), in W. Stokes and J. Strachan, *Thesaurus Palaeohibernicus*, 3 vols. (Cambridge, England: Cambridge University Press, 1901-1903), 2:246-7. Ryan takes white martyrdom to signify the monk's first step of renouncing the world, and green martyrdom to mean a further, more severe degree of ascetic austerity.
29 *Life of Antony* 47; tr. Gregg, 66. The authorship of the work has been much disputed, but there seems to be no conclusive reason to reject the traditional ascription to Athanasius.
30 *AP*, alphabetical collection, Longinus 5 (*PG* 65:257B); tr. Ward, *Sayings*, 123.
31 *Questions and Answers*, §254.
32 *On prayer* 136 (*PG* 79:1196C); tr. *Philokalia*, 1:69.

martyrs.[33] The sharing of a common life between husband, wife and children involves precisely that cutting off of self-will which St Barsanuphius terms a shedding of blood. Mutual love, while joyful and self-fulfilling, needs also to be sacrificial. All this is made clear in the Orthodox marriage service. The prayers speak of joy, but what they envisage is the joy *of the cross*, "the joy which blessed Helena felt when she found the precious cross." In the culminating action of the sacrament, the coronation of bridegroom and bride, the crowns are understood as emblems of victory, athletes' garlands destined for those who have proved triumphant in the contest against sinful passions. But they are at the same time martyrs' crowns; for without inward martyrdom, without willingly accepted suffering, there can be no true marriage. As the newly crowned couple go processionally three times round in a circle, the priest carries the cross in front of them,[34] and the choir sings a hymn in honor of the holy martyrs, "You who have fought the good fight and have received your crowns."

Husbands and wives, then, as well as monks and nuns, are cross-bearers, martyrs of conscience. So also are those in the single life: those, that is to say, who have not deliberately adopted the vocation of virginity but who find themselves celibate because the opportunity to marry has never actually occurred. In contemporary western society this is an increasingly large group, strongly represented in our church congregations. Orthodoxy has a rich theology of the monastic life, and an equally rich—although often neglected—theology of marriage; but it has so far given little thought to the theology of the single life. What, then, should we say to those in the third situation?

By way of beginning we might reflect on the two aspects of martyrdom underlined earlier: acceptance and solidarity. The single man or woman may not at the outset have chosen to be unmarried; but if he or she learns inwardly to accept the position, then what seems at first a deprivation can become a fulfillment. Likewise the apparent isolation of the single person can be turned into an occasion for sharing. The freedom from immediate family ties which he or she commonly enjoys, while at

---

33   See Paul Evdokimov, *The Sacrament of Love. The Nuptial Mystery in the Light of the Orthodox Tradition*, 65-84, where the two vocations of marriage and monasticism are rightly treated as complementary.

34   In the Russian practice.

first sight a loss, can be transformed if this leisure time is used for practical compassion towards others, for acts of personal or community service. Developing a wide circle of friends—though not necessarily a "social life" in the secular sense—devoting special attention to the prayer of intercession, the single person can be like Cicero, *numquam minus solus quam cum solus*, never so little alone as when seemingly in solitude. But it is sometimes bitterly hard. For nothing of value comes without suffering; as St Seraphim warns us, "Without sorrows, there is no salvation."[35] St Theophan the Recluse says the same: "A soul untried by sorrows is good for nothing."[36]

Between red martyrdom and the other forms there is this obvious difference. The martyr in a persecution is called to make, once for all, a single, all-embracing sacrifice. The martyr of conscience—monastic, married or single—is called to make a lifelong self-giving, continually renewed; not one great sacrifice, but a multitude of small ones. In the words of St Methodius of Olympus, the virgin life is a martyrdom, "not in one brief moment of time, but extended over the whole of life."[37] As St Luke's Gospel insists, we are to take up our cross *daily* (9:23).

Expressed in that way, the prospect may seem daunting. Yet daily death is at the same time daily resurrection. "Something in me has been killed" means also "something in me has come to life." In St Paul's phrase, "dying, and behold we live...sorrowful, yet always rejoicing" (2 Cor 6:9-10).

Joyful sorrow

Let this, then, be our final reflection. The martyr is a witness—a witness not only to the Crucifixion but to the Resurrection. Martyrdom involves anguish, both physical and mental, of a most acute kind; yet the suffering of the martyrs is a joy-creating sorrow, both for others and for themselves. Repeatedly in the eyewitness accounts it is stated that the martyr goes to meet death, not grim-faced or terrified, but eager and expectant. When the proconsul condemns St Polycarp to be burnt alive, he answers, "Why

35 Archimandrite Lazarus Moore, *St. Seraphim of Sarov*, 126.
36 Quoted in Igumen Chariton, *The Art of Prayer*, 231.
37 *Banquet* 7.3.

do you delay? Do what you will"; and then, so we are told, "he was inspired with courage and joy, and his face was filled with grace."[38] The New Martyr Nicolas the Grocer, on his way to execution, "was like someone going to a marriage, not to his death";[39] Jordan of Trebizond, as he was led out to be killed, "ran through the streets joyfully, as a thirsty deer that seeks the water-springs."[40]

The Church has good reason to begin so many of its hymns to the martyrs with the word "Rejoice!"

38 *Martyrdom of Polycarp* 11.2; 12.1.
39 *Neon Martyrologion*, 87.
40 *Ibid.*, 72; tr. Papadopoulos and Lizardos, 46.

9

THE SPIRITUAL GUIDE IN
ORTHODOX CHRISTIANITY

More important than all possible books

If we are climbing a mountain for the first time, we need to follow a
known route; and we also need to have with us, as companion and guide,
someone who has been up before and is familiar with the way. To serve as
such a companion and guide is precisely the role of the "abba" or spiritual
father—of the one whom the Greeks call *geron* or *geronta* and the Russians
starets, a title which in both languages means "old man" or "elder."[1]

---

1 On spiritual fatherhood in the Christian East, the standard work is by Irénée Hausherr, *Direction spirituelle en Orient autrefois,* Orientalia Christiana Analecta 144 (Rome: Pont. Institutum
Studiorum Orientalium, 1955); English translation, *Spiritual Direction in the Early Christian
East*, Cistercian Studies Series 116 (Kalamazoo, MI: Cistercian Publications, 1990). Consult
also I. Hadot, "The Spiritual Guide," in A. H. Armstrong (ed.), *Classical Mediterranean Spirituality: Egyptian, Greek, Roman* (London: Routledge & Kegan Paul, 1986), 436-59; Graham
Gould, *The Desert Fathers on Monastic Community* (Oxford: Clarendon Press, 1993), especially
26-87; Stephan B. Clark, *Unordained Elders and Renewal Communities* (New York/Paramus/
Toronto: Paulist Press, 1976); John Chryssavgis, *Ascent to Heaven. The Theology of the Human
Person according to Saint John of the Ladder* (Brookline, MA: Holy Cross Orthodox Press,
1989), 211-30; H. J. M. Turner, *St. Symeon the New Theologian and Spiritual Fatherhood*
(Leiden: E. J. Brill, 1990). For a comparison between Climacus and Symeon, see my introduction to the English translation of Hausherr, *Spiritual Direction*, vii-xxxiii. On the Russian tra-
dition, consult J. B. Dunlop, *Staretz Amvrosy: Model for Dostoevsky's Staretz Zossima* (Belmont,
MA: Nordland, 1972); I. de Beausobre (ed.), *Macarius, Starets of Optino: Russian Letters of Di-
rection 1834-1860* (Westminster: Dacre, 1944); Archimandrite Sophrony (Sakharov), *Saint
Silouan the Athonite* (Tolleshunt Knights: Monastery of Saint John the Baptist, 1991). For
modern Greek examples, see Elder Paisios of Mount Athos, *Athonite Fathers and Athonite
Matters* (Thessalonica: Holy Convent of the Evangelist John the Theologian, Souroti, 1999).
On Romania, see [Hieromonk Seraphim Rose], *Blessed Paisius Velichkovsky* (Platina, CA: Saint
Herman of Alaska Brotherhood, 1976); Romul Joantă (now Metropolitan Seraphim of Ger-
many and Central Europe), *Roumanie: tradition et culture hésychastes*, Spiritualité orientale 46
(Bégrolles: Abbaye de Bellefontaine, 1987); English translation, *Romania: Its Hesychast Tradi-
tion and Culture* (Wildwood, CA: St Xenia Skete, 1992).

The importance of obedience to a *geron* is underlined from the very first beginnings of Eastern Christian monasticism. It is clearly evident, for example, in the sayings attributed to St Antony of Egypt:

> I know of monks who fell after much toil and lapsed into madness, because they trusted in their own works and did not give due heed to the command-ment of him who says, "Ask your father, and he will tell you" (Deut 32:7). If possible, for every step that a monk takes, for every drop of water that he drinks in his cell, he should entrust the decision to the old men, to avoid mak-ing some mistake in what he does.[2]

The need for spiritual guidance is a master-theme throughout the *Apophthegmata* or *Sayings of the Desert Fathers*:

> The old men used to say: "If you see a young monk climbing up to heaven by his own will, grasp him by the feet and throw him down, for this is to his profit… If a person places his faith in someone else and surrenders himself to the other in full submission, he has no need to attend to the commandment of God, but he needs only to entrust his entire will into the hands of his father. Then he will be blameless before God, for God requires nothing from begin-ners so much as self-stripping through obedience."[3]

This figure of the *starets*, so prominent in the first generations of Egyp-tian monasticism, has retained its full significance up to the present day in Orthodox Christendom. "There is one thing more important than all possible books and ideas," states a Russian layman of the nineteenth cen-tury, the Slavophil Ivan Kireyevsky, "and that is the example of an Ortho-dox *starets*, before whom you can lay each of your thoughts and from whom you can hear, not a more or less valuable private opinion, but the judgement of the Holy Fathers. God be praised, such *startsi* have not yet disappeared from our Russia."[4] And a priest of the Russian emigration in the twentieth century, Father Alexander Elchaninov, writes: "Their field of action is unlimited…they are undoubtedly saints, recognized as such by the people. I feel that in our tragic days it is precisely through this

2   *AP*, alphabetical collection, Antony 37, 38 (*PG* 65:88B); tr. Ward, 8-9 (the translation needs correcting).

3   *AP*, anonymous collection, 244, 290: ed. Nau, *ROC* 14 (1909), 364, 376; tr. Ward, *Wisdom*, §§112, 158 (34, 45).

4   Cited by Ivan Tschetwerikow, in Metropolitan Seraphim (ed.), *L'Eglise Orthodoxe* (Paris: Payot, 1952), 219.

means that faith will survive and be strengthened in our country."[5]

The spiritual guide as a "charismatic" figure

What entitles someone to act as spiritual guide? How and by whom is he or she appointed?

To this there is a simple answer. The elder or *starets* is essentially a "charismatic" and prophetic figure, accredited for her or his task by the direct action of the Holy Spirit. Spiritual guides are ordained, not by human hands, but by the hand of God. They are an expression of the Church as "event" or "happening," rather than of the Church as institution.[6]

There is, however, no sharp line of demarcation between the prophetic and the institutional elements in the life of the Church; each grows out of the other and is intertwined with it. The ministry of the *starets*, itself charismatic, is related to a clearly-defined function within the institutional framework of the Church, the office of priest-confessor. In the Orthodox tradition, the right to hear confessions is not granted automatically at ordination. Before acting as confessor, a priest requires authorization from his bishop; and in the Greek Church, at any rate, only a minority of the clergy are so authorized. Yet, although the sacrament of confession is certainly an appropriate occasion for spiritual direction, the ministry of the *starets* is by no means identical with that of a confessor. The *starets* gives advice, not only at confession, but on many other occasions. Moreover, while the confessor must always be a priest, the *starets* may be a simple monk, not in holy orders, or even a layman; the ministry of eldership may also be exercised by a nun or a laywoman, for in the Orthodox tradition there are spiritual mothers as well as spiritual fathers.[7] The *starets*, whether

---

5   Elchaninov, *The Diary of a Russian Priest*, 54.

6   I use "charismatic" in the restricted sense customarily given to it by contemporary writers. But if that word indicates (as properly it should) someone who has received the gifts or *charismata* of Holy Spirit, then the ministerial priest, ordained through the episcopal laying on of hands, is as genuinely "charismatic" as one who speaks with tongues.

7   In the alphabetical collection of the *Sayings of the Desert Fathers,* alongside 127 "abbas" there are three "ammas" or spiritual mothers: the women are in a minority, but they have their place in the *Gerontikon*. See Sister Benedicta Ward, "'Apophthegmata Matrum,'" *Studia Patristica* 16:2, Texte und Untersuchungen 129 (Berlin: Akademie Verlag, 1985), 63-66; Joseph M. Soler, "Les Mères du désert et la maternité spirituelle," *Collectanea Cisterciensia* 48(1986), 235-50.

ordained or lay, frequently speaks with an insight and authority that only a very few confessor-priests possess.

If, however, spiritual fathers or mothers are not appointed by an official act of the hierarchy, how then do they come to embark on their ministry? Sometimes an existing *starets* will designate his own successor. In this way, at certain monastic centers such as Optino in nineteenth-century Russia, there was established an "apostolic succession" of spiritual masters. In other cases, the *starets* emerges spontaneously, without any act of external authorization. As Elchaninov says, they are "recognized as such by the people." Within the continuing life of the Christian community, it becomes plain to the believing people of God—which is the true guardian of Holy Tradition—that this or that person has the gift of spiritual fatherhood or motherhood. Then, in a free and informal fashion, others begin to come to him or her for advice and direction.

It will be noted that the initiative comes, as a rule, not from the master but from the disciples. It would be perilously presumptuous for someone to say in his own heart or to others, "Come and submit yourselves to me; I am a *starets*, I have the grace of the Spirit." What happens, rather, is that—without any claims being made by the person himself—others approach him, seeking his advice or asking to live permanently under his care. At first, he will probably send them away, telling them to consult someone else. Eventually the moment comes when he no longer sends them away but accepts their coming to him as a disclosure of the will of God. Thus it is his spiritual children who reveal the elder to himself.

The figure of the *geronta* or *starets* illustrates the two interpenetrating levels on which the earthly Church exists and functions. On the one hand, there is the external, official and hierarchical level, with its geographical organization into dioceses and parishes, its great centers—Rome, Constantinople, Moscow, and Canterbury—and its "apostolic succession" of bishops. On the other hand, there is the inner, spiritual and "charismatic" level, to which the *startsi* primarily belong. Here the chief centers are, for the most part, not the great primatial and metropolitan sees but certain remote hermitages, in which there shine forth a few personalities richly endowed with spiritual gifts. Most *startsi* have possessed no exalted status in the formal hierarchy of the Church; yet the influence of a simple priest-monk such as St Seraphim of Sarov exceeded that of any patriarch or bishop in nineteenth-century Orthodoxy. In this fashion, alongside the apostolic succession of the episcopate, there exists also the apostolic succession of the saints and Spirit-bearers. Both types of succession are essential for the true functioning of the Body of Christ, and it is through their interaction that the life of the Church on earth is accomplished.

Flight and return: the preparation of the spiritual guide

Although spiritual guides are not ordained or appointed for their task, it is certainly necessary that they should be *prepared*. There is a classic pattern for this preparation, a movement of flight and return such as may be clearly discerned in the lives of St Antony the Great and St Seraphim of Sarov, to take but two examples separated from each other by fifteen centuries.

St Antony's life falls sharply into two halves, with his fifty-fifth year as the watershed. The years from early manhood to the age of fifty-five were his time of preparation, spent in an ever-increasing seclusion from the world as he withdrew further and further into the desert. According to his biographer, he eventually passed twenty years in an abandoned fort, meeting no one whatsoever. When he had reached the age of fifty-five, his friends could contain their curiosity no longer, and broke down the entrance. St Antony came out and, for the remaining half century of his long life, without abandoning the life of a hermit he made himself freely available to others, acting as "a physician given by God to Egypt," to use the phrase of his biographer, St Athanasius. "He was beloved by all," Athanasius states, "and all desired to have him as their father."[8] Observe that the transition from enclosed anchorite to spiritual father came about, not through any initiative on St Antony's part, but through the action of others. It should also be noted that Antony was a lay monk, never ordained to the priesthood.

St Seraphim followed a comparable path. After sixteen years spent in the ordinary life of the monastic community, as novice, professed monk, deacon, and priest, he withdrew for twenty years of solitude, first as a hermit in the forest and then for the last three years, after being ordered by

---

8   *Life of Antony*, 87 and 81; tr. Gregg, 94, 90.

the abbot to return to the monastery, as a recluse enclosed in his cell. During part of these twenty years he met occasional visitors, but at other times his isolation was almost total: at the start of his time in the forest he spent a thousand days on the stump of a tree and the thousand nights of those days on a rock, devoting himself to unceasing prayer; for the last three years in his forest hut he spoke to no one; and during his three years of enclosure in the monastery he did not go to church even to receive Holy Communion, but the sacrament was brought to him at the door of his cell. Then in 1813, at the age of fifty-three, he ended his seclusion, devoting the last two decades of his life to the ministry of *starchestvo* (eldership) and receiving all who came to him, whether monks or laypeople. He did nothing to advertise himself or to call others to him; it was the others who took the initiative in approaching him, but when they came—sometimes hundreds or even thousands in a single day—he did not send them empty away.[9]

Without this intense ascetic preparation, without this radical flight into solitude, would St Antony or St Seraphim have been able to guide and inspire their contemporaries to the same degree? Not that they withdrew with the specific and conscious purpose of becoming the teachers and guides of others. They fled, not in order to prepare themselves for any such task, but simply out of a consuming desire to be alone with God. God accepted their love, but then He sent them back as instruments of healing in the world from which they had withdrawn. Even had He never sent them back, their flight would still have been supremely creative and valuable to society; for nuns and monks help the world not primarily by anything that they do and say but by what they are, by the state of unceasing prayer which—for some at any rate among them—has become identical with their innermost being. Had St Antony and St Seraphim done nothing but pray in solitude they would still have been serving others to the highest degree. As things turned out, however, God ordained that

9　I follow here the generally accepted chronology of St Seraphim's life. But there is evidence to suggest that he may have begun his ministry as *starets* at a much earlier point, before his withdrawal into the forest in 1794. Yet even so the pattern of flight and return still holds good in Seraphim's case, at any rate in general terms; for, prior to 1813, his ministry as *starets* was restricted and sometimes totally interrupted. See Vsévolod Rochcau, *Saint Séraphim: Sarov et Divéyevo. Études et Documents,* Spiritualité Orientale 45 (Bégrolles: Abbaye de Bellefontaine, 1987), 53-84.

they should also serve them in a more direct fashion. Yet this direct and visible service was not their original aim: it was a side-effect that they had not themselves intended or initially envisaged, an outward consequence of the inner and invisible service which they were already rendering through their prayer.

"Acquire a peaceful spirit," said St Seraphim, "and then thousands of others around you will be saved."[10] Such is the pattern of spiritual father-hood or motherhood. Establish yourself in God; then you can bring oth-ers to His presence. Each must learn to be alone, and so in the stillness of their own heart they will begin to hear the wordless speech of the Spirit, thus discovering the truth about themselves and about God. Then their word to others will be a word of power, because it is a word out of silence.

Shaped in this way by the encounter with God in solitude, the *starets* is able to heal by his very presence. He guides and forms others, not primar-ily by words of advice but by his companionship, by the living and specific example which he sets. He teaches as much by his stillness as by his speech, by his very presence as much as by any word of counsel that he utters. That is why Abba Pambo saw no reason to say anything to Arch-bishop Theophilus of Alexandria: "If he isn't edified by my silence," ob-served the old man, "then he won't be edified by my words."[11] A story with the same moral is told of St Antony. "It was the custom of three Fathers to visit the Blessed Antony once each year, and two of them used to ask him questions about their thoughts (*logismoi*) and the salvation of their soul; but the third remained completely silent, without putting any questions. After a long while, Abba Antony said to him, 'See, you have been in the habit of coming to me all this time, and yet you do not ask me any ques-tions.' And the other replied, 'Father, it is enough for me just to look at you.'"[12]

The real journey of the *starets,* however, is not spatially into the desert, but spiritually into the heart. External solitude, however valuable, is not indispensable, and a person may learn to stand alone before God while yet continuing to pursue a life of active service in the midst of society. The story of the Alexandrian doctor who was the equal of St Antony, and who

10 Archimandrite Lazarus Moore, *St. Seraphim of Sarov,* 126.
11 *AP,* alphabetical collection, Theophilus 2; quoted above, 89.
12 *AP,* alphabetical collection, Antony 27 (84D); tr. Ward, *Sayings,* 7.

all day long sang the Thrice-Holy Hymn with the angels,[13] shows us that the mystical and "angelic" life is possible in the city as well as the desert. Unceasing prayer of the heart is no monopoly of the eremitic solitary; for people such as the Alexandrian doctor have accomplished the inner journey without severing their outward links with the community.

This pattern of flight and return, then, is not to be understood in too literal and clear-cut a way. The two stages need not necessarily be expressed in external and spatial terms; and by the same token the flight and return are not always sharply distinguished in temporal sequence. Take, for example, the case of St Seraphim's younger contemporary, St Ignaty Brianchaninov. Trained originally as an army officer, he then withdrew to a monastery; but after only four years in monasticism he was appointed at the early age of twenty-six to take charge of a busy and influential community close to the heart of St Petersburg. After twenty-four years as abbot, he was consecrated bishop. Four years later he resigned, to spend the remaining six years of his life as a hermit. Thus in St Ignaty's case a long period of active pastoral work and spiritual fatherhood preceded the period of his anachoretic seclusion. When he was originally made abbot, he must surely have felt ill-prepared. His secret withdrawal into the heart was undertaken continuously during the many years in which he administered a monastery and a diocese; but it did not receive an exterior expression until the very end of his life. The life of St Theophan the Recluse followed the same pattern: first an active pastorate, then the hermit's cell.[14]

St Ignaty's career may serve as a paradigm to many of us at the present time, even though we are conscious of falling far short of his level of spiritual achievement. Under the pressure of outward circumstances and probably without clearly realizing what is happening to us, we assume the responsibilities of teaching, preaching and pastoral counseling, while lacking any deep knowledge of the desert and its creative silence. But through instructing others we ourselves perhaps begin to learn. Slowly we recognize our powerlessness to heal the wounds of humanity solely

13 *AP,* alphabetical collection, Antony 24 (84B); see above, 86.
14 On Ignaty and Theophan, see the introduction to Igumen Chariton, *The Art of Prayer,* 11-15. St Tikhon of Zadonsk is yet another example of one who, after many years of active pastorate, only became a recluse at the end of his life.

through philanthropic programs, common sense and psychoanalysis. Our self-dependence is broken down, we appreciate our own inadequacy, and so we start to understand what Christ meant by the "one thing that is necessary" (Lk 10:42). That is the moment when a person may by the divine mercy start to advance along the path of the *starets*. Through our pastoral experience, through our anguish over the pain of others, we are brought to undertake the journey inwards and to seek the hidden treasure-house of the Kingdom, where alone a genuine solution to the world's problems can be found. No doubt few if any among us would venture to think of ourselves as a *starets* in the full sense, but provided we seek with humble sincerity to enter into the "secret chamber" of our heart, we can all share to some degree in the grace of spiritual fatherhood or motherhood. Perhaps we shall never outwardly lead the life of a monastic recluse or a hermit—that often rests with circumstances outside our own control—but what is supremely important is that each should see the need to be a hermit of the heart.

The three gifts of the spiritual guide

Three gifts in particular distinguish the spiritual guide. The first is *insight and discernment* (*diakrisis*), the ability to perceive intuitively the secrets of another's heart, to understand the hidden depths of which the other does not speak and is usually unaware. The spiritual father or mother penetrates beneath the conventional gestures and subterfuges whereby we conceal our true personality from others and from ourselves; and, beyond all these trivialities, she or he comes to grips with the unique person made in the image and likeness of God. This power of discernment is spiritual rather than psychic; it is not simply a happy knack of hitting the nail on the head, nor yet a kind of extra-sensory perception or clairvoyance, but it is the fruit of grace, presupposing concentrated prayer and an unremitting ascetic struggle.

With this gift of insight there goes the ability to use words with power. As each person comes before him, the *starets* or *geronta* knows immediately and specifically what it is that this particular individual needs to hear. Today, by virtue of computers and photocopying machines, we are inundated with words as never before in human history; but alas! for the most part these are conspicuously *not* words uttered with power.[15] The *starets,* on the other hand, uses few words, and sometimes none at all; but, by these few words or by his silence, he is often able to alter the entire direction of another's life. At Bethany Christ used three words only: "Lazarus, come out" (Jn 11:43); and yet these three words, spoken with power, were sufficient to bring the dead back to life. In an age when language has been shamefully trivialized, it is vital to rediscover the power of the word; and this means rediscovering the nature of silence, not just as a pause in the midst of our talk, but as one of the primary realities of existence. Most teachers and preachers surely talk far too much; the true *starets* is distinguished by an austere economy of language.[16]

Yet, for a word to possess power, it is necessary that there should be not only one who speaks with the genuine authority of personal experience, but also one who listens with attention and eagerness. If we question a *geronta* out of idle curiosity, it is likely that we will receive little benefit; but if we approach him with ardent faith and deep hunger, the word that we hear may transfigure our whole being. The words of the *startsi* are for the most part simple in verbal expression and devoid of literary artifice; to those who read them in a superficial way, they will seem jejune and banal.

The elder's gift of insight is exercised primarily through the practice known as the "disclosure of thoughts" (*logismoi*). In early Eastern monasticism the young monk used to go daily to his spiritual father and lay before him all the thoughts which had come to him during the day. This disclosure of thoughts includes far more than a confession of sins, since the novice also speaks of those ideas and impulses which may seem innocent to him, but in which the spiritual father may discern secret dangers or significant signs. Confession is retrospective, dealing with sins that have already occurred; the disclosure of thoughts, on the other hand, is prophylactic, for it lays bare our *logismoi* before they have led to sin and so

15 If the chairmen of committees and others in seats of authority were forced to write out personally in longhand everything they wanted to communicate, might they not choose their words with greater care?

16 See the perceptive discussion in Douglas Burton-Christie, *The Word in the Desert: Scripture and the Quest for Holiness in Early Christian Monasticism* (New York/Oxford: Oxford University Press, 1993), especially chapter 5; and compare Max Picard, *The World of Silence* (London: Harvill Press, n.d.).

deprives them of their power to harm. The purpose of the disclosure is not juridical, to secure absolution from guilt, but its aim is self-knowledge, that we may see ourselves as we truly are.

The principle underlying the disclosure of thoughts is clearly summed up in the *Sayings of the Desert Fathers*: "If unclean thoughts trouble you, do not hide them but tell them at once to your spiritual father and condemn them. The more we conceal our thoughts, the more they multiply and gain strength... [But] once an evil thought is revealed, it is immediately dissipated... Whoever discloses his thoughts is quickly healed."[17]

If we cannot or will not bring out into the open a *logismos*, a secret fantasy or fear or temptation, then it possesses power over us. But if, with God's help and with the assistance of our spiritual guide, we bring the thought out from the darkness into the light, its influence begins to wither away. Having exposed the *logismos*, we are then in a position to deal with it, and the process of healing can begin. The method proposed here by the early monks has interesting similarities with the techniques of modern psychoanalysis and psychotherapy. But the early monks had worked out this method fifteen centuries before Freud and Jung! There is, of course, an important difference: the early monks did not employ the notion of the unconscious in the way that modern psychology does, even though they recognized that with our conscious understanding we are usually aware of only a small part of ourselves.

Endowed as he is with discernment, the spiritual father does not merely wait for a person to reveal himself, but takes the initiative in revealing to the other many thoughts of which the other is not yet aware. When people came to St Seraphim of Sarov, he often answered their difficulties before they had time to put their perplexities before him. On many occasions the answer at first seemed quite irrelevant, and even absurd and irresponsible; for what St Seraphim answered was not the question his visitor had consciously in mind, but the one which the visitor ought to have been asking. In all this St Seraphim relied on the inner light of the Holy Spirit. He found it important, he explained, not to work out

---

17 For the Greek text of this *apophthegma*, see *Evergetinos* 1.20.11, ed. Victor Matthaiou, 4 vols. (Athens: Monastery of the Transfiguration of the Savior at Kronize Kouvara, 1957-66), 1:168-9; French translation in Lucien Regnault (ed.), *Les Sentences des Pères du Désert, serie des anonymes* (Sablé-sur-Sarthe/Bégrolles: Solesmes/Bellefontaine, 1985), 227.

in advance what he was going to say; in that case, his words would represent merely his own human judgment, which might well be in error, and not the judgment of God.[18]

In St Seraphim's eyes, the relationship between *starets* and spiritual child is stronger even than death, and he therefore urged his children to continue their disclosure of thoughts to him after his departure to the next life. These are the words which, by his own instructions, were written on his tomb: "When I am no more, come to me at my grave, and the more often, the better. Whatever weighs on your soul, whatever may have happened to you, whatever sorrows you have, come to me as if I were alive and, kneeling on the ground, cast all your bitterness upon my grave. Tell me everything and I shall listen to you, and all the sorrow will fly away from you. And as you spoke to me when I was alive, do so now. For to you I am alive, and I shall be forever."[19]

The second gift of the spiritual father or mother is *the ability to love others and to make others' sufferings their own*. Of one elder mentioned in the *Sayings of the Desert Fathers*, it is briefly and simply recorded: "He possessed love, and many came to him."[20] He possessed love—this is indispensable in all spiritual motherhood and fatherhood. Insight into the secrets of people's hearts, if devoid of loving compassion, would not be creative but destructive; if we cannot love others, we will have little power to heal them.

Loving others involves suffering with and for them; such is the literal sense of the word "compassion." "Bear one another's burdens, and so fulfill the law of Christ" (Gal 6:2): the spiritual father or mother is the one *par excellence* who bears the burdens of others. "A *starets*," writes Dostoevsky in *The Brothers Karamazov*, "is one who takes your soul, your will into his soul and into his will."[21] It is not enough for him merely to offer advice in a detached way. He is also required to take up the soul of his spiritual children into his own soul, their life into his life. It is his task to pray for them, and his constant intercession on their behalf is more important to them than

18   Archimandrite Lazarus Moore, *St. Seraphim of Sarov*, 217-20.
19   *Op. cit.*, 436-7.
20   *AP*, alphabetical collection, Poemen 8 (321C); tr. Ward *Sayings*, 167.
21   *The Brothers Karamazov*, tr. Richard Pevear and Larissa Volokhonsky (New York: Vintage Classics, 1991), 27.

any words of counsel.[22] It is his task likewise to assume their sorrows and their sins, to take their guilt upon himself, and to answer for them at the Last Judgment. St Barsanuphius of Gaza insists to his spiritual children, "As God Himself knows, there is not a second or an hour when I do not have you in my mind and in my prayers... I take upon myself the sentence of condemnation against you, and by the grace of Christ, I will not abandon you, either in this age or in the Age to come."[23] In the words of Dostoevsky's *starets* Zosima, "There is only one way of salvation, and that is to make yourself responsible for the sins of all...to make yourself responsible in all sincerity for everything and everyone."[24] The ability of the elder to support and strengthen others is measured exactly by the extent of his willingness to adopt this way of salvation.

Yet the relation between the spiritual father and his children is not one-sided. Though he takes the burden of their guilt upon himself and answers for them before God, he cannot do this effectively unless they themselves are struggling wholeheartedly on their own behalf. Once a brother came to St Antony of Egypt and said: "Pray for me." But the old man replied: "Neither will I take pity on you nor will God, unless you make some effort of your own."[25]

When considering the love of the guide for the disciple, it is important to give full meaning to the word "father" or "mother" in the title "spiritual father" or "spiritual mother." As the father and mother in an ordinary family are joined to their offspring in mutual love, so it should also be within the "charismatic" family of the elder. Needless to say, since the bond between elder and disciples is a relationship not according to the flesh but in the Holy Spirit, the wellspring of human affection, without being ruthlessly repressed, has to be transfigured; and this transfiguration

---

22 See, for example, the story in *AP*, anonymous collection 293: ed. Nau, *ROC* 14 (1909), 377; tr. Ward, *Wisdom*, §160 (45-46). The monk is delivered as soon as he says, "Lord, by the prayers of my father, save me in this hour."

23 *Questions and Answers*, ed. Schoinas §§208, 239; tr. Regnault and Lemaire, §§113, 239. On the spiritual father as burden-bearer, see above, 119-20, especially the quotations from Barsanuphius. In general, the 850 questions and answers that make up the Book of Barsanuphius and John show us, with a vividness not to be found in any other ancient source, exactly how the ministry of pastoral guidance was exercised in the Christian East.

24 *The Brothers Karamazov*, tr. Pevear and Volokhonsky, 320.

25 *AP*, alphabetical collection, Antony 16 (80c); tr. Ward, *Sayings*, 4.

may sometimes take forms which, to an outside observer, seem somewhat inhuman. It is recounted, for example, how a young monk looked after his elder, who was gravely ill, for twelve years without interruption. Never once in that period did his elder thank him or so much as speak one word of kindness to him. Only on his death-bed did the old man remark to the assembled brethren, "He is an angel and not a man."[26] Such stories are valuable as an indication of the need for spiritual detachment, but they are hardly typical. An uncompromising suppression of all outward tokens of affection is not characteristic of the *Sayings of the Desert Fathers*, still less of the two Old Men of Gaza, Barsanuphius and John.

A third gift of the spiritual father and mother is *the power to transform the human environment*, both the material and the non-material. The gift of healing, possessed by so many of the *startsi*, is one aspect of this power. More generally, the *starets* helps his disciples to perceive the world as God created it and as God desires it once more to be. The true elder is one who discerns the universal presence of the Creator throughout creation, and assists others to discern it likewise. He brings to pass, in himself and in others, the transformation of which William Blake speaks: "If the doors of perception were cleansed every thing would appear to man as it is, infinite."[27] For the one who dwells in God, there is nothing mean and trivial: he or she sees everything in the light of Mount Tabor. A momentary glimpse of what this signifies is provided in the account by Nicolas Motovilov of his conversation with St Seraphim of Sarov, when Nicolas saw the face of the *starets* shining with the brilliancy of the mid-day sun, while the blinding light radiating form his body illuminated the snow-covered trees of the forest glade around them.[28]

Obedience and freedom

Such are, by God's grace, the gifts of the *starets*. But what of the spiritual child? How does he or she contribute to the mutual relationship between guide and disciple?

26 *AP*, alphabetical collection, John the Theban 1 (240A); tr. Ward, *Sayings*, 109.

27 "The Marriage of Heaven and Hell," in Geoffrey Keynes (ed.), *Poetry and Prose of William Blake* (London: Nonesuch Press, 1948), 187.

28 "A Wonderful Revelation to the World," in Archimandrite Lazarus Moore, *St. Seraphim of Sarov*, 197.

Briefly, what the disciple offers is sincere and willing obedience. As a classic example, there is the story in the *Sayings of the Desert Fathers* about the monk who was told to plant a dry stick in the sand and to water it daily. So distant was the spring from his cell that he had to leave in the evening to fetch the water and he only returned in the following morning. For three years he patiently fulfilled his abba's command. At the end of this period, the stick suddenly put forth leaves and bore fruit. The abba picked the fruit, took it to the church, and invited the monks to eat, saying, "Take and eat the fruit of obedience."[29]

Another example of obedience is the monk Mark, who while copying a manuscript was suddenly called by his abba; so immediate was his response that he did not even complete the circle of the letter O that he was writing. On another occasion, as they walked together, his abba saw a small pig; testing Mark, he said, "Do you see that buffalo, my child?" "Yes, father," replied Mark. "And you see how elegant its horns are?" "Yes, father," he answered once more without demur.[30] Abba Joseph of Panepho, following a similar policy, tested the obedience of his disciples by assigning paradoxical and even scandalous tasks, and only if they complied would he then give them sensible commands.[31] Another *geron* instructed his disciple to steal things from the cells of the brethren;[32] yet another told his disciple (who had not been entirely truthful with him) to throw his son into the furnace.[33]

At this point it is surely necessary to state clearly certain serious objections. Stories of the kind that we have just reported are likely to make a deeply ambivalent impression upon a modern reader. Do they not describe the kind of behavior that we may perhaps reluctantly admire but would scarcely wish to imitate? What has happened, we may ask with some indignation, to "the glorious liberty of the children of God" (Rom 8:21)?

---

29 *AP*, alphabetical collection, John the Dwarf 1 (204C); tr. Ward, *Sayings*, 85-86.

30 *AP*, alphabetical collection, Mark the Disciple of Silvanus 1, 2 (293D-296B); tr., 145-46.

31 *Ibid.*, Joseph of Panepho 5 (229BC); tr., 103.

32 *Ibid.*, Saio 1 (420AB); tr., 229. The *geron* subsequently returned the things to their rightful owners.

33 *AP*, anonymous series 295: ed. Nau, *ROC* 14 (1909), 378; tr. Ward, *Wisdom*, §162 (47). Miraculously the child was preserved unharmed. For a parallel story, see *AP*, alphabetical collection, Sisoes 10 (394C-396A); tr. Ward, *Sayings*, 214; and compare Abraham and Isaac (Gen 22).

Few of us would doubt the value of seeking guidance from someone else, whether man or woman, who has a greater experience than we do of the spiritual way. But should such a person be treated as an infallible oracle, whose every word is to be obeyed without any further discussion? To interpret the mutual relationship between the disciple and the spiritual mother or father in such a manner as this seems dangerous for both of them. It reduces the disciple to an infantile and even subhuman level, depriving her or him of all power of judgment and moral choice; and it encourages the teacher to claim an authority which belongs to God alone. Earlier we quoted the statement from the *Sayings of the Desert Fathers* that someone under obedience to an elder "has no need to attend to the commandment of God."[34] But is such an abdication of responsibility desirable? Should the *geronta* be allowed to usurp the place of Christ?

In response, it needs to be said first of all that "charismatic" elders, such as St Anthony the Great or St Seraphim of Sarov, have always been exceedingly rare. The kind of relationship that they had with their disciples, whether monastic or lay, has never been the standard pattern in the Orthodox tradition. The great *startsi,* whether of the past or of the present day, do indeed constitute a guiding light, a supreme point of reference; but they are the exception, not the norm.

In the second place, there is clearly a difference between monastics, who have taken a special vow of obedience, and lay people who are living in the "world." (Even in the case of monastics, there are extremely few communities where the ministry of eldership is to be found in its full form, as described in the *Sayings of the Desert Fathers* or as practiced in nineteenth-century Optino.) A contemporary Russian priest, Father Alexander Men—himself much revered as a spiritual father before his tragic and untimely death at unknown hands in 1990—has wisely insisted that monastic observances cannot be transferred wholesale to parish life:

> We often think that the relation of spiritual child to spiritual father requires that the former be always obedient to the latter. In reality, this principle is an essential part of the monastic life. A monk promises to be obedient, to do whatever his spiritual father requires. A parish priest cannot impose such a model on lay people and cannot arrogate to himself the right to give peremptory orders. He

34 See above, 128.

must be happy recalling the Church's rules, orienting his parishioner's lives, and helping them in their inner struggles.[35]

Yet, when full allowance has been made for these two points, there are three further things that need to be said if a text such as the *Sayings of the Desert Fathers* or a figure such as *Starets* Zosima in *The Brothers Karamazov* are to be interpreted aright. First, the obedience offered by the spiritual child to the abba is not forced but willing and voluntary. It is the task of the *starets* to take up our will into his will, but he can only do this if by our own free choice we place it in his hands. He does not break our will, but accepts it from us as a gift. A submission that is forced and involuntary is obviously devoid of moral value; the *starets* asks of each one that we offer to God our heart, not our external actions. Even in a monastic context the obedience is voluntary, as is vividly emphasized at the rite of monastic profession: only after the candidate has three times placed the scissors in the abbot's hand does the latter proceed to tonsure him.[36]

This voluntary offering of our freedom, however, even in a monastery, is obviously something that cannot be made once and for all, by a single gesture. We are called to take up our cross *daily* (Lk 9:23). There has to be a continual offering, extending over our whole life; our growth in Christ is measured precisely by the increasing degree of our self-giving. Our freedom must be offered anew each day and each hour, in constantly varying ways; and this means that the relation between *starets* and disciple is not static but dynamic, not unchanging but infinitely diverse. Each day and each hour, under the guidance of his abba, the disciple will face new situations, calling for a different response, a new kind of self-giving.

In the second place, the relation between *starets* and spiritual child, as we have already noted, is not one-sided, but mutual. Just as the *starets* enables the disciples to see themselves as they truly are, so it is the disciples who reveal the *starets* to himself. In most instances, someone does not realize that he is called to be a *starets* until others come to him and insist on placing themselves under his guidance. This reciprocity continues throughout the relationship between the two. The spiritual father does not possess an exhaustive program, neatly worked out in advance and im-

---

35 Quoted in Yves Hamant, *Alexander Men: A Witness for Contemporary Russia* (Torrance, CA: Oakwood Publications, 1995), 124.

36 See above, 115-16.

posed in the same manner upon everyone. On the contrary, if he is a true *starets*, he will have a different word for each; he proceeds on the basis not of abstract rules but of concrete human situations. He and his disciple enter each situation together, neither of them knowing beforehand exactly what the outcome will be, but each waiting for the illumination of the Spirit. Both of them, the spiritual father as well as the disciple, have to learn as they go.

The mutuality of their relationship is indicated by stories in the *Sayings of the Desert Fathers* where an unworthy abba is saved through the patience and humility of his disciple. A brother, for example, has an elder who is given to drunkenness, and is sorely tempted to leave him; but, instead of doing so, he remains faithfully with his abba until the latter is eventually brought to repentance. As the narrator comments, "Sometimes it is the young who guide their elders to life."[37] The disciple may be called to give as well as to receive; the teacher may often learn from his pupils. As the Talmud records, "Rabbi Hanina used to say, 'Much have I learnt from my teachers, more from my fellow-students, but from my pupils most of all.'"[38]

In reality, however, the relationship is not two-sided but triangular, for in addition to the abba and his disciple there is also a third partner, God. Our Lord insisted that we should call no one "father," for we have only one Father, who is in heaven (Mt 13:8-10). The abba is not an inerrant judge or an ultimate court of appeal, but a fellow-servant of the living God; not a tyrant, but a guide and companion on the way. The only true "spiritual director," in the fullest sense of the word, is the Holy Spirit.

This brings us to the third point. In the Orthodox tradition at its best, spiritual guides have always sought to avoid any kind of constraint and spiritual violence in their relations with their disciples. If, under the guidance of the Spirit, they speak and act with authority, it is with the authority of humble love. Anxious to avoid all mechanical constraint, they may sometimes refuse to provide their disciples with a rule of life, a set of external commands to be applied automatically. In the words of a contemporary Romanian monk, the spiritual father is "not a legislator but a

---

37   *AP*, anonymous collection 340: ed. Nau, *ROC* 17 (1912), 295; tr. Ward, *Wisdom*, §209 (56-57).
38   C. G. Montefiore and H. Loewe (ed.), *A Rabbinic Anthology* (London: Macmillan, 1938), §494.

mystagogue."[39] He guides others, not by imposing rules, but by sharing his life with them. A monk told Abba Poemen, "Some brethren have come to live with me; do you want me to give them orders?" "No," said the old man. "But, Father," the monk persisted, "they themselves want me to give them orders." "No," repeated Poemen, "be an example to them but not a lawgiver."[40] The same moral emerges from a story told by Isaac the Priest. As a young man, he remained first with Abba Kronios and then with Abba Theodore of Pherme; but neither of them told him what to do. Isaac complained to the other monks and they came and remonstrated with Theodore. "If he wishes," Theodore replied eventually, "let him do what he sees me doing."[41] When Barsanuphius was asked to supply a detailed rule of life, he declined, saying: "I do not want you to be under the law, but under grace." And in other letters he wrote: "You know that we have never imposed chains upon anyone... Do not force people's free will, but sow in hope; for our Lord did not compel anyone, but He preached the good news, and those who wished hearkened to Him."[42]

Do not force people's free will. The task of our spiritual father is not to destroy our freedom, but to assist us to see the truth for ourselves; not to suppress our personality, but to enable us to discover our own true self, to grow to full maturity and to become what we really are. If on occasion the spiritual father requires an implicit and seemingly "blind" obedience from his disciple, this is never done as an end in itself, nor with a view to enslaving him. The purpose of this kind of "shock treatment" is simply to deliver the disciple from his false and illusory "self," so that he may enter into true liberty; obedience is in this way the door to freedom. The spiritual father does not impose his personal ideas and devotions, but he helps the disciple to find his own special vocation. In the words of a seventeenth-century Benedictine, Dom Augustine Baker: "The director is not to teach his own way, nor indeed any determinate way of prayer, but to instruct his disciples how they may themselves find out the way proper for

---

39 Father André Scrima, "La tradition du père spirituel dans l'Église d'Orient," *Hermès*, 1967, No. 4, 83.

40 *AP,* alphabetical collection, Poemen 174 (364C); tr. Ward, *Sayings,* 191.

41 *Ibid.,* Isaac the Priest 2 (224CD); tr., 99-100.

42 *Questions and Answers,* §§25, 51, 35.

them... In a word, he is only God's usher, and must lead souls in God's way, and not his own."[43]

Such was also the approach of Father Alexander Men. In the words of his biographer Yves Hamant, "Father Alexander wanted to lead each person to the point of deciding for himself; he did not want to order or to impose. He compared his role to that of a midwife who is present only to help the mother give birth herself to her baby. One of his friends wrote that Father Alexander was 'above us yet right beside us.'"[44]

In the last resort, then, what the spiritual mother or father gives to the disciple is not a code of written or oral regulations, not a set of techniques for meditation, but a personal relationship. Within this personal relationship the abba grows and changes as well as the disciple, for God is constantly directing them both. The abba may on occasion provide his disciple with detailed verbal instructions, with precise answers to specific questions. On other occasions he may fail to give any answer at all, either because he thinks that the question does not need an answer, or because he himself does not yet know what the answer should be. But these answers—or this failure to answer—are always given within the framework of a personal relationship. Many things cannot be said in words, but can only be conveyed through a direct personal encounter. As the Hasidic master Rabbi Jacob Yitzhak affirmed, "The *way* cannot be learned out of a book, or from hearsay, but can only be communicated from person to person."[45]

Here we touch on the most important point of all, and that is the *personalism* that inspires the encounter between disciple and spiritual guide. This personal contact protects the disciple against rigid legalism, against slavish submission to the letter of the law. He learns the way, not through external conformity to written rules, but through seeing a human face and hearing a living voice. In this way the spiritual mother or father is the guardian of evangelical freedom.

---

43 Quoted by Thomas Merton, *Spiritual Direction and Meditation* (Collegeville, MN: Liturgical Press, 1960), 12.
44 *Alexander Men*, 124.
45 Buber, *Tales of the Hasidim: The Early Masters*, 256.

In the absence of a starets

And what are we to do, if we cannot find a spiritual guide? For, as we have noted, guides such as St Antony or St Seraphim are few and far between.

We may turn, in the first place, to *books*. Writing in fifteenth-century Russia St Nil Sorsky laments the extreme scarcity of qualified spiritual directors; yet how much more frequent they must have been in his day than in ours! Search diligently, he urges, for a sure and trustworthy guide. Then he continues: "However, if such a teacher cannot be found, then the Holy Fathers order us to turn to the Scriptures and listen to our Lord Himself speaking."[46] Since the testimony of Scripture should never be isolated from the continuing witness of the Spirit in the life of the Church, we may add that the inquirer will also want to read the works of the Fathers, and above all the *Philokalia*. But there is an evident danger here. The *starets* adapts his guidance to the inner state of each; books offer the same advice to everyone. How are we to discern whether or not a particular text is applicable to our own situation? Even if we cannot find a spiritual father in the full sense, we should at least try to find someone more experienced than ourselves, able to guide us in our reading.

It is possible to learn also from visiting *places* where divine grace has been exceptionally manifest and where, in T. S. Eliot's phrase, "prayer has been valid." Before making a major decision, and in the absence of other guidance, many Orthodox Christians will go on pilgrimage to Jerusalem or Mount Athos, to some monastery or the shrine of a saint, where they will pray for illumination. This is the way in which I myself have reached certain of the more difficult decisions in my life.

Thirdly, we can learn from *religious communities* with an established tradition of the spiritual life. In the absence of a personal teacher, the monastic environment can itself serve as abba; we can receive our formation from the ordered sequence of the daily program, with its periods of liturgical and silent prayer, with its balance of manual labor, study and recreation. This seems to have been the chief way in which St Seraphim of Sarov gained his spiritual training. A well-organized monastery embodies, in an accessible and living form, the inherited wisdom of many *startsi*.

46 "The Monastic Rule," in G. P. Fedotov, *A Treasury of Russian Spirituality* (London: Sheed & Ward, 1950), 95-96.

Not only monks but those who come as visitors, remaining for a longer or shorter period, can be formed and guided by the experience of community life.

It is indeed no coincidence that, when the kind of "charismatic" spiritual fatherhood that we have been describing first emerged in fourth century Egypt, this was not within the fully organized communities under St Pachomius, but among the hermits and in the semi-eremitic milieu of Nitria and Scetis. In the Pachomian *koinonia*, spiritual direction was provided by Pachomius himself, by the superiors of each monastery, and by the heads of individual "houses" within the monastery. The *Rule* of St Benedict also envisages the abbot as spiritual father, and there is virtually no provision for further direction of a more "charismatic" type.[47] In time, it is true, the cenobitic communities incorporated many of the traditions of spiritual fatherhood as developed among the hermits, but the need for those traditions has always been less intensely felt in the *cenobia*, precisely because direction is provided by the corporate life pursued under the guidance of the monastic rule.

Finally, before leaving this question of the absence of a *starets*, it is important for us to emphasize the extreme flexibility in the relationship between spiritual guide and disciple. Some may see their spiritual guide daily or even hourly, praying, eating and working with him, perhaps sharing the same cell, as often happened in the Egyptian desert. Others may see him only once a month or once a year; others, again, may visit an abba on but a single occasion in their entire life, yet this will be sufficient to set them on the right path. There are, furthermore, many different types of spiritual father or mother; few will be wonder-workers like St Seraphim of Sarov. There are numerous priests and laypeople who, while lacking the more spectacular endowments of the famous *startsi*, are certainly able to provide others with the guidance that they require. Furthermore, let us never forget that, alongside spiritual fatherhood and motherhood, there is also spiritual brotherhood and sisterhood. At school or university we often learn more from our fellow students than from our teachers; and the same may happen also in our life of prayer and inner exploration.

---

47 Except that in the *Rule,* §46, it is said that monks may confess their sins in confidence, not necessarily to the abbot, but to one of the senior monks possessing spiritual gifts (*tantum abbati, aut spiritalibus senioribus*).

When people imagine that they have failed in their search for a guide, often this is because they expect him or her to be of a particular type; they want a St Seraphim, and so they close their eyes to the guides whom God is actually sending to them. Often their supposed problems are not so very complicated, and in reality they already know in their own heart what the answer is. But they do not like the answer, because it involves patient and sustained effort on their part; and so they look for a *deus ex machina* who, by a single miraculous word, will suddenly make everything easy. Such people need to be helped to an understanding of the true nature of spiritual direction.

Contemporary examples

In conclusion, I wish to recall two elders of our own day, whom I have had the privilege and happiness of knowing personally. The first is Father Amphilochios (†1970), at one time abbot of the Monastery of St John on the Island of Patmos, and subsequently *geronta* to a community of nuns which he had founded not far from the Monastery. What most distinguished his character was his gentleness, his humor, the warmth of his affection, and his sense of tranquil yet triumphant joy. His smile was full of love, but devoid of all sentimentality. Life in Christ, as he understood it, is not a heavy yoke, a burden to be carried with sullen resignation, but a personal relationship to be pursued with eagerness of heart. He was firmly opposed to all spiritual violence and cruelty. It was typical that, as he lay dying and took leave of the nuns under his care, he should urge the abbess not to be too severe on them: "They have left everything to come here, they must not be unhappy."[48]

Two things in particular I recall about him. The first was his love of nature and, more especially, of trees. "Do you know," he used to say, "that God gave us one more commandment, which is not recorded in Scripture? It is the commandment *Love the trees*." Whoever does not love trees, he was convinced, does not love Christ. When hearing the confessions of the local farmers, he assigned to them as a penance (*epitimion*) the task of planting a tree; and through his influence many hill-sides of Patmos,

---

48 See I. Gorainoff, "Holy Men of Patmos," *Sobornost* 6:5 (1972), 341-44.

which once were barren rock, are now green with foliage every summer.[49]

A second thing that stands out in my memory is the counsel which he gave me when, as a newly-ordained priest, the time had come for me to return from Patmos to Oxford, where I was to begin teaching in the university. He himself had never visited the west, but he had a shrewd perception of the situation of Orthodoxy in the *diaspora*. "Do not be afraid," he insisted. Do not be afraid because of your Orthodoxy, he told me; do not be afraid because, as an Orthodox in the west, you will be often isolated and always in a small minority. Do not make compromises but do not attack other Christians; do not be either defensive or aggressive; simply be yourself.

My second example of a twentieth-century *starets* known to me personally is St John Maximovitch (†1966), Russian bishop in Shanghai, then in Western Europe, and finally in San Francisco. Little more than a dwarf in height, with tangled hair and beard, and with an impediment in his speech, at first sight he seemed to possess more than a touch of the "fool in Christ." From the time of his profession as a monk, except when ill he did not lie down on a bed; he went on working and praying all night, snatching his sleep at odd moments in the twenty-four hours. He wandered barefoot through the streets of Paris, and once he celebrated a memorial service in the port of Marseilles on the exact spot where King Alexander of Yugoslavia had been assassinated, in the middle of the road among the tram lines. Punctuality had little meaning for him. Baffled by his behavior, the more conventional among his flock judged him unsuited for the public position and the administrative work of a bishop. But, if unpredictable, he was also practical and realistic. With his total disregard of normal formalities he succeeded where others, relying on worldly influence and expertise, had failed entirely—as when, against all hope and in the teeth of the "quota" system, he secured the admission of thousands of homeless Russian refugees to the USA.

In private conversation he was abrupt yet kindly. He quickly won the confidence of small children. Particularly striking was the intensity of his intercessory prayer. It was his practice, whenever possible, to celebrate the Divine Liturgy daily, and the service often took twice the normal space of

---

49 See my lecture, *Through the Creation to the Creator*, 5.

time, such was the multitude of those whom he commemorated individually by name. As he prayed for them, they were never mere entries on a list, but always persons. One story that I was told is typical. It was his custom each year to visit Holy Trinity Monastery in Jordanville, NY. As he made his departure after one such visit, a monk gave him a slip of paper with four names of those who were gravely ill. St John received thousands upon thousands of such requests for prayer in the course of each year. On his return to the monastery some twelve months later, at once he beckoned to the monk and, much to the latter's surprise, from the depths of his cassock St John produced the identical slip of paper, now crumpled and tattered. "I have been praying for your friends," he said, "but two of them"—he pointed to their names—"are now dead, while the other two have recovered." And so indeed it was.

Even at a distance he shared in the concerns of his spiritual children. One of them, Father (later Archbishop) Jacob, superior of a small Orthodox monastery in Holland, was sitting at a late hour in his room, unable to sleep from anxiety over the financial and other problems which faced him. In the middle of the night the phone rang; it was St John, speaking from several hundred miles away. He had telephoned to say that it was time for Father Jacob to go to bed: "Go to sleep now, what you are asking of God will certainly be all right."[50]

Such is the role of the spiritual father. As St Barsanuphius expressed it, "I care for you more than you care for yourself."

---

50 Bishop Savva of Edmonton, *Blessed John: The Chronicle of the Veneration of Archbishop John Maximovich* (Platina, CA: Saint Heman of Alaska Brotherhood, 1979), 104; Father Seraphim Rose and Abbot Herman, *Blessed John the Wonderworker. A Preliminary Account of the Life and Miracles of Archbishop John Maximovitch,* 3rd edn. (Platina, CA: Saint Herman of Alaska Brotherhood, 1987), 163. I heard the story from Father Jacob himself.

10

THE FOOL IN CHRIST
AS PROPHET AND APOSTLE

He is nobody's son, nobody's brother, nobody's father, and has no home... From a practical point of view, no useful purpose is served by anything that the *iurodivyi* does. He achieves nothing.

Iulia de Beausobre

The fool is the symbol of the lost ones of this world who are destined to inherit eternal life. The fool is not a philosophy, but a quality of consciousness of life, an endless regard for human identity...not the product of intellectual achievement, but a creation of the culture of the heart.

Cecil Collins

The fool has nothing to lose. He dies daily.

Mother Maria of Normanby

Breakdown or breakthrough?

Within the spiritual tradition of the Christian East there is no figure more paradoxical and, in the eyes of many, more scandalous than the holy fool, the fool in Christ, known in Greek as *salos* and in Russian as *iurodivyi*. Any reader of Tolstoy's childhood memories will recall the vivid description that he gives of "God's fool," Grisha. The portrait is by no means flattering, and Tolstoy does not attempt to conceal the ambivalence that surrounds the person of the fool:

> The door opened and there stood a figure totally unknown to me. Into the room walked a man of about fifty with a long pale pock-marked face, long gray hair and a scanty reddish beard... He wore a tattered garment, something between a peasant tunic and a cassock; in his hand he carried a huge staff. As he entered the room he used the staff to strike the floor with all his might and then, wrinkling his brow and opening his mouth extremely wide, he burst into

a terrible and unnatural laugh. He was blind in one eye, and the white iris of that eye darted about incessantly and imparted to his face, already ill-favored, a still more repellent expression... His voice was rough and hoarse, his movements hasty and jerky, his speech devoid of sense and incoherent (he never used any pronouns)... He was the saintly fool and pilgrim Grisha.

One feature strikes us at once: the *freedom* of the fool. Grisha is at liberty to enter the house of the local gentry and to wander about in it as he wishes. Tolstoy goes on to indicate a mysterious, almost "apophatic," quality in Grisha's personality. No one knows exactly who he is:

Where had he come from? Who were his parents? What had induced him to adopt the wandering life he led? No one knew. All I know is that from the age of fifteen he had been one of "God's fools," who went barefoot in winter and summer, visited monasteries, gave little icons to those he took a fancy to, and uttered enigmatic sayings which some people accepted as prophecies.

The fool, we notice, is a *stranger*. He is free from the normal ties of family life—"nobody's son, nobody's brother, nobody's father"—homeless, a wanderer, often an exile. Usually he is not a hermit, but spends his life constantly in the company of his fellow humans. And yet he remains somehow an alien, an expatriate, on the margin of organized society, in the midst of the world yet not of it. The fool is free, a stranger—and therefore capable, as we shall see, of fulfilling a *prophetic* role.

Significantly, Tolstoy speaks of the sharply conflicting opinions that others held about Grisha: "Some said he was the unfortunate son of wealthy parents, a pure soul, while others held that he was simply a lazy peasant."[1] The fool is equivocal, enigmatic, always a disturbing question mark. When dealing with the vocation of folly for Christ's sake, it is an exceptionally delicate task to distinguish genuine from counterfeit, the holy innocent from the unholy fraud, the man of God from the drop-out, the hippie or the streaker. How are we to "test the spirits"? The frontier between breakdown and breakthrough is not clearly marked.

Let us move back in time three hundred years from the Russia of Tolstoy to the Russia of Ivan the Terrible and Boris Godunov. In his book *Of the Russe Commonwealth*, the English traveler Giles Fletcher describes the

---

1   L. N. Tolstoy, *Childhood, Boyhood, Youth*, tr. R. Edmonds (Harmondsworth: Penguin, 1964), 26-27.

fools whom he saw wandering through the streets of Moscow during his visit in 1588-89:

> They use to go stark naked save a clout about their middle, with their hair hanging long and wildly about their shoulders, and many of them with an iron collar or chain about their necks or middle, even in the very extremity of winter. These they take as prophets and men of great holiness, giving them a liberty to speak what they list without any controlment, though it be of the very highest himself. So that if he reprove any openly in what sort soever, they answer nothing but that it is *po grekham*, that is, for their sins. And if any of them take some piece of sale ware from any man's shop as he passeth by to give where he list, he thinketh himself much beloved of God and much beholding to the holy man for taking it in that sort.

With a touch of English common sense Fletcher adds: "Of this kind there are not many because it is a very hard and cold profession to go naked in Russia, specially in winter."[2]

The *nakedness* of the fool is important: it is not simply a mark of eccentricity, but has a theological meaning. The fool has returned in some measure to the *status ante peccatum*, to the innocence of Adam in Paradise before the fall, when he was naked and unashamed. In this the fool resembles the *boskoi*, the "browsers" or grass-eating ascetics of early Christian monasticism, who lived in the open air, naked among the herds of antelope, at peace with the animal creation. Such naked ascetics are still to be found on the Holy Mountain today: one of them is described by the French visitor Jacques Valentin in his book *The Monks of Mount Athos*. When Valentin questioned another monk about the naked ascetic, the reply was: "We're free, and that's his way of loving God."[3] Once more we hear the note of freedom.

Significant also is Fletcher's allusion to the prophetic function of the fool: "These they take as prophets." By virtue of his utter poverty, of his voluntary rejection of all outward status or security, the fool is free to speak when others, afraid of the consequences, choose to keep silent—free to tell the truth "without any controlment," even about "the very highest himself," the autocratic tsar. We shall look at an example of this in due course. Here the fool makes us think of the prisoner Bobynin

2   L. E. Berry and R. O. Crummey (eds.), *Rude and Barbarous Kingdom: Russia in the Accounts of Sixteenth-Century English Voyagers* (Madison: University of Wisconsin Press, 1968), 218-19.

3   *The Monks of Mount Athos* (London: A. Deutsch, 1960), 37.

in Solzhenitsyn's novel *The First Circle*. Interrogated by Abakumov, Stalin's all-powerful Minister of State Security, Bobynin says: "You need me, but I don't need you." Abakumov is astonished: as head of the secret police, he can have Bobynin exiled, tortured, liquidated, whereas the latter has no possible way of retaliating. But Bobynin sticks to his point. Abakumov, he says, can frighten only those who have "plenty to lose":

> I've got nothing, see? Nothing! You can't touch my wife and child—they were killed by a bomb. My parents are dead. I own nothing in the world except a handkerchief... You took my freedom away a long time ago and you can't give it back to me because you haven't got it yourself... You can tell old You-know-who—up there—that you only have power over people so long as you don't take *everything* away from them. But when you've robbed a man of *everything* he's no longer in your power—he's free again.[4]

The fool in Christ is likewise free, because he has "nothing to lose": not that he has been robbed of everything, but he has renounced everything by his own choice. Like Bobynin he has no possessions, no family, no position, and so can speak the truth with a prophetic boldness. He cannot be exploited, for he has no ambition; and he fears God alone.

This vocation of folly for Christ's sake is not limited only to Russia, but is also a characteristic of Greek and Syriac Christianity from the fourth century onwards. Holy fools are to be found likewise in the Christian West and, indeed, altogether outside the Christian tradition among, for instance, the Jewish Hasidim, the Sufis of Islam, and the Zen Buddhists.[5] The fool is a universal figure. One of the earliest examples in East-

---

4   A. I. Solzhenitsyn, *The First Circle*, tr. M. Guybon (London: Fontana, 1970), 106-7.

5   There is an admirable and scholarly treatment of the subject by John Saward, *Perfect Fools: Folly for Christ's Sake in Catholic and Orthodox Spirituality* (Oxford: Oxford University Press, 1980), which concentrates mainly on the West; see also his article, "The Fool for Christ's Sake in Monasticism, East and West," in A. M. Allchin (ed.), *Theology and Prayer,* Studies Supplementary to *Sobornost* 3 (London: Fellowship of St Alban and St Sergius, 1975), 29-55. Saward's article can also be found in M. Basil Pennington (ed.), *One Yet Two: Monastic Tradition in East and West,* Cistercian Studies Series 29 (Kalamazoo, MI: Cistercian Publications, 1976) 48-80. Irina Gorainoff, *Les fols en Christ dans la tradition orthodoxe* (Paris: Desclée de Brouwer, 1983), deals chiefly with Russia; a vivid and sympathetic account, but regrettably without detailed references to the sources. For a useful general survey, see T. Spidlik (for the Christian East) and F. Vandenbroucke (for the Christian West), in *DS* 5:752-70. Consult also Elizabeth Behr-Sigel, *Prière et sainteté dans l'Eglise russe* (1950), 2nd edn. (Bégrolles: Abbaye de Bellefontaine, 1982), 98-108; G. P. Fedotov, *The Russian Religious Mind*, 2 vols. (Cambridge, MA: Harvard University Press, 1946-1966), 2:316-43; Lennart Rydén, "The Holy Fool," in Sergei Hackel (ed.), *The Byzantine Saint*, Studies Supplementary to *Sobornost* 5 (London: Fel-

ern Christendom—perhaps the earliest of all—is not a man but a woman: the unnamed nun described by Palladius in the *Lausiac History*, who lived in Upper Egypt at a women's community under the Pachomian rule in the late fourth century. Feigning madness, she worked in the kitchen, with rags wrapped round her head instead of the monastic cowl. She undertook all the most menial tasks and was treated with general contempt, kicked and insulted by the other nuns. One day the renowned ascetic Pitiroum visited the community. To the consternation of everyone he knelt at her feet and asked for a blessing. "She is mad (*salē*)," the nuns protested. "It's you who are mad," retorted Pitiroum. "She is our *amma* [spiritual mother]—mine and yours." A few days later, to avoid the honors she was now receiving, the nun disappeared and was never heard of again. "And where she went," Palladius adds, "or where she disappeared to, or how she died, no one knows." He seems to be ignorant even of her name.[6]

As before, we note the elusiveness of the fool: he or she is unknown, hidden, a stranger.

In the Greek tradition two holy fools enjoy especial prominence: St Symeon of Emesa and St Andrew of Constantinople. Symeon may well be an historical figure, active in the middle or late sixth century; for he is mentioned by the church historian Evagrius, writing only a few years later.[7] Symeon's *Life*, composed by St Leontius of Neapolis in Cyprus, probably during the 640s, may have been based in part on an earlier written source, now lost, but this remains a disputed question.[8] How far the

lowship of St Alban and St Sergius, 1981), 106-13; Ewa M. Thompson, *Understanding Russia: The Holy Fool in Russian Culture* (Lanham, MD: University Press of America, 1987). On the partial secularization of the fool in the West, see Enid Welsford, *The Fool: His Social and Literary History* (London: Faber, 1935); Sandra Billington, *A Social History of the Fool* (Brighton: Harvester Press, 1984).

6 *Lausiac History* 34. In later sources she is sometimes identified with St Isidora (May 1st). See Kari Vogt, "La moniale folle du monastère des Tabbenésiotes. Une interprétation du chapitre 34 de l'Historia Lausiaca de Pallade," *Symbolae Osloenses* 62 (1987), 95-108.

7 *Ecclesiastical History* 4:34.

8 Critical Greek text, ed. Lennart Rydén, *Das Leben des Heiligen Narren Symeon von Leontios von Neapolis*, Studia Graeca Upsaliensia 4 (Stockholm: Almqvist & Wiksell, 1963); revised text in A. J. Festugière and L. Rydén, *Vie de Syméon le Fou et Vie de Jean de Chypre*, Bibliothèque archéologique et historique 95 (Paris: P. Geunther, 1974); my own citations are made from this latter. There is an English translation of the *Life* in Derek Krueger, *Symeon the Holy Fool: Leontius's Life and the Late Antique City*, The Transformation of the Classical Heritage 25

Life by Leontius is historically reliable is a matter that I shall leave on one side; for my present purposes it is sufficient simply to treat the *Life* as an "icon" of the holy fool, offering a typical picture of what, in the Orthodox tradition, the holy fool is supposed to be. The historicity of the *Life* of Andrew is far more questionable than that of Symeon. The work is attributed to Nicephorus, presbyter at Hagia Sophia in Constantinople, but it is unclear exactly when it was written,[9] and almost all modern scholars are agreed in regarding it as little more than a "hagiographical romance."[10] Yet, even if fictional, the *Life* of Andrew is nevertheless important, like that of Symeon, as an "icon" or type. Andrew is remembered above all in Russia, where he is linked with the feast of *Pokrov* or the Protecting Veil of the Mother of God (October 1st). Symeon was a monk, Andrew a layman; both pursued their vocation of folly in cities—Symeon in Emesa, Andrew in Constantinople—and in both cases the folly was feigned.

The earliest holy fool known to us in Russia is Isaac (eleventh century), a monk of the Monastery of the Caves in Kiev, whose madness, for at any rate part of the time, was genuine rather than feigned. It is curious to observe how many of the Russian fools were foreigners. St Prokopy of Ustiug (*ca.* early fourteenth century) was a German convert to Ortho-

---

(Berkeley/Los Angeles/London: University of California Press, 1996), 131-71. The earlier part of Krueger's work discusses the historicity of the *Life*, and in particular compares the Christian "holy fool" with the pagan Cynic philosopher. See also L. Rydén, *Bemerkungen zum Leben des heiligen Narren Symeon von Leontios von Neopolis*, Studia Graeca Upsaliensia 6 (Stockholm: Almqvist & Wiksell, 1970).

9 Greek translation in *PG* 111:628-888; there is an independent edition, sometimes fuller, by Archimandrite Andreas Polyetopoulos (Athens: Taygetos, 1911), which I have consulted. The fullest discussion of this work is by Panagiotis S. Martines, *Ho Salos Hag. Andreas kai he Saloteta sten Orthodoxe Ekklesia* (Athens: Ekdoseis Tenos, 1988), who considers (contrary to the prevailing view) that Andrew may have been an historical figure, living in the second half of the ninth century. See also José Grosdidier de Matons, "Les thèmes d'édification dans la Vie d'André Salos," *Travaux et Mémoires* 4 (1970), 277-328; John Wortley, "The Life of St. Andrew the Fool," *Studia Patristica* 10, Texte und Untersuchungen 107 (Berlin, 1970), 315-19; *idem*, "The *Vita Sancti Andreae Sali* as a Source of Byzantine Social History," *Societas* 4 (1974), 1-20; Cyril Mango, "The Life of Saint Andrew the Fool Reconsidered," *Rivista di Studi Bizantini e Slavi* 2 (1982), 297-313; L. Rydén, "Style and Historical Fiction in the Life of St. Andreas Salos," *Jahrbuch der Österreichischen Byzantinistik* 32 (1982), 175-83. I have not had access to Sara Murray, *A Study of the Life of Andreas, the Fool for the Sake of Christ* (Borna-Leipzig: R. Noske, 1910). The date of the *Life* of Andrew is uncertain: Mango places it in the years 674-95, while Rydén and others prefer a date around 950-59.

10 H.-G. Beck, *Kirche und theologische Literatur im Byzantinischen Reich* (Munich: C. H. Beck, 1959), 568.

doxy; St Isidore *Tverdislov* of Rostov (thirteenth century) was supposedly also a German; St John "the Hairy," likewise of Rostov (†1581), was certainly a foreigner, and his Psalter, still preserved on his tomb in the eighteenth century, was written in Latin. All this illustrates the point already made, that the fool is a stranger and a pilgrim. Is folly for Christ's sake, one wonders, especially a vocation for Western converts to Orthodoxy? I can think of some examples among the present-day English Orthodox...

The golden age of the Russian *iurodivye* was in the sixteenth century, the period of which Fletcher speaks. Two of the best known fools of that time, St Basil the Blessed of Moscow (†1552) and St Nicolas of Pskov (†1576), were both in contact with Ivan the Terrible. After the seventeenth century fools became less frequent, and the westernized Russia of Peter the Great and his successors had little use for them. But the tradition continues: in the eighteenth century, Blessed Xenia of St Petersburg, widow of a colonel who died suddenly at a drinking party (students still pray at her tomb before taking their examinations); in the nineteenth century, Theophil of Kitajevo, visited by Emperor Nicolas I, and Pelagia, St Seraphim's disciple, who rebuked a bishop by slapping him on the face;[11] in the twentieth century, Pasha of Sarov, with whom Nicolas II talked in 1903, immediately after the canonization of St Seraphim. It was Pasha's practice to put plenty of sugar in the tea of those visitors for whom she foresaw misfortunes; in the case of the future imperial martyr she put in so many lumps that the tea overflowed. And what of the Soviet Union? According to an *émigré* from the 1970s, holy fools were still at that time to be found in Russia: "They keep hidden and others hide them"—if discovered, they were interned in psychiatric asylums.[12] Modern tyrannies have reason to be afraid of the fool's freedom.

---

11 The incident occurred in 1861 at the Diveyevo Convent, of which St Seraphim had been spiritual father until his death. The local hierarch, Bishop Nektary of Nizhni-Novgorod, had been conducting a visitation of the community, at which he illegally deposed the abbess, installing in her place someone acceptable only to a small minority of the nuns. On being struck by Pelagia on one cheek, Bishop Nektary—doubtless recalling the Sermon on the Mount (Mt 5:39)—offered the other cheek also. But Pelagia turned away, remarking in tones of contempt, "One slap is enough." The bishop, to his credit, insisted that she should not be punished. See Rochcau, *Saint Séraphim*, 100; also [anon.], *Seraphim's Seraphim. The Life of Pelagia Ivanovna Serebrenikova, Fool for Christ's Sake of the Seraphim-Diveyevo Convent* (Boston, MA: Holy Transfiguration Monastery, 1979), 57-58.

12 See Gorainoff, *Les fols en Christ*, 191.

What is to be learnt from this vocation, seemingly so bizarre, yet in reality so profoundly Christian? Let us take as our paradigm the *Life* of St Symeon of Emesa the Fool in Christ, written by St Leontius; for this, as well as being the earliest full-length *Life* devoted to a holy fool, has the advantage of possessing a certain historical basis. It has also the further merit of presenting folly for Christ in its most shocking and provocative form. Extreme cases, by posing the issues with the sharpest clarity, have often the most to teach us.

From the desert to the city

St Symeon the Fool in Christ was born, so we are told, in Edessa the "blessed city" (the modern Urfa, in south-eastern Turkey), the chief center of Syriac-speaking Christianity. The child of wealthy parents, he received a good education and was fluent in both Greek and Syriac. Aged about twenty, still unmarried, he went on pilgrimage to Jerusalem with his elderly mother; he was apparently her only child, and his father was already dead. In the Holy City he met another young man from Syria, John by name, recently married, who had come on pilgrimage with both his parents. Symeon and John at once became firm friends. Having visited the shrines, they set off homewards together, accompanied by Symeon's mother and John's parents. Descending into the valley of the Dead Sea and passing through Jericho, they gazed at the monasteries in the distance close to the river Jordan. On a sudden impulse—the initiative came from John—they decided not to continue the journey home but to turn aside and become monks. Parting from their companions by a subterfuge, they disappeared without a word of explanation, Symeon abandoning his old mother, John his parents and the young wife waiting for him at home. The others simply did not know what had happened to the two of them.

This part of Leontius' narrative somewhat resembles a fairy tale in atmosphere, and seemingly possesses an historical foundation far less firm than that which may perhaps underlie the later sections of the *Life*, dealing with Symeon's time in Emesa. What is interesting is that the *Life* makes no attempt to gloss over the harshness and cruelty of what Symeon and John were doing to others—and, indeed, to themselves. On the con-
tius goes out of his way to emphasize that neither of them was
They were both warmly affectionate by character. John loved

his wife, Symeon was devoted to his mother, and for a long time both of them grieved most bitterly over the separation. Why, then, should they have acted as they did? The *Life* offers a simple explanation. Monasticism is the way to salvation:

> By chance they found themselves on the side road, leading back to the holy Jordan. They both stopped, and John, pointing with his finger, said to Symeon, "Behold the road that leads to life!" and he showed him the road to the holy Jordan. "And behold the road which leads to death!" (cf. Mt 7:13-14), he said, showing him the main road on which their parents had already gone ahead.[13]

The modern reader is scarcely likely to rest satisfied with this. Is not the vocation of the married Christian in the "world" also a path that leads to eternal life? As St Andrew of Crete affirms in the *Great Canon*:

> Marriage is honorable, and the marriage bed undefiled.
> For on both Christ has bestowed His blessing,
> Present incarnate and eating at the wedding in Cana.[14]

There are, however, texts in the New Testament that Symeon and John could have quoted in support of their action. Christ tells us to "hate" father and mother, wife and children (Lk 14:26), and He forbids a prospective disciple so much as to say farewell to his family (Lk 9:61-2): such is the overriding force of the divine call. The incident in the Jordan valley reveals in this way a feature present throughout Symeon's life: his desire to take literally the "hard sayings" in the Gospel, his refusal of all compromise, his *maximalism*.

Having parted from their parents, Symeon and John went down to the monastery of Abba Gerasimos, close to the Jordan; and here, on the very same day, the abbot gave them the monastic tonsure. Two days later they resolved to leave the *cenobium* and to go out into the desert to live as *boskoi* or "browsers." Significantly they came to this decision without asking the abbot's permission; obedience to any authority on earth is not a prominent feature in the life of the fool in Christ. The nun described by Palladius possessed humility, but did she also display obedience? She sought no blessing from the abbess before feigning madness, and none before fleeing from the monastery. In the case of Symeon and John, the ab-

13 Ed., Rydén, 125.2-7; tr. Krueger, 135.
14 Mother Mary and Archimandrite Kallistos Ware, *The Lenten Triodion*, 412.

bot was in fact warned in a dream of their impending departure, and he intercepted them at the monastery gate to give them his blessing. But, even if he had not been there to bless them, they would still have left.

The two settled on the far side of the Jordan, close to the Dead Sea, where they found a deserted cell. Thus, even though the term *boskos* is applied to them in the *Life*,[15] they were not in fact such in the strict sense, since unlike the true "browser" they had a dwelling, however primitive. They rapidly attained continual prayer. It was their custom each to pray alone, about a stone's throw from one another: "But when distractive thoughts (*logismoi*) or a sense of sadness (*acedia*) assailed one of them, he would go to the other and together they would call on God to be delivered from the temptation."[16] Even amid the savage austerity of the desert, the element of companionship and mutual affection—the warmth of friendship that Symeon and John felt towards each other when they first met in the Holy City—was still allowed some place.

So matters continued for thirty-one years. Symeon was now in his early fifties. One day he said to John: "What do we gain, brother, by spending our days in this desert? But, if you will hearken to me, arise, let us go and save others as well."[17] Filled with dismay at this proposal, John did his utmost to dissuade Symeon, but the other continued to insist: "Believe me, I won't stay, but in the power of Christ I will go and mock the world."[18] In an illuminating variant, an Armenian version of Symeon's *Life* says here, "I will go to bring peace on the earth."[19] John, however, felt that the path now chosen by Symeon—to return from the desert to the city, with the aim of "mocking the world"—was altogether too arduous for him:

> I beg you in the Lord's name, dear brother, do not abandon me in my wretchedness. For I have not yet reached so high a level as this, to be able to mock the world. But, for the sake of Christ who joined us together, do not seek to be

15 Ed., Rydén, 133.3; tr. Krueger, 141.
16 Ed., Rydén, 139.17-19; tr. Krueger, 146.
17 Ed., Rydén, 142.14-15; tr. Krueger, 148.
18 Ed., Rydén, 142.25-26; tr. Krueger, 148.
19 From the Armenian *Synaxarion* compiled by Ter Israel (thirteenth century), on the basis of older sources: *PO* 21 (1930), 753. The Armenian version is summarized by Festugière in *Vie de Syméon*, 41-43.

parted from your brother. You know that, after God, I have no one except you, my brother.[20]

John also warned Symeon against the possibility of demonic deception. But Symeon replied that he had received a special call directly from God: "Do not fear, brother John; for it is not by my own choice that I wish to do this, but because God commands me."[21] So they parted, both of them weeping bitterly.

Now began the distinctive period of Symeon's life, the period about which we are best informed, when he assumed the mask of folly. First he went on pilgrimage to Jerusalem, and in the Holy Places this was his prayer: "…that all his works might remain hidden until his departure from life, so that he might escape human glory, which gives rise to arrogance and conceit."[22] Thus his motive for adopting the path of feigned madness was, first of all, to avoid being honored as a holy man; it was a way of preserving humility. But, as we shall see, he had other reasons as well.

From Jerusalem he traveled to Emesa (the modern Homs, in western Syria), and at once began to act the fool:

> The manner of his entry to the city was as follows. The blessed one, finding a dead dog on a dunghill outside the city, untied the rope belt he was wearing, attached one end to the dog's leg and dragged it after him as he ran. So he entered through the city gate. There was a school nearby, and when the children saw him they began to shout, "Hey, a crazy abba!" And they started to run after him and box him on the ears. On the next day, which was Sunday, he took some nuts and went into the church at the start of the Liturgy, and he began to throw the nuts and to put out the lamps. When they chased after him to drive him out, he climbed up into the pulpit and from there pelted the women with nuts. With the utmost difficulty they expelled him, but as he went out he overturned the stalls of the pastry sellers, who beat him up so severely that he nearly died.[23]

His life in Emesa continued as it had begun. Deliberately and continually he provoked others with his absurd and shameless actions. He flouted

---

20 Ed., Rydén, 142.27-143.1; tr. Krueger, 148.
21 Ed., Rydén, 144.5-6; tr. Krueger, 149.
22 Ed., Rydén, 144.23-25; tr. Krueger, 150.
23 Ed., Rydén, 145.20-146.3; tr. Krueger, 150-51. The women would have been in the gallery of the church; the pastry sellers were presumably in the courtyard outside. Compare Christ in the Temple (Mt 21:12).

the church rules by eating meat in public during Holy Week; all the time, it should be remembered, he went about dressed as a monk. He hopped and jumped in the streets, tripping people up and pretending to be an epileptic. A merchant employed him to look after his refreshment stall; at the earliest opportunity Symeon distributed all the food and drink free to the poor.[24] He was given a job in a tavern; one day when the innkeeper's wife was asleep alone, Symeon entered her room and made as if he was going to undress, to the fury of her husband who entered just at that moment.[25] (But, as we shall note shortly, he had a special reason for doing this.) On another occasion, when his friend John the Deacon—not to be confused with the John who had been Symeon's companion in the desert—suggested that they should go to the public baths to wash, he replied with a laugh, "Yes, let's go, let's go." Then, in the middle of the street, he removed all his clothes, wrapped them round his head like a turban, and rushed straight into the women's part of the baths.[26]

Throughout Leontius' narrative we hear the echo of Symeon's laugh. He follows his chosen path of folly with a light and joyful heart: "Sometimes he pretended to have a limp, sometimes he jumped around, sometimes he dragged himself along on his buttocks."[27] Again and again the *Life* uses such words as "game" and "play"; Simeon *plays* the fool, in the full and true sense of the word. Here, in the playfulness of the fool in Christ, in his purifying laughter, we have perhaps a genuine christianization of irony, the basis for a theology of jokes.

Symeon consorted above all with those who had been marginalized by society, with the disreputable and the rejected. He spent his time with actors and actresses—on the whole, a far from honorable profession in the ancient world. He visited prostitutes, forming special links with particular women whom he called his "girlfriends."[28] The "respectable" and self-important were of course scandalized by the activities of this unusual monk. But the poor and the outcasts quickly came to see in him a true friend, and they showed towards him, not merely an amused and tolerant con-

24 Ed., Rydén, 146.5-17; tr. Krueger, 151-52.
25 Ed., Rydén, 148.1-10; tr. Krueger, 153.
26 Ed., Rydén, 148.24-149.9; tr. Krueger, 153-54.
27 Ed., Rydén, 155.20-21; tr. Krueger, 159.
28 Ed., Rydén, 155.15; 156.5; tr. Krueger, 159, 160.

tempt, but also in many instances a genuine affection; they found him lovable and cherished him. Utterly destitute, he rested each night in a tiny abandoned hut. Andrew of Constantinople and many of the Russian fools lacked even that, and usually slept in a porch or doorway, like the homeless in the affluent yet cruel London of the 1990s.

Leontius makes it entirely clear that, throughout his time in Emesa, Symeon's folly was deliberate. He was never actually mad, but was merely putting on an act. While talking nonsense with others, when he was alone with John the Deacon he spoke seriously and coherently. All day long he went about in public, behaving as a fool; but at night he withdrew to secret places, known only to John, where he spent the hours of darkness in prayer. He was not only a fool but a hesychast—an urban hesychast. Watching him on one occasion, John saw "globes of fire ascending from him to heaven, and all around him it was like a baker's oven full of flames, with him in the middle, so that I did not dare to approach him."[29] The account reminds us of St Arsenius in the *Apophthegmata*,[30] or of St Seraphim talking with Motovilov.[31]

Outrageous though the fool's behavior may appear, there are limits set to it. Publicly Symeon defied the regulations of fasting, but in private he observed throughout Lent a fast far stricter than the rules required. The fool is not a schismatic or a heretic, but a faithful child of the Church: he may throw nuts during the Divine Liturgy, but he also receives Holy Communion, and he does not call into doubt Christ's Virgin Birth or His bodily Resurrection. He is eccentric, but not immoral. Although Symeon passed his days and nights in taverns and brothels, he himself remained entirely chaste and pure, preserving true virginity of spirit; when caressed by prostitutes, he felt no sexual desire and was never for a moment separated in his heart from God.[32] After Symeon had been thrown out of the women's bathhouse which he had entered in such a startling manner, his friend John asked him how he had felt among so many naked women. Symeon replied: "Like a block of wood among other blocks of wood, that was how I felt then. I wasn't conscious of having a body or being sur-

29 Ed., Rydén, 160.10-12; tr. Krueger, 163.
30 *AP*, alphabetical collection, Arsenius 27 (*PG* 65:96c); tr. Ward, *Sayings*, 13.
31 See above, 140.
32 Ed., Rydén, 154.28-155.4; tr. Krueger, 159.

rounded by other bodies, but my intellect was wholly occupied with God's work and never departed from Him."[33] The continual prayer conferred on him in the solitude of the desert remained with him wherever he went in the city; and, along with this continual prayer, he possessed *apatheia* or dispassion—purity of the passions, inner freedom, integration and integrity of both soul and body.

The path of self-humiliation that Symeon had made his own, he followed up to the very end. He died alone in his hut, covered by branches, for he had no bed or blanket. It was two days before his friends found him. He was buried in a perfunctory way, "without psalm-singing and candles or incense," in the cemetery for foreigners.[34] Even in his death the fool remains a stranger.

"I am going to mock the world"

Such is Symeon's life: what, if any, is its spiritual value? Are we simply to repeat with Lucretius, *Tantum religio potuit suadere malorum*, "How great are the evils that religion can inspire"? Are we to see in Symeon's feigned madness no more than a deplorable aberration, of limited interest to the student of religious psychopathology, but otherwise best passed over in silence? Or does the Fool of Emesa have something to teach us today?

Let us begin by noting a basic feature in Symeon's vocation as a fool. He was, as we have seen, a monk, a solitary, who after a prolonged period in the desert then felt the call to return to the city. After the "flight of the alone to the Alone," he came back to live out his final years in the streets and public places, surrounded by activity and noise. In common with St Antony of Egypt, although in a different way, his spiritual journey takes the form of flight followed by a return.[35] Andrew and most of the Russian fools, on the other hand, were not monks and had never been solitaries; in their case there was no return from the desert, but their whole life was

---

33 Ed., Rydén, 149.13-16; tr. Krueger, 154.
34 Ed., Rydén, 168.12-13; tr. Krueger, 169. John the Deacon, we are told, arrived shortly after this hasty funeral; he had the tomb opened, but found it empty (ed., Rydén, 168.26-27; tr. Krueger, 170). Those inclined to dismiss this as mere legend should read J. A. T. Robinson, *The Human Face of God* (London: SCM Press, 1973), 139.
35 See above, 131.

lived out in the "world." In yet other cases, as with the nun described by Palladius, the fool lives in a cenobitic monastery. Underlying these variations, then, there is a common feature: the fool pursues his or her chosen path in close proximity with other humans. There are, it is true, occasional examples of fools living throughout their life in solitude, but they are an exception. In almost all instances the pattern is this. The fool may have an inner life of prayer disclosed to very few or to no one at all; but, so far as the daily ordering of his outer life is concerned, it is his vocation to be *in the midst of society*, constantly meeting others, sharing himself with those around him. His is a *communal* vocation, lived with and for his neighbor.

A communal vocation, but also a very strange one. What, then, are Symeon's reasons for making the return from the desert to the city, and there assuming the mask of folly? Three motives emerge. First, there is the reason that Symeon gave to John his fellow solitary: "I am going to mock the world." Two further reasons are also mentioned by Leontius: "Some of the things that he did were done for the salvation of humankind and out of compassion (*sympatheia*), others he did so that his own spiritual achievements should remain hidden."[36] Such are the factors leading Symeon into the path of folly:

> The fool *mocks the world*;
> The fool seeks the way of *humility and humiliation*;
> The fool desires to *save others by means of compassion*.

Let us look at these three features in order, and then ask a final question: In Symeon's case the folly was feigned and deliberate, but need this always be so? Could someone be really mad, and yet still be regarded as a fool *for Christ's sake*?

"I am going to mock the world." This aspect of the fool's vocation can best be understood by recalling what St Paul says in the opening chapters of the First Epistle to the Corinthians. His words, quoted by Leontius in the prologue to the *Life* of Symeon,[37] constitute the royal charter of the fool in Christ: "God's foolishness is wiser than human wisdom... If any-

---

36 Ed., Rydén, 149.16-18; tr. Krueger, 154.
37 Ed., Rydén, 122.29-123.1; tr. Krueger, 133.

one among you seems to be wise in this age, let him become a fool that he may become wise… We are fools for Christ's sake (1 Cor 1:25; 3:18; 4:10)."

Earlier, describing how Symeon abandoned his mother without a word of farewell, we spoke of his maximalism, of his desire to take the Gospel literally. Here the same maximalism confronts us. The fool takes the apostle's words literally. And is he really so very foolish in assuming that when Paul wrote, "Let him become a fool," he meant precisely what he said? As G. P. Fedotov observes:

> We are so accustomed to the paradox of Christianity that we hardly see in the tremendous words of Paul anything but a rhetorical exaggeration. But Paul insists here upon the radical irreconcilability of the two orders—that of the world and that of God. In the kingdom of God reigns a complete inversion of our earthly values.

Folly for Christ's sake, Fedotov continues, expresses "essentially the need to lay bare the radical contradiction between the Christian truth and both the common sense and the moral sense of the world."[38]

Such exactly is the fool's purpose in "mocking the world." Through his entire manner of life, he testifies to the "irreconcilability," the fundamental disparity, existing between two orders or levels of being: between this present age and the Age to come, between the kingdoms of this world and the Kingdom of heaven, between—in St Augustine's terminology—the "earthly city" and the "city of God." He insists upon a "complete inversion of values"; in God's Kingdom the perspective is reversed, the pyramid stood upon its head. That, indeed, is the proper meaning of repentance: *metanoia*, a "change of mind"—not a feeling of guilt, but an entire transposition of priorities, a radically new understanding. The fool is in this sense *par excellence* the one who has repented. In the words of Irina Gorainoff, he "lives life in reverse"; he is a "living witness to the anti-world, to the possibility of the impossible."[39] He makes his own the world-in-reverse manifested by Christ in the Beatitudes.

The fool's "life in reverse" is a challenge, says Fedotov, to both the "common sense" and the "moral sense" of our fallen world. By virtue of his inner freedom, through his laughter and his playfulness, he "mocks"

---

38 *The Russian Religious Mind,* 2:322.
39 *Les fols en Christ,* 27.

and calls in question any attempt to reduce the Christian life to the level of respectability and conventional moral standards. He mocks all the forms of legalism that turn Christianity into a code of "rules." He is fiercely opposed to those who, in the words of Christos Yannaras, "have identified faith and truth with the secularized concept of moral upright-ness and conventional decorum." The fool, adds Yannaras, "is the incar-nation of the Gospel's fundamental message: that it is possible for someone to keep the whole of the Law without managing to free himself from his biological and psychological ego, from corruption and death."[40] It is significant that, in his prologue to the *Life* of Symeon, Leontius in-sists upon the supreme importance of the personal conscience:[41] the fool is guided, not by objectivized "laws," but by the voice of God speaking di-rectly in the heart. In this way the fool expresses, in the phrase of Cecil Collins, "an endless regard for human identity." He bears witness to the preeminent value of *persons* rather than *rules*.

Mocking the world, the fool strips off the masks of hypocrisy, demystifies roles, and reveals the presence of the human, the all-too-hu-man, behind the facade of dignity and honor. He is the one who dares to say that the emperor has no clothes. To awaken others from their "pious" complacency, he often employs shock tactics. Yet the purpose, even when he breaks the fast or causes a disturbance at the Divine Liturgy, is never to create confusion in the faith of others or to obscure the truth of the Church. The fool, as we have said of Symeon, is neither schismatic nor heretic. He does not mock Holy Scripture or the Creed, the sacraments or the icons. He mocks only the pompous and self-satisfied who hold high office in the Church and the humorless ritualists who confuse outer ges-ture with inner life. His protest is not destructive but liberating and cre-ative. By "mocking" the world, as the Armenian version of Symeon's *Life* so rightly says, the fool is also "bringing peace" to the world.

In his mockery of this fallen world, the fool may be seen as an eschato-logical figure, affirming the primacy of the Age to come. He is a "sign," bearing witness that Christ's Kingdom is not of this world. This helps us to understand why fools should have been prominent mainly during peri-ods when Christianity was firmly "established" within the fabric of the so-

40 *The Freedom of Morality* (Crestwood: NY: St Vladimir's Seminary Press, 1984), 74, 75.
41 Ed., Rydén, 122.1-3; tr. Krueger, 132.

cial order, and when there was a close identification between the things of
Caesar and the things of God. In the first three centuries of our era, when
Christianity was oppressed and persecuted, there was no special need for
the fool's testimony: *all* Christians were at that time considered fools by
the dominant classes in society. But when, as in the christianized Empire
of East Rome from the fourth century onwards or in the sacral autocracy
of sixteenth-century Moscow, people were in danger of confusing an
earthly kingdom with the Kingdom of God, then there was an urgent
need of the fool's mockery. Like the monk, the fool acts as an essential
counterbalance to a "Christendom" that has too readily come to terms
with the world.

As sign and witness pointing to the Kingdom, the fool has much in
common with the child. The special link between the two is expressed in
the Greek proverb, "If you want to know the truth, ask a child or a fool."[42]
In Russia it used to be the custom to bring children to the fool to be
blessed. St Isaac, the holy fool of Kiev, loved to gather children round him
and to play with them; and in our own day St John Maximovitch, who
had about him many characteristics of the fool in Christ, likewise showed
a particular love for children.[43] In his freedom, in his innocence and virginity of spirit, the fool is precisely one who has become "as a little child"
(cf. Mt 18:3), and has learnt the secrets "hidden from the wise and pru-
dent" but "revealed to babes" (Mt 11:25). "Before the divine, man is as a
child," says Heraclitus;[44] the fool takes this to heart and, as a child before
the divine, he *plays*. The fool expresses something present in all of us as
children, something all too often killed as we grow up, which we need to
rediscover and bring back to life. But, if the fool plays, he is also serious:
his laughter is close to tears, for he is sensitive to the tragedy in this world
as well as to the comedy. He embodies both the joy of life and the sorrow
of life.

Because of his childlikeness, his playfulness, the fool is sometimes
loved, as Symeon of Emesa was loved. But at other times he is feared and
hated. It is painful to observe, in the lives of many fools, with what sadis-

---

42 Cited by Saward, *Perfect Fools*, ix.
43 See Bishop Savva of Edmonton, *Blessed John*, 106-7.
44 Fragment 79; cf. Hugo Rahner, *Man at Play* (New York: Herder & Herder, 1972), especially
     58-60.

tic violence they are treated. Why should the world so fear and hate the fool? Because he is free, and so the world is disturbed by him; because he is useless and does not seek power, and so it cannot exploit him.

Such, then, is the first meaning of folly for Christ's sake. The fool bears witness to the basic discrepancy between human and divine wisdom. "Mocking" all forms of conventional morality based on rules, he affirms the cardinal worth of the person. As a little child, he points to the Kingdom of heaven that is utterly different from every earthly kingdom.

Imitators of the Divine Fool

The second feature of the fool's vocation is the desire to preserve humility, the willing acceptance of humiliation. Returning from solitude to society, apprehensive of the honors he might receive as an ascetic, Symeon prayed at Jerusalem that "all his works might remain hidden."[45] Feigned madness was a way, precisely, of avoiding honors and of keeping his "works" hidden. This factor emerges particularly in the story of the innkeeper's wife: Symeon pretended to rape her, because her husband was beginning to honor him as a saint.[46] Folly, then, ensures contempt and acts as a safeguard for humility.

There is also, however, a deeper motive behind the fool's acceptance of humiliation. He desires to be associated as closely as possible with the humiliated Christ, who was "despised and rejected by others" (Is 53:3). The fool is to be seen as a Christ-like figure, as an imitator of the Lord Jesus. As Cecil Collins states, "The greatest fool in history was Christ...the Divine Fool."[47] It is true that the parallel between Christ and the holy fool is not exact. Christ did not interrupt the temple worship by throwing nuts, He did not trip people up in the street, He did not pretend to be an epileptic, and He did not feign madness. But such was His behavior in other ways that His close relatives concluded that He was in fact mad: in Mark's words, "When His own people heard about this, they went out to lay hold of Him, for they said, 'He is out of His mind'" (Mk 3:21)—a sentence

---

45 Ed., Rydén, 144.23-24; tr. Krueger, 150.
46 Ed., Rydén, 147.24; tr. Krueger, 153.
47 Cecil Collins, *The Vision of the Fool*, rev. edn. (Chipping Norton: Kedros, 1981), 4. This beautiful essay was originally written in 1944.

that, not surprisingly, has been omitted by Matthew and Luke. Even though Jesus was not mad and did not pretend to be, He purposely did many things that offended both the common sense and the moral sense of His contemporaries. Like Symeon eating meat in Holy Week, He broke the rules of the Sabbath in an obvious and pointed way (Mk 2:23). Like Symeon, He consorted with those whom "respectable" society spurned as sinners (Mk 2:15-16; Lk 7:34; 19:7), and He showed a special gentleness towards women of doubtful repute, such as the sinful woman with the flask of myrrh (Lk 7:37), the Samaritan woman at the well (Jn 4:7-26), or the woman taken in adultery (Jn 8:11). Like Symeon, He overturned the tables of those who bought and sold in the precincts of God's house (Mt 21:12; Jn 2:15). In refusing to become the leader of a political party, in deliberately renouncing the path of human popularity and secular influence, in choosing the way of the Cross, Jesus acted in a manner that most of His followers could only regard as willful folly.

Here, then, is a deep similarity between the Savior and the fool. The fool accepts the paradox and folly of the Cross, which is at the same time true wisdom (1 Cor 1:23-4). As an icon of the humiliated Christ, unreservedly he makes his own the *kenosis* of the Lord, accepting every form of reproach and mockery so as to be as close as possible to his Savior. For Jesus, glory meant vulnerability and abasement, victory meant weakness and failure: that is true likewise of the fool. In worldly, secular terms nothing of practical value is achieved by the fool; but in worldly terms nothing of practical value was achieved by the Cross. In his kenotic maximalism, the fool is a profoundly evangelical figure. He dies daily and therefore, because crucifixion and resurrection constitute a single event, daily he rises again from the dead; an icon of the humiliated Christ, he is therefore an icon also of the great joy of the Transfiguration.

Prophet and apostle

"Sign" of the heavenly kingdom, icon of the One who was "despised and rejected," the fool has also, in the third place, a prophetic and apostolic function. "The prophet is a fool," says Hosea (9:7); but the statement may also be reversed—the fool is a prophet. His folly is a way of awakening the conscience of others. Through his feigned madness he acts as a missionary, preaching the Good News of salvation to those who cannot be reached in any other way.

Symeon, it will be remembered, speaking with John his fellow solitary, gave this as his reason for returning to the world: "What do we gain, brother, by spending our days in this desert? ...Let us go and *save others*."[48] Folly, for Symeon, was a way of showing love for others. He was conscious of an apostolic vocation; it was not sufficient for him to intercede on the world's behalf as a hermit, but in love he had to return to the world. Leontius underlines the meaning of his loving self-sacrifice in the prologue to the *Life*: "After being so much honored and exalted by God" as a solitary in the desert, Symeon

> did not think it right to neglect the salvation of his fellow humans; but, remembering Christ's words, "You shall love your neighbor as yourself," and recalling how Christ, while remaining Himself unchanged, did not refuse to be clothed in the form of a servant for the servant's salvation, he imitated his Master by truly laying down his own soul and body so as to save others.[49]

Symeon lays down his life. The fool, like the monk, is a martyr: not an outward martyr of blood but an inner martyr of the heart and conscience.[50]

The fool saves others, not so much through anything that he says, but through what he is, through his entire manner of life. He is a living parable. He preaches the faith, not by his eloquence or ingenious arguments, but by his compassion. As Leontius says of Symeon: "He returned to the world, wishing to *show his compassion* for those under assault and to save them."[51] The fool follows the path not of exhortation and reproof but of *solidarity*. That is why Symeon spends his time with prostitutes and those whom the pharisaic dismiss as the "dregs" of society. He unites himself to the despised and unloved, the misfits and deformed: "my brethren and companions in poverty," to use the phrase that Nicephorus puts in Andrew's mouth.[52] And through this act of total participation he brings hope and healing. Like Christ, the fool goes out in search of the lost sheep and

48 Ed., Rydén, 142.14-15; tr. Krueger, 148.
49 Ed., Rydén, 123.20-24; tr. Krueger, 133-34.
50 See above, 115-16, 122.
51 Ed., Rydén, 155.13-14; tr. Krueger, 159.
52 *Life* 28 (*PG* 111:661A).

brings it back on his shoulders. He goes down into the pit to draw others out of it.

But, it may be asked, could not Symeon have converted sinners in a less eccentric way, without pretending to be mad? Perhaps not. Folly opened before him doors that otherwise would have remained closed. Had he simply gone into the taverns and brothels and delivered homilies, who would have listened? It was through his vulnerability and his gentle companionship, through his playfulness and joy, that he moved the hearts of drunkards and prostitutes. When Cecil Collins speaks of the fool's "wild painful gestures of tenderness before the suffering of all the living ones in the Universe,"[53] his words are surely applicable to Symeon: underneath the laughter and the outrageous absurdities, there is in him an immense tenderness for all who are rejected. Without condoning sin he loves the sinner, and avoids any suggestion of moral superiority. "Neither do I condemn you" (Jn 8:11): like Christ, the fool does not curse or condemn, and therein lies his power of attraction. For, according to Leontius, Symeon's apostolate of folly did in fact prove highly effective: "Through his jokes he often brought impure women and prostitutes to lawful marriage... Others he filled with contrition through his own purity, and induced them to adopt the monastic life."[54] *Through his jokes*—not through his reproaches or righteous indignation.

One particular group of outcasts, apart from prostitutes, towards whom Symeon showed especial love were the "demoniacs"—often treated with great cruelty in the ancient world: "He had extraordinary compassion for those possessed by demons. Often he went and joined them, behaving as if he were himself one of them; and, passing his time with them, he healed many of them through his prayers."[55]

He shared in their suffering: the fool's vocation is the way of compassion, in the full sense of that often debased word—an "enigmatic and universal compassion," as Collins puts it.[56] Symeon does not proffer aid from a secure distance, detached and uninvolved, but he goes and lives with the possessed, entering totally into their situation. The fool's prayers confer

---

53 *The Vision of the Fool*, 8.
54 Ed., Rydén, 145.11-14; tr. Krueger, 150.
55 Ed., Rydén, 162.12-14; tr. Krueger, 165.
56 *The Vision of the Fool*, 7.

healing because he has made his own all the anguish of those for whom he intercedes. His path is indeed what Charles Williams called the "way of exchange" and "substituted love."

All this is powerfully expressed by Iulia de Beausobre. When she says "Russian," may we not simply say "Christian"?

> How does the Russian pity, then, strive to mend the ill, to heal the wound, to bridge the gap? On the grand scale it simply cannot be done; it cannot be done at all without losing caste. It can only be done from man to man; by no amount of organization or subscriptions, but only through a complete dedication of oneself...
>
> He who pities another must leave his own place among the good people on the sunny side of the gap, must go out and find the other where he is—in the darkness, on the side of evil—and be ready to stay with him there; if he returns at all, it is with the other and at his pace...
>
> Evil can be overcome by man only through knowledge, the knowledge of evil; and it seems to the Russian that man can know a thing, as man, only through participation...
>
> The aim of the *iurodivyi* is to participate in evil through suffering. He makes of this his life's work because, to the Russian, good and evil are, here on earth, inextricably bound up together. This is, to us, the great mystery of life on earth. Where evil is at its most intense, there too must be the greatest good. To us this is not even an hypothesis. It is axiomatic.[57]

Such is the axiom that the fool lives out: no healing without solidarity, no salvation without participation. The same axiom is presupposed at the Incarnation and in Gethsemane.

If the fool wishes to prophesy or preach in a more specific way, commonly he does this not through words but through symbolic gestures. In this he is heir to a long tradition. The Old Testament prophets frequently performed acts of a startling or even shocking nature, yet with a hidden meaning: Isaiah went about barefoot and naked (20:2), Jeremiah wore a yoke like a beast of burden (27:2), Ezekiel baked his bread on human excrement (4:12), and Hosea married a prostitute (3:1). Similar actions of a symbolic type occur in Symeon's life. Before a great earthquake at Emesa, he went round striking the pillars of the buildings: to some he said "Stand," and in the earthquake none of these collapsed; to one he said,

---

57 *Creative Suffering*, 32-33, 34.

"Neither fall nor stand," and this was split down the middle. Shortly before a plague, he visited the schools and kissed some of the children, saying "Happy journey, my dear," but he did not do this to them all; and he
told the schoolmaster, "Don't beat the children I kiss, for they have a long
way to go." When the epidemic came, all those whom he had kissed fell
victim to it.[58]

Striking symbolic actions are also a characteristic of the Russian fools.
Prokopy of Ustiug carried about three pokers in his left hand; according
to the way in which he held them, the farmers could predict whether it
would be a good or bad harvest. Basil the Blessed had behind his strange
behavior a prophetic purpose: he destroyed the goods of certain mer-
chants, because they were trading dishonestly; he hurled stones at the
houses of the virtuous, because the devils, expelled from within, were
clinging to the outside; he kissed the corner-stones of houses in which
"blasphemies" were being committed, because the angels, unable to enter
such houses, were standing round them weeping. Most terrifying of all,
he smashed with a stone the miraculous icon of the Virgin at the Barbar-
ian Gates, because unknown to everyone a devil had been drawn on the
board behind the holy picture.[59]

In this fashion the wild, inconsequential gestures of the fool have a
deeper meaning: they warn others of future peril or convict them of secret
sin. His nonsense is pointed and purposeful; beneath an exterior of idiocy,
he displays insight and foresight. Many of the stories told of Symeon emphasize his *diakrisis*, his gift of discernment or sanctified clairvoyance. He
smashed a vessel of wine that, unnoticed by all, had been poisoned by a
snake;[60] he understood the secret thoughts in the hearts of others;[61] he
knew what people were doing or saying at a distance.[62] So the fool acts as
the living conscience of the community. He is a mirror, showing people
their true face, making the implicit explicit, causing the unconscious to
rise to the surface. He is a catalyzer: remaining himself detached, he re-
leases reactions in others.

58 Ed., Rydén, 150.20-151.9; tr. Krueger, 155.
59 Fedotov, *The Russian Religious Mind*, 2:329, 337-38.
60 Ed., Rydén, 147.12-24; tr. Krueger, 152-53.
61 Ed., Rydén, 156.20-21; tr. Krueger, 160.
62 Ed., Rydén, 159.4-15; tr. Krueger, 162.

In particular the fool, combining audacity with humility, uses his prophetic *charisma* by denouncing the great and the powerful. Because he is free, a stranger, inured to pain and hardship, having nothing to lose, he can speak boldly without fear of reprisals. Symeon's life contains no instances of such social protests directed against those in authority, but there are examples in the *Life* of St Andrew the Fool,[63] and more especially among the sixteenth-century *iurodivye* under Ivan the Terrible. Fletcher refers, for example, to the occasion when the tsar entered Pskov during the Lenten fast, and was met by Nicolas the fool who offered him a lump of raw meat. Ivan recoiled in disgust:

> "And doth Ivashka (which is as much to say, as Jack) think," quoth Nikola, "that it is unlawful to eat a piece of beast's flesh in Lent and not to eat up so much man's flesh as he hath done already?" So threatening the emperor with a prophecy of some hard adventure to come upon him except he left murdering of his people and departed the town, he saved a great many men's lives at that time.[64]

Not without reason did Nicolas Fyodorov describe Russia as an autocracy limited by fools in Christ.[65]

Unwitting prophets?

Must the madness of the fool in Christ be always feigned and deliberate, or may it be sometimes a genuine instance of mental illness? The question assumes that there is a clear differentiation between sanity and insanity; but is this always the case? In labeling some persons "normal" and others "abnormal," are we not assuming—perhaps without good reason—that we know exactly what "normality" is? But, insofar as a distinction is to be made, then it can be argued that in principle the madness of the fool must necessarily be feigned; only so can it be regarded as freely chosen folly for Christ's sake, and not just an involuntary affliction.[66] Yet in practice it is less easy to impose rigid lines of demarcation. In Symeon's case, certainly, the folly was feigned, although a neurologist who has made a special study of the *Life* of Leontius has commented that, if so, Symeon was remarkably

63 See, for example, *Life* 205 (*PG* III:849B).

64 Berry and Crummey (eds.), *Rude and Barbarous Kingdom*, 220.

65 Gorainoff, *Les fols en Christ*, 92.

66 See V. Rochcau, "Que savons-nous des Fous-pour-le-Christ?," *Irénikon* 53 (1980), 343-44.

ingenious and accurate in counterfeiting the symptoms of genuine
mania.[67] Andrew's folly is also presented by Nicephorus as feigned. But in
other instances the evidence is less easy to interpret: Isaac of Kiev, for at
any rate part of his life, and some of the other Russian fools, seem to be
truly deranged. Alongside those who are consciously playing a part, so it
seems, some place should also be found for holy fools who are involun-
tarily subject to psychic maladies. Is it not possible that the grace of Christ
may likewise be at work among them? A man or woman may be psycho-
logically ill, and yet spiritually well; mentally sick, but of deep moral
purity. Such persons may surely be included among the holy fools, and
may be seen as inspired by God to fulfill a prophetic role.

For the prophet is not always consciously aware of what he is saying.
As the Fourth Gospel states of Caiaphas: "Now this he did not say on his
own authority; but being high priest that year he prophesied that Jesus
would die for the nation" (Jn 11:51). Caiaphas is an unwitting and involuntary prophet: he does not appreciate, with his conscious mind, the real
meaning of the truth that he proclaims, but he says more than he intends
or realizes. If God, without depriving the prophet of his free will, may yet
use him as the mouthpiece of a message greater than his own understanding, cannot the same be true also of the holy fool? Even when actually un-
balanced on the psychological level, his mental disabilities may yet be
employed by the Holy Spirit as a way of healing and saving others.

The perils of folly

The fool, it has been said, walks on a tightrope stretched above an infernal
abyss. Instead of transfiguring his folly into a prophetic innocence, he
may simply lapse into willful crankiness. It is only too easy to opt out
from conventional social life without thereby choosing the heavenly
Kingdom. Genuine instances of folly for Christ's sake are exceedingly
rare, and the spiritual tradition is unanimous in regarding this as a singu-
larly perilous vocation. Many of the fools had personal disciples, but it is
hard to find even a single instance where the fool encouraged his follower
to adopt the same path. When Symeon of Emesa felt the call to return

---

67 See Grosdidier de Matons, "Les thèmes d'édification dans la Vie d'André Salos," *Travaux et
    Mémoires* 4 (1970), 303.

from the desert to "mock" the world, his companion John chose to stay where he was: he felt that he lacked the strength to adopt the arduous path that Symeon had chosen—"I have not yet reached so high a level as this." The solitude of the hermit is an easier way than folly in Christ. Many in fact doubted the authenticity of Symeon's vocation, saying: "His prophecies came from Satan."[68] And Symeon himself would never have chosen to be a fool had he not been conscious of a specific call from God.[69]

St Seraphim of Sarov insisted equally on the need for a special call from God. In general he gave little encouragement to would-be fools:

> Others came to the *starets* to ask his blessing and approval on their desire to become fools in Christ. Not only did he fail to recommend this, but he would angrily exclaim: "All those who take upon themselves the way of being fools in Christ without a special call from God fall into temptation. Scarcely one fool in Christ can be found who did not fall into temptation, perish, or return to the world. The *starets* [in the monastery of Sarov] never allowed anyone to be a fool in Christ. In my time, only one of the monks gave symptoms of folly; he started to mew like a cat in church. *Starets* Pakhomy [the abbot] immediately ordered him to be led out of the church and taken to the monastery gates."[70]

It is scarcely surprising that the church authorities should have expressed repeated reservations about the fool in Christ. The Council in Trullo (692), in its sixtieth canon, severely censures those "who pretend to be possessed by demons, and in their depraved behavior copy such persons with feigned mimicry." The twelfth-century canonist Theodore Balsamon, commenting on this text, concludes that it refers to fools in Christ, even though he is anxious to limit the scope of the canon by insisting on the possibility of genuinely holy fools as well as "depraved counterfeits."[71] It is interesting to note the date of the canon: it was promulgated about half a century later than the *Life* of Symeon of Emesa, and may well express an official reaction against the widespread popular influence exer-

---

68 Ed., Rydén, 152.4; tr. Krueger, 156. But the same was said of Christ (Mk 3:22)!

69 Ed., Rydén, 144.5-6; tr. Krueger, 149.

70 "Fragments from the Life of Saint Seraphim," in Fedotov, *A Treasury of Russian Spirituality*, 261. There are, however, three cases in which St Seraphim blessed people to become fools in Christ: see Archimandrite Lazarus Moore, *St. Seraphim of Sarov*, 319.

71 G. A. Rallis and M. Potlis (ed.), *Syntagma ton Theion kai Ieron Kanonon*, 6 vols. (Athens: G. Chartophylax, 1852-1859), 2:440-42.

cised by Leontius' work.[72] Another canonical source that condemns folly for Christ's sake, the *Interpretations* of Nikon of the Black Mountain (eleventh century), refers explicitly to Symeon: "The divine laws condemn those who practice folly after the manner of the great Symeon and of Andrew, and today such things are altogether forbidden."[73]

Despite all the dangers, however, up to the present time such things have not been in fact "altogether forbidden." On the contrary, the Orthodox Church has continued to allow a place for this unconventional but life-giving vocation. And we may be glad that this is so. For while the fools in Christ certainly do not belong to the institutional and hierarchical ministry of the Chruch, they have nonetheless a place within the "apostolic succession" of prophets and seers, of spiritual fathers and mothers, who belong to the Church's free, unregulated, "charismatic" life.[74] May we always find room for the holy fool within our church communities; for the community that excludes the fool may find that it has also shut the door in the face of the Divine Fool, Christ Himself.

---

72 See John Wortley, "The Sixtieth Canon of the Council in *Troullo*," *Studia Patristica* 15, Texte und Untersuchungen 128 (Berlin: Akademie Verlag, 1984), 255-60.

73 *PG* 106:1372B.

74 On the two forms of "apostolic succession," see above, 130-31.

II

Time: prison or
path to freedom?

See then that you walk circumspectly, not as fools but as wise,
redeeming the time.

Ephesians 5:15-16

Circle, line, spiral

It is a striking fact, easily overlooked, that in the New Testament Jesus
Christ begins His public ministry by speaking of time, and that He likewise refers to time in the last conversation that He has with His disciples at
the very end of His earthly life. "The time is fulfilled" (Mk 1:15): so Christ
commences His preaching, while immediately before his Ascension He
says to the eleven, "It is not for you to know the times or seasons which the
Father has fixed by His own authority" (Acts 1:7). Both at the outset and at
the conclusion of the story, the question of time confronts us: time as
fulfilled in Christ, time as a mystery still hidden in God. What, then, do we
mean by time?

Since the theme of time is in this way deeply embedded in the Gospel
narrative, we cannot dismiss the question as no more than a speculative issue, of interest merely to the professional philosopher. It is a matter that
concerns each one of us personally. Philip Larkin's query is posed to us all:

What are days for?
Days are where we live.
They come, they wake us
Time and time over...
Where can we live but days?[1]

---

1   Philip Larkin, *Collected Poems* (London/Boston: Marvell Press, Faber, 1988), 67.

"What are days for?" The question is not simply "What is time?" but "What is time *for*?" We are concerned not just with the abstract essence of time but with its practical effect on our lives. What are we to do about time, what are we to make of it?

Oscar Cullmann, in his classic work *Christ and Time*, offers two basic images. Time may be seen as cyclical, as a circle, ring or wheel; or else it may be seen as linear, as a straight path, a river or an arrow. Without asserting too sharp a dichotomy between Hellenism and Judaism, it may be said that the first manner of envisaging time is characteristically Greek—in Aristotle's words, "For indeed time itself seems to be a sort of circle"[2]—while the second approach predominates in Hebraic and Iranian thought. Not that the two symbols need be mutually exclusive, for they both embody an aspect of the truth. The image of the circle reflects the recurrent rhythms in the world of nature, the line expresses our sense of time as direction, progress and evolution. What strikes us at once is that these symbols are both alike double-edged. The circle of time may be felt as redemptive, as the means of our return to the golden age, to the lost paradise; or it may be viewed as meaningless repetition, as boredom and futility. It may serve as an image of celestial eternity—Henry Vaughan's "great ring of pure and endless light"—or it may be a sign of hell, a closed and vicious circle. So it is also with linear time. It is true that the line may be strictly horizontal, and therefore neutral. But equally it may be seen as oblique or sloping, and in that case inclined either upward or downward. Interpreted positively, the line of time becomes a path of ascent to the summit of the holy mountain; understood negatively, it signifies deterioration and decline, "downhill all the way": *Facilis descensus Averni…* Once more the image is equivocal.

A better symbol of time than either the circle or the line is surely the spiral, combining elements from both the other figures, yet avoiding their more blatant defects. The spiral, more truly than the circle or the line, reflects the basic patterns in the physical universe, from the movement of the galaxies to the folds in the human cerebral cortex. It includes the cyclic rhythms of nature, yet in the case of the spiral the circle is not closed but suggests continuous advance towards a goal. Above all, the spiral has

---

2   *Physics* 4.14 (223b29).

the advantage of being—at any rate in some instances—three-dimensional, thus expressing our post-Einsteinian sense of living in a space-time continuum. St Dionysius the Areopagite regarded the spiral as the highest type of movement, the form most befitting the angelic powers,[3] and that strange prophetic figure of twelfth-century Italy, Joachim of Fiore, thought the same; and I am inclined to agree with them. Once more, however, the question confronts us: what kind of spiral? For spirals can be either descending or ascending, or rather they may be both these things at once, as the sailor discovered in Poe's story, *A Descent into the Maelstrom*. What, then, is to be our perception of time's spiral: a descending vortex, sucking us down into annihilation, or the never-ending dance of love, drawing us "farther up and farther in"?[4]

Enemy or friend?

Our experience of time, as these three symbols indicate, is deeply ambivalent. How are we to regard time: as enemy or friend, as our prison or our path to freedom? Which aspect do we find predominant in its double-edged impact upon us: anguish or healing, terror or hope, decay or growth, separation or relationship? If the second edition of *The Oxford Dictionary of Quotations* can be trusted as a guide, time has commonly been seen more as a threat than as an enrichment. We find Shakespeare castigating "envious and calumniating time...that bald sexton, Time"; in Ben Jonson's eyes time is "that old bald cheater"; "Time with a gift of tears," writes Swinburne, while Tennyson calls time "a maniac scattering dust." Others, it is true, refer to time in more constructive terms as a "gardener" or a "physician," but they are minority voices. For Isaac Watts, time with its irreversible flow brings about a sense of loss and unreality:

> Time, like an ever-rolling stream,
> Bears all its sons away:
> They fly forgotten, as a dream
> Dies at the opening day.

An equally somber view is to be found in the main biblical work devoted to the theme of time, Ecclesiastes. In the opening chapter the

---

3   *The Divine Names* 4.8 (*PG* 3:704D); ed. Suchla, 153.4-9. On the symbolism of the spiral, see Jill Purce, *The Mystic Spiral: Journey of the Soul* (London: Thames and Hudson, 1974).
4   See the title of chapter 15 in C. S. Lewis, *The Last Battle* (London: Bodley Head, 1956).

Preacher sees time as vain repetition, as the cause of "weariness" and disil-
lusion (Eccl 1:2-9):

> All is vanity…
> One generation passes away,
> and another generation comes…
> The wind blows to the south,
> and goes round to the north;
> round and round goes the wind,
> and on its circuits the wind returns.
> All streams run to the sea,
> but the sea is not full;
> to the place where the streams flow,
> there they flow, again.
> All things are full of weariness…
> and there is nothing new under the sun.

Taken as a whole, however, the Scriptural attitude towards time is
markedly less hostile than this. The Preacher himself in a later section
links time with beauty and with eternity: "For everything there is a time,
and an appointed moment for every matter under heaven… He has made
everything beautiful in its time; also he has put eternity into man's mind"
(Eccl 3: 1, 11). In the New Testament this positive approach is reaffirmed.
"The time is fulfilled" (Mk 1:15): time is not pointless but purposive;
Christ comes in the fullness of time. So far from being meaningless and
arbitrary, time is something which "the Father has fixed by His own
authority" (Acts 1:7). St Paul speaks of "the accepted time" or "time of
God's favor" (2 Cor 6:2); time can be "redeemed" (Eph 5:16). God has
made the "ages" or "aeons" of time (Heb 1:12), and He is "the king of the
ages" (1 Tim 1:17). There is no doubt about the Biblical view: time is part
of God's creation, and as such it is "altogether good and beautiful" (Gen
1:31, LXX).

Bisecting the world of time

If we are to appreciate the beauty of time at its full value, then there are
two basic truths that need to be kept in view. First, time and eternity are
not opposed but interdependent, not mutually exclusive but complementary. Second, the meaning of time is to be found in relationship, in personal communion, in response and openness to others. Time is not to be

interpreted merely in privative terms as a reflection of human finitude and a restriction on our liberty, but it is a positive expression of what it signifies to be a person, an indispensable precondition of human freedom and love. As regards both of these truths, the key to the right understanding of time is provided by Christ's Incarnation.

Time and eternity are not opposed. When Spinoza maintains, "Eternity cannot be defined by time or have any relation to it,"[5] the second part of this statement, at any rate, is definitely open to question. Indeed, the Incarnation involves precisely an "intersection of the timeless with time," to use T. S. Eliot's phrase in *The Four Quartets*.[6] As he puts it in *The Rock*, Christ's birth is an event within time and yet transforming time:

> Then came, at a predetermined moment, a moment in time
>   and of time,
> A moment not out of time, but in time, in what we call
>   history: transecting, bisecting the world of time, a
>   moment in time but not like a moment of time,
> A moment in time but time was made through that moment:
>   for without the meaning there is no time, and
>   that moment of time gave the meaning.[7]

"Transecting, bisecting the world of time": Eliot's point is brought out vividly in the *Protevangelion* or *Book of James*, when Joseph speaks of time as standing still at the moment of the Nativity:

> Now I Joseph was walking about, and yet I did not walk. And I looked up into the vault of heaven, and saw it standing still, and I looked up to the air, and saw the air in amazement, and the birds of heaven remain motionless. And I looked at the earth, and saw a dish placed there and workmen lying round it with their hands in the dish. But those who chewed did not chew, and those who lifted up anything lifted up nothing, and those who put something to their mouth put nothing to their mouth, but all had their faces turned upwards. And behold, sheep were being driven, and yet they did not come forward, but stood still; and the shepherd raised his hand to strike them with his staff, but his hand remained up. And I looked at the flow of the river, and saw

5   Spinoza, *Ethics*, Part 5, proposition 23, note; tr. A. Boyle (London: Everyman's Library, 1910), 24. Quoted in Maurice Nicoll, *Living Time and the Integration of Life* (Boulder/London: Shambhala, 1984), 132.

6   T. S. Eliot, 'The Dry Salvages,' *The Complete Poems and Plays* (London: Faber, 1969), 189-90.

7   *Ibid.*, 160.

the mouths of the kids over it and yet they did not drink. And then all at once everything went on its course again.[8]

What can be affirmed to a supreme degree concerning the time of the Incarnation is likewise true, at least potentially, of every moment of time. At the Incarnation eternity transects time in a unique manner. Yet each moment of time is also open to eternity; at each moment it is possible for eternity to break into the temporal sequence, assuming time into itself and so transforming it. Eternity is not simply outside the moments of time but at the heart of each moment; and this eternity, present within time, gives to time its true value. "Eternity is as much in time as it is above time," writes the contemporary Romanian Orthodox theologian, Archpriest Dumitru Staniloae, who has devoted particular attention to the Christian significance of time.[9]

Plato was not far from the truth when he spoke of time as a moving image of eternity.[10] Time and eternity—and, by the same token, space and infinity—do not contradict but complete one another. Time and space, while modalities of the created order, are rooted in God's eternal, uncreated life and find their fulfillment there. Between time and eternity there exists, to use the phrase of the French Orthodox author Olivier Clément, "a marriage bond," *un rapport proprement nuptial*.[11] In the words of St Maximus the Confessor, "The inner principles (*logoi*, "reasons") of time abide in God."[12] "The divine eternity," writes Staniloae, "…carries within itself the possibility of time, while time carries within itself the possibility of participating in eternity."[13] Eternity is turned towards time and goes out to meet it; and time, when taken up into eternity, is not annihilated but transfigured.

---

8   *Protevangelion* 18.2: ed. C. Tischendorf, *Evangelia Apocrypha* (Leipzig: H. Mendelssohn, 1876), 34-35; ed. Wilhelm Schneemelcher, *New Testament Apocrypha*, 2 vols. (Cambridge: James Clarke, 1991-92), 1:433.

9   *The Experience of God* (Brookline, MA: Holy Cross Orthodox Press, 1994), 158.

10 Cf. Plato, *Timaeus* 37d.

11 *Transfigurer le temps. Notes sur le temps à la lumière de la tradition orthodoxe* (Neuchâtel/Paris: Delachaux and Niestlé, 1959), 54.

12 *Difficulties* (PG 91:1164B).

13 *The Experience of God*, 153.

Time as the freedom to love

Let us turn now to our second point. Time from a Christian perspective is one of the means whereby God evokes and guarantees our created human freedom, our freedom to love. The notion of freedom—both divine freedom and human freedom—is fundamental to the Christian doctrine of creation. "God is truly present and operative only in freedom," claims Nicolas Berdyaev. "Freedom alone should be recognized as possessing a sacred quality."[14] As Søren Kierkegaard has rightly insisted, "The most tremendous thing granted to humans is choice, freedom."[15] God created the world in freedom, and He willed that the beings whom He formed in His image should likewise be free. As a Trinitarian God, a God of shared interpersonal love, He desired that we humans in our turn should be joined to Him in a relationship of mutual love. Mutual love, however, presupposes freedom, for where there is no voluntary choice there can be no love. Love cannot be constrained, but can only be tendered willingly; God is able to do anything except *compel* us to love him. Love comes always as an offer to which the beloved is invited to respond in freedom.

By creating in this way a world of persons capable of freely responding to Him in love, God accepted to restrict, in some measure, the exercise of His omnipotence. He "withdrew" as it were from His creation, "distancing" Himself so that His creatures might have room to love. Creation involves a divine self-limitation, what the sixteenth-century Jewish Kabbalist, Isaac Luria, termed *zimzum*, "contraction" or "concentration."[16] In thus bringing into existence free persons with the power of rejecting him, God inevitably took a risk. But had He not taken this risk, there would have been a universe without love. As Vladimir Lossky observes, "This divine risk, inherent in the decision to create beings in the image and likeness of God, is the summit of almighty power, or rather a surpassing of that summit in a voluntarily undertaken powerlessness... He who takes no risks does not love."[17]

14 *Dream and Reality,* 46.
15 *The Journals of Søren Kierkegaard,* tr. A. Dru (New York/London: Oxford University Press, 1938), 372.
16 See Jürgen Moltmann, *The Trinity and the Kingdom of God* (London: SCM Press, 1981), 108-111.
17 *In the Image and Likeness of God* (Crestwood, NY: St Vladimir's Seminary Press, 1974), 214.

This risk-taking or *kenosis* on God's part, inaugurated at the creation, came to its full expression at the Incarnation. In choosing to become a creature, the divine Creator embraced a situation of complete vulnerability, an entire and unreserved solidarity with us humans in our pain and brokenness. He willed to effect our salvation, not through any exercise of transcendent power, but through the utter powerlessness of His incarnate state: "My strength is made perfect in weakness" (2 Cor 12:9). Such exactly is the supreme paradox of Christology: God is never so strong as when He is most weak, never so truly divine as when He empties himself. St Gregory of Nyssa saw this clearly: "The fact that the omnipotent nature should have been capable of descending to the humiliated condition of humanity provides a clearer proof of power than great and supernatural miracles… His descent to our lowliness is the supreme expression of His power."[18] Nestorius made the same point: "All greatness grows great by self-abasement, and not by exalting itself."[19] And the reason why God chose to save us not by force but with our voluntary consent is specifically that He loves us and therefore desires us to be free.

It is in this context of freedom and love that the meaning of time can best be appreciated. Time is part of the "distancing" or "contraction" on God's side which makes it possible for us humans freely to love. It is, as it were, the interspace which enables us to move towards God unconstrained and by our voluntary choice. "Behold I stand at the door and knock," says Christ; "if anyone hears My voice and opens the door, I will come in to him and eat with him and he with Me" (Rev 3:20). God knocks, but does not break down the door; He waits for us to open. This *waiting* on God's part is exactly the essence of time: in Staniloae's words, "For God, time means the duration of the expectant waiting between His knocking on the door and our act of opening it."[20] God issues His appeal to human freedom: "Whom shall I send, and who will go for us?" After that He awaits the voluntary response from our side: "Then I said, 'Here am I! Send me'" (Is 6:8). Time is the interval between God's appeal and our answer. We humans need this interval of time so as freely to love God

---

18   *Catechetical Oration* 24: ed. Mühlenberg, 61.4-8, 13-15.

19   *The Bazaar of Heraclides*, tr. G. R. Driver and L. Hodgson (Oxford: Clarendon Press, 1925), 69.

20   *The Experience of God*, 160.

and one another; without the interval we cannot engage in the dialogue of love. On the level of uncreated divine freedom, the mutual love of the Trinity is an expression of the *totum simul,* of eternal simultaneity, and so it is without any interval of time. But on the level of created human freedom love has to be learnt; and learning takes time, as those who teach or study in a university are only too well aware. Blake has well described our human condition in his *Songs of Innocence*:

> And we are put on earth a little space,
> That we may learn to bear the beams of love.[21]

Time is thus an all-important dimension of our created personhood, the setting that makes it possible for us to choose love. It is time that allows us to respond to God by our own free consent, that enables our love to mature, that permits us to grow in love. Space is to be understood in similar terms, as an expression of God's self-distancing so that we may be free to respond to Him in love. It affords us, says Staniloae, the possibility of "free movement...the freedom to draw near or to move away."[22] Without time and space we cannot experience the "between" that unites in love the "I" and the "Thou."

If in our daily life we commonly apprehend time very differently—not as relationship but as separation, not as freedom but as fetters upon our liberty—then that is because we are part of a fallen world in which time has become linked with mortality and death. Yet, although fallen, time is not totally so; even in our present condition we still glimpse its primal significance as a "time of gifts" and a continual miracle. And, because it is God's creation and as such is "altogether good and beautiful," time is not to be repudiated or ignored, but redeemed. Our goal is not timelessness but time transfigured. It is true that in the Apocalypse the angel proclaims, "There shall be time no longer" (Rev. 10:6)—some would render it "There shall be no more delay"—but the time that is to be abolished is the fallen time of death (cf. Rev. 21:4). For the Apocalypse also states that within the heavenly Jerusalem there will be "the tree of life with its twelve kinds of fruit, yielding its fruit *each month*" (Rev 22:2). This can only

---

21 *Poetry and Prose of William Blake*, ed. Keynes, 54.
22 *The Experience of God,* 172.

mean that, in the eternal Kingdom of the Age to come, the rhythms of cyclic time are not abolished but transformed.[23]

If the significance of time is to be found in relationship and love, it follows that true time is not simply that which is assessed mechanically by the clock or the calendar. True time is living, personal, existential, measured not by mere succession but by intention. True time is *kairos* rather than *chronos*, characterized not by the predetermined swing of the pendulum but by unpredictable yet decisive moments of opportunity, moments of disclosure filled with meaning when clock time stands still, as Joseph found in the *Protevangelion*, and when eternity breaks in. Time is not just a fixed, unvarying pattern imposed upon us from outside, but it can be recreated from within and used as an expression of our inner selves. We are in time, but time is also in us. We speak of "wasting time" and "killing time," but let us also give full value to the habitual phrases "make time," "give time" and "save time."

Without the meaning there is no time

In my reflections on time, as perhaps you will have noticed, a transition has taken place. Seeking to answer the question "What is time?" I have been led to speak not just about time itself but about personhood, freedom and love. If time is discussed in the abstract and treated as a "thing" that exists by itself, it proves ever more baffling and more elusive. St Augustine voices a difficulty familiar to us all: "What is time? If no one asks me, I know; if I try to explain to an inquirer, I do not know."[24] We can only begin to understand the nature of time when we take into account a whole series of other matters as well, such as our experiences of growth and decay, of being in relation, of learning to respond. *Without the meaning there is no time*: and there is no such thing as absolute time, for all time is related to persons and their inner experience. Time becomes intelligible only when set in the total context of life (and death)—indeed, the two terms "time" and "life" are in many respects virtually interchangeable.

It is the Incarnation, we have found, that provides us with a clue to the meaning of time. As "the moment in and out of time," to use Eliot's

23 Compare Clément, *Transfigurer le temps*, 72.
24 *Confessions* 11.14.

words,[25] it shows us the interdependence of time and eternity; only *sub specie aeternitatis* does time acquire its authentic resonance and depth. And the Incarnation, as an act of love addressed to our human freedom, also indicates how time is to be understood in terms of personal relationship, of reciprocity and dialogue. Time, whether we choose to picture it as circle, line or spiral, is not a sexton or jailer, but the safeguard of our human personhood, the protector of liberty and love.

There are two moments in the Divine Liturgy which sum up these two aspects of time. The first is when the celebrant, immediately prior to the opening blessing, uses the words of the angels at the Incarnation, "Glory be to God in the highest, and on earth peace…" (Lk 2:14); and then the deacon says to him, "It is time for the Lord to act" (Ps 118 [119]:126). It is the vocation of time to be open to eternity; time is fulfilled when God's eternity, God's action, breaks into the temporal sequence, as happened supremely at Christ's birth in Bethlehem, as happens also at every Eucharist. The second moment comes just before the Creed, when the deacon says to the people, "Let us love one another…," and the people reply affirming their faith in the Father, Son and Holy Spirit. Such exactly is the true rationale of time: mutual love after the image of the Trinity.

---

25 "The Dry Salvages," *The Complete Poems and Plays*, 190.

12

DARE WE HOPE
FOR THE SALVATION OF ALL?

*Origen, St Gregory of Nyssa and
St Isaac the Syrian*

God is not one who requites evil, but He sets aright evil.

St Isaac the Syrian

"Love could not bear that"

There are some questions which, at any rate in our present state of knowledge, we cannot answer; and yet, unanswerable though these questions may be, we cannot avoid raising them. Looking beyond the threshold of death, we ask: How can the soul exist without the body? What is the nature of our disembodied consciousness between death and the final resurrection? What is the precise relationship between our present body and the "spiritual body" (1 Cor 15:44) which the righteous will receive in the Age to come? Last, but not least, we ask: Dare we hope for the salvation of all? It is upon this final question that I wish to concentrate. Unanswerable or not, it is a question that decisively affects our entire understanding of God's relationship to the world. At the ultimate conclusion of salvation history, will there be an all-embracing reconciliation? Will every created being eventually find a place within the Trinitarian *perichoresis*, within the movement of mutual love that passes eternally among Father, Son, and Holy Spirit?

Sin is Behovely, but
All shall be well, and
All manner of thing shall be well.

Have we the right to endorse that confident affirmation of Julian of Norwich, as T. S. Eliot does in the last of his *Four Quartets*?

Let us pose the question more sharply by appealing first to the words of a twentieth-century Russian Orthodox monk and then to the opening chapter of Genesis. The dilemma that disturbs us is well summed up in a conversation recorded by Archimandrite Sophrony, the disciple of St Silouan of Mount Athos:

> It was particularly characteristic of Staretz Silouan to pray for the dead suffering in the hell of separation from God... He could not bear to think that anyone would languish in "outer darkness." I remember a conversation between him and a certain hermit, who declared with evident satisfaction, "God will punish all atheists. They will burn in everlasting fire."
>
> Obviously upset, the Staretz said, "Tell me, supposing you went to paradise, and there looked down and saw somebody burning in hell-fire—would you feel happy?"
>
> "It can't be helped. It would be their own fault," said the hermit.
>
> The Staretz answered him with a sorrowful countenance. "Love could not bear that," he said. "We must pray for all."[1]

Here exactly the basic problem is set before us. St Silouan appeals to divine compassion: "Love could not bear that." The hermit emphasizes human responsibility: "It would be their own fault." We are confronted by two principles that are apparently conflicting: first, *God is love*; second, *human beings are free*.

How are we to give proper weight to each of these principles? First, *God is love,* and this love of His is generous, inexhaustible, infinitely patient. Surely, then, He will never stop loving any of the rational creatures whom He has made; He will continue to watch over them in His tender mercy until eventually, perhaps after countless ages, all of them freely and willingly turn back to Him. But in that case what happens to our second principle, *human beings are free*? If the triumph of divine love is inevitable, what place is there for liberty of choice? How can we be genuinely free if in the last resort there is nothing for us to choose between?

Let us restate the issue in a slightly different way. On the first page of the Bible it is written, "God saw everything that He had made, and be-

---

1   Archimandrite Sophrony (Sakharov), *Saint Silouan the Athonite*, 48.

hold, it was altogether good and beautiful" (Gen 1:31, LXX). In the beginning, that is to say, there was unity; all created things participated fully in the goodness, truth and beauty of the Creator. Are we, then, to assert that at the end there will be not unity but duality? Is there to be a continuing opposition between good and evil, between heaven and hell, between joy and torment, that remains forever unresolved? If we start by affirming that God created a world which was wholly good, and if we then maintain that a significant part of His rational creation will end up in intolerable anguish, separated from Him for all eternity, surely this implies that God has failed in His creative work and has been defeated by the forces of evil. Are we to rest satisfied with such a conclusion? Or dare we look, however tentatively, beyond this duality to an ultimate restoration of unity when "all shall be well"?

Rejecting the possibility of universal salvation, C. S. Lewis has stated: "Some will not be redeemed. There is no doctrine which I would more willingly remove from Christianity than this, if it lay in my power. But it has the full support of Scripture and specially of Our Lord's own words; it has always been held by Christendom; and it has the support of reason."[2] Is Lewis right? Does universalism in fact contradict Scripture, tradition, and reason in such a stark and clear-cut way?

Two strands of Scripture

It is not difficult to find texts in the New Testament that warn us, in what seem to be unambiguous terms, of the prospect of never-ending torment in hell. Let us take but three examples, each consisting of words attributed directly to Jesus.

Mark 9:43, 47-48. "If your hand causes you to stumble, cut it off; it is better for you to enter life maimed than to have two hands and to go to hell, to the unquenchable fire... And if your eye causes you to stumble, tear it out; it is better for you to enter the Kingdom of God with one eye than to have two eyes and to be thrown into hell, where their worm does not die, and the fire is not quenched" (cf. Mt 18:8-9; Is 66:24).

---

2   *The Problem of Pain* (London: Geoffrey Bles, 1940), 106.

Matthew 25:41 (from the story of the sheep and the goats). "Then He will say to those at His left hand, 'You that are accursed, depart from Me into the eternal fire.'"

Luke 16:26 (the words of Abraham to the rich man in hell). "Between you and us a great chasm has been fixed, so that those who might want to pass from here to you cannot do so, and no one can cross from there to us."

It is difficult, if not impossible, to speak about the life after death except through the use of metaphors and symbols. Not surprisingly, then, these three passages employ a metaphorical "picture language": they speak in terms of "fire," the "worm," and a "great chasm." The metaphors doubtless are not to be taken literally, but they have implications that are hard to avoid: the fire is said to be "unquenchable" and "eternal"; the worm "does not die"; the gulf is impassable. If "eternal" (*aionios*, Mt 25:41) in fact means no more than "age-long"—lasting, that is, throughout this present aeon but not necessarily continuing into the Age to come—and if the gulf is only temporarily impassable, then why is this not made clear in the New Testament?

Yet these and other "hell-fire" texts need to be interpreted in the light of different, less frequently cited passages from the New Testament, which point rather in a "universalist" direction.

There is a series of *Pauline texts* which affirm a parallel between the universality of sin on the one hand and the universality of redemption on the other. The most obvious example is *1 Corinthians 15:22*, where Paul is working out the analogy between the first and the second Adam: "As all die in Adam, so all will be made alive in Christ." Surely the word "all" bears the same sense in both halves of this sentence. There are similar passages in Romans: "Just as one man's trespass led to condemnation for all, so one man's act of righteousness leads to justification and life for all" (5:18); "God has imprisoned all in disobedience, that He may be merciful to all" (11:32). It might be argued that in these three cases Paul's meaning is simply that Christ's death and Resurrection extend to all the *possibility* of redemption. It does not follow that all will or must be saved, for that depends upon the voluntary choice of each one. Salvation, that is to say, is offered to everyone, but not everyone will actually accept it. In fact, however, Paul suggests more than a mere possibility; he expresses a confident expectation. He does not say, "All *may* perhaps be made alive," but "All *will* be made alive." At the very least this encourages us to *hope* for the salvation of all. C. S. Lewis therefore contradicts St Paul when he asserts as an established fact, "Some will not be redeemed."

The same note of expectant confidence is also to be heard, yet more distinctly, in *1 Corinthians 15:28* (this was Origen's key text). Christ will reign, says Paul, until "God has put all things in subjection under His feet... And when all things are made subject to the Son, then the Son himself will also be made subject to the Father, who has subjected all things to Him; and thus *God will be all in all*." The phrase "all in all" (panta en pasin) definitely suggests not ultimate dualism but an ultimate reconciliation.

There is also the text from the *Pastoral Epistles* that influenced the Arminians and John Wesley: "It is the will of God our Savior... that all should be saved and come to the knowledge of the truth" (1 Tim 2:4). It can of course be pointed out that the author does not here state as a certainty that all will be saved, but merely says that this is what God wants. Are we to assert, however, that God's will is going to be eventually frustrated? As before, we are being encouraged at least to hope for universal salvation.

It is important, therefore, to allow for the complexity of the Scriptural evidence. It does not all point in the same direction, but there are two contrasting strands. Some passages present us with a *challenge*. God invites but does not compel. I possess freedom of choice: am I going to say "yes" or "no" to the divine invitation? The future is uncertain. To which destination am I personally bound? Might I perhaps be shut out from the wedding feast? But there are other passages which insist with equal emphasis upon *divine sovereignty*. God cannot be ultimately defeated. "All shall be well," and in the end God will indeed be "all in all." Challenge and sovereignty: such are the two strands in the New Testament, and neither strand should be disregarded.

God the cosmic physician

Turning now from Scripture to tradition, let us look first at the author who, more than anyone else in Christian history, has been associated with the universalist standpoint, Origen of Alexandria. He is someone who, over the centuries, has been greatly commended and greatly reviled, in almost equal measure. He is praised, for instance, by his fellow Alexandrian Didymus the Blind, who calls him "the chief teacher of the Church after the Apostles."[3] "Who would not rather be wrong with Origen than right with anyone else?" exclaims St Vincent of Lérins.[4] A striking but typical expression of the opposite point of view is to be found in a story told of St Pachomius, the founder of cenobitic monasticism in Egypt. While conversing one day with some visiting monks, Pachomius was puzzled because he noticed an "exceedingly nasty smell," for which he could find no explanation. Suddenly he discovered the reason for the odor: the visitors were Origenists. "Behold, I testify to you before God," he admonished them, "that everyone who reads Origen and accepts his writings will go down to the depth of hell. The inheritance of all such persons is the outer darkness, where there is weeping and gnashing of teeth… Take all the works of Origen that are in your possession, and throw them into the river."[5] Alas! All too many have heeded Pachomius' advice, burning and destroying what Origen wrote, with the result that several of his chief works survive only in translation, not in the original Greek. This is true in particular of the treatise *On First Principles*, where Origen expounds most fully his teaching about the end of the world. Here we have to rely largely on the Latin version (not always accurate) made by Rufinus.[6]

Origen, to his credit, displays a humility not always apparent in his leading critics, Jerome and Justinian. Again and again in his treatment of the deeper issues of theology, Origen bows his head in reverent wonder before the divine mystery. Not for one moment does he imagine that he has all the answers. This humility is evident in particular when he speaks about the Last Things and the future hope. "These are matters hard and difficult to understand," he writes. "…We need to speak about them with

---

3   See Jerome's preface to Origen, *Homilies on Ezekiel*: ed. Baehrens, 318.

4   *Commonitorium* 17 (23): tr. C. A. Huertley, Nicene and Post-Nicene Fathers, second series, 11 (Oxford: James Parker, 1894), 144.

5   *Paralipomena* 7: ed. Halkin, 130-32; tr. Armand Veilleux, *Pachomian Koinonia*, Cistercian Studies Series 45-47, 3 vols. (Kalamazoo, MI: Cistercian Publications, 1980-82), 2:28-29.

6   By the same token, how far can we depend upon the total accuracy of the Greek quotations found in Justinian's *Letter to Menas* and used by Koetschau in his edition of Origen's *On First Principles*?

great fear and caution, discussing and investigating rather than laying down fixed and certain conclusions."[7]

Yet, humble or not, Origen was condemned as a heretic and anathematized at the time of the Fifth Ecumenical Council, held at Constantinople under the Emperor Justinian in 553. The first of the fifteen anathemas directed against him states: "If anyone maintains the mythical preexistence of souls, and the monstrous *apocatastasis* that follows from this, let him be anathema."[8] This seems entirely explicit and definite: belief in a final "restoration" (*apocatastasis*) of all things and all persons— belief in universal salvation, not excluding that of the devil—has apparently been ruled out as heretical in a formal decision by what is for the Orthodox Church the highest visible authority in matters of doctrine, an Ecumenical Council.

There is, however, considerable doubt whether these fifteen anathemas were in fact formally approved by the Fifth Ecumenical Council. They may have been endorsed by a lesser council, meeting in the early months of 553 shortly before the main council was convened, in which case they lack full ecumenical authority; yet, even so, the Fathers of the Fifth Council were well aware of these fifteen anathemas and had no intention of revoking or modifying them.[9] Apart from that, however, the precise wording of the first anathema deserves to be carefully noted. It does not speak only about *apocatastasis* but links together two aspects of Origen's theology: first, his speculations about the beginning, that is to say, about

---

7   *On First Principles* 1.6.1; tr. Butterworth, 52.

8   For Greek text, see Franz Diekamp, *Die origenistischen Streitigkeiten im sechsten Jahrhundert und das fünfte allgemeine Concil* (Münster: Verlag Aschendorff, 1899), 90; French translation in Antoine Guillaumont, *Les "Képhalaia Gnostica" d'Évagre le Pontique et l'histoire de l'Origénisme chez les Grecs et chez les Syriens,* Patristica Sorbonensia 5 (Paris: Editions du Seuil, 1962), 144; English translation in Aloys Grillmeier and Theresia Hainthaler, *Christ in Christian Tradition* 2:2 (London: Mowbray, 1995), 404-5. Origen took the term *apocatastasis* from Acts 3:21.

9   See Grillmeier and Hainthaler, *op. cit.,* 403-4. It should be noted that there are two sets of anathemas against Origen: the ten anathemas attached to the letter of Justinian to Patriarch Menas of Constantinople in 543, and the fifteen anathemas attached to Justinian's letter of 553, addressed to the bishops gathered in Constantinople before the opening of the Fifth Ecumenical Council. Distinct from these fifteen anathemas against Origen, there are also fourteen other anathemas dealing with the question of the "Three Chapters," which were formally endorsed by the Fifth Ecumenical Council; and in the eleventh of these there is a general condemnation of Origen, although without any specific reference to *apocatastasis*.

the preexistence of souls and the precosmic fall; second, his teaching about the end, about universal salvation and the ultimate reconciliation of all things. Origen's eschatology is seen as following directly from his protology, and both are rejected together.

That the first of the fifteen anathemas should condemn protology and eschatology in the same sentence is entirely understandable, for in Origen's thinking the two form an integral unity. At the beginning, so he believed, there was a realm of *logikoi* or rational intellects (*noes*) existing prior to the creation of the material world as minds without a body. Originally all these *logikoi* were joined in perfect union with the Creator Logos. Then followed the precosmic fall. With the exception of one *logikos* (which became the human soul of Christ), all the other *logikoi* turned away from the Logos and became, depending on the gravity of their deviation, either angels or human beings or demons. In each case they were given bodies appropriate to the seriousness of their fall: lightweight and ethereal in the case of angels; dark and hideous in the case of demons; intermediate in the case of human beings. At the end, so Origen maintained, this process of fragmentation will be reversed. All alike, whether angels, human beings, or demons, will be restored to unity with the Logos; the primal harmony of the total creation will be reinstated, and once more "God will be all in all" (1 Cor 15:28). Origen's view is in this way circular in character: the end will be as the beginning.

Now, as we have noted, the first of the fifteen anti-Origenist anathemas is directed not simply against Origen's teaching concerning universal reconciliation, but against his total understanding of salvation history—against his theory of preexistent souls, of a precosmic fall and a final *apocatastasis*—seen as a single and undivided whole. Suppose, however, that we separate his eschatology from his protology; suppose that we abandon all speculations about the realm of eternal *logikoi*; suppose that we simply adhere to the standard Christian view whereby there is no preexistence of the soul, but each new person comes into being as an integral unity of soul and body, at or shortly after the moment of the conception of the embryo within the mother's womb. In this way we could advance a doctrine of universal salvation—affirming this, not as a logical certainty (indeed, Origen never did that), but as a heartfelt aspiration, a visionary hope—which would avoid the circularity of Origen's view and so would escape the condemnation of the anti-Origenist anathemas. We shall return to this possibility in a moment when considering St Gregory of Nyssa, but let us first explore further Origen's reasons for affirming a final *apocatastasis*.

It is often claimed that belief in universal salvation, because it considers the eventual triumph of divine love to be inevitable, fails to properly allow for our liberty of choice. This is an objection to which Origen is consistently sensitive. However confident his hope that God's love will in the end prevail, he is careful never to undermine the vital significance of human free will. While affirming that "God is love," he does not lose sight of the correlative principle, "Human beings are free." Thus, when speaking of the subjection of all things to Christ, and of Christ to the Father (1 Cor 15:28), he observes: "This subjection will be accomplished in accordance with various assured methods and disciplines and times; yet it should not be thought that there is some necessity which compels all things into subjection, or that the whole world will be subdued by force to God."[10] Origen is altogether definite here: there is no compulsion, no force. If God's love is finally victorious, this will be because it is freely and willingly accepted by the whole of rational creation. Origen's *apocatastasis* is not simply a deduction from some abstract system; it is a *hope*.

Here we touch upon a difficulty that is frequently felt not only in connection with the final reconciliation at the end of the world but also throughout our Christian experience in this present life. It is tempting to regard divine grace and human freedom as two contrasting principles, the one excluding the other; and as a result we often assume that the stronger the action of grace, the more restricted is the exercise of our human freedom. But is this not a false dilemma? In the words of John A. T. Robinson:

> Everyone may point to instances in which he has been constrained to thankful response by the overmastering power of love. And yet, under this strange compulsion, has anyone ever felt his freedom infringed or his personality violated? Is it not precisely at these moments that he becomes conscious, perhaps only for a fleeting space, of being himself in a way he never knew before, of attaining a fullness and integration of life which is inextricably bound up with the decision drawn from him by another's love? Moreover, this is true however

10   *On First Principles* 3.5.8; tr. Butterworth, 243.

strong be the constraint laid upon him: or, rather, it is truer the stronger it is. Under the constraint of the love of God in Christ this sense of self-fulfillment is at its maximum. The testimony of generations is that here, as nowhere else, service is perfect freedom.[11]

Surely this is true *par excellence* of the victory of God's love in the age to come. The power that is victorious is the power of loving compassion, and so it is a victory that does not overrule but enhances our human freedom.

Origen's caution is evident in particular when he refers to the salvation of the devil and his angels. He makes it abundantly clear that he regards this not as a certainty but as a possibility. In his *Commentary on John* he does no more than pose a question: "Since human beings can display repentance and turn from unbelief to faith, shall we shrink back from asserting something similar about the angelic powers?"[12] In his treatise *On Prayer*, Origen limits himself to saying that God has a plan for the devil in the age to come, but we have at present no idea what this plan may be: "God will make arrangements for him, I know not how."[13] In the work *On First Principles*, the matter is left to the judgment of the reader:

> Whether certain of those orders, which are under the leadership of the devil and are obedient to his wickedness, can at some point in future ages be converted to goodness, inasmuch as there still exists in them the power of free will; or whether the evil has become so permanent and deep-rooted that it has become through habit part of their nature: let my reader decide this for himself.[14]

Here Origen suggests two possibilities: either the demons still possess the power of free will, or else they have reached the point of no return, after which repentance is impossible. But he expresses no judgment; both possibilities are left open.

This raises an interesting question, which I once put to a Greek archbishop at the beginning of a four-hour car journey, in the hope that it would help us while away the time. If it is possible that the devil, who must surely be a very lonely and unhappy person, may eventually repent

---

11   *In the End God* (London: Fontana Books, Collins, 1968), 122.

12   *Commentary on John* 13.59: ed. Preuschen, 291.1-3.

13   *On Prayer* 27.15; tr. Greer, 146.

14   *On First Principles* 1.6.3; tr. Butterworth, 56-57. I have followed Rufinus here; the Greek (from Justinian) is less clear, but the sense is basically the same.

and be saved, why do we never pray for him? To my disappointment (for I could not at the moment think of other topics of conversation), the archbishop settled the matter with a sharp and brief rejoinder: "Mind your own business." He was right. So far as we humans are concerned, the devil is always our adversary; we should not enter into any kind of negotiations with him, whether by praying for him or in other ways. His salvation is quite simply none of our business. But the devil has also his own relationship with God, as we learn from the prologue of the book of Job, when Satan makes his appearance in the heavenly court among the other "sons of God" (Job 1:6-2:7). We are, however, altogether ignorant of the precise nature of this relationship, and it is futile to pry into it. Yet, even though it is not for us to pray for the devil, we have no right to assume that he is totally and irrevocably excluded from the scope of God's mercy. We do not know. In Wittgenstein's words, *Wovon man nicht reden kann, darüber muß man schweigen.*[15]

The strongest point in Origen's case for universalism is his analysis of punishment. We may summarize his view by distinguishing three primary reasons that have been advanced to justify the infliction of punishment.

First, there is the *retributive* argument. Those who have done evil, it is claimed, themselves deserve to suffer in proportion to the evil that they have done. Only so will the demands of justice be fulfilled: "an eye for an eye and a tooth for a tooth" (Ex 21:24). But in the Sermon on the Mount Christ explicitly rejects this principle (Mt 5:38). If we humans are forbidden by Christ to exact retribution in this way from our fellow humans, how much more should we refrain from attributing vindictive and retributive behavior to God. It is blasphemous to assert that the Holy Trinity is vengeful. In any case, it seems contrary to justice that God should inflict an infinite punishment in requital for what is only a finite amount of wrongdoing.

The second line of argument insists upon the need for a *deterrent*. It is only the prospect of hell-fire, it is said, that holds us back from evil-doing. But why then, it may be asked, do we need an unending, everlasting punishment to act as an effective deterrent? Would it not be sufficient to

---

15 "Whereof one cannot speak, thereof one must be silent" (from the preface of the *Tractatus Logico-Philosophicus*).

threaten prospective malefactors with a period of painful separation from
God that is exceedingly prolonged, yet not infinite? In any case, it is only
too obvious, especially in our own day, that the threat of hell-fire is almost
totally ineffective as a deterrent. If in our preaching of the Christian faith
we hope to have any significant influence on others, then what we need is
not a negative but a positive strategy: let us abandon ugly threats, and attempt rather to evoke people's sense of wonder and their capacity for love.

There remains the *reformative* understanding of punishment, which
Origen considered to be the only view that is morally acceptable. Punishment, if it is to possess moral value, has to be not merely retaliatory or dissuasive but remedial. When parents inflict punishment on their children,
or the state on criminals, their aim should always be to heal those whom
they punish and to change them for the better. And such, according to
Origen, is precisely the purpose of the punishments inflicted upon us by
God; He acts always as "our physician."[16] A doctor may sometimes be
obliged to employ extreme measures which cause agony to his patients.
(This was particularly so before the use of anesthetics.) He may cauterize a
wound or amputate a limb. But this is always done with a positive end in
view, so as to bring about the patient's eventual recovery and restoration
to health. So it is with God, the physician of our souls. He may inflict
suffering upon us, both in this life and after our death; but always He does
this out of tender love and with a positive purpose, so as to cleanse us
from our sins, to purge and heal us. In Origen's words, "The fury of God's
vengeance avails to the purging of our souls."[17]

Now, if we adopt this reformative and therapeutic view of punishment—and this is the only reason for inflicting punishment that can wor-
thily be attributed to God—then surely such punishment should not be
unending. If the aim of punishment is to heal, then once the healing has
been accomplished there is no need for the punishment to continue. If,
however, the punishment is supposed to be everlasting, it is difficult to see
how it can have any remedial or educative purpose. In a never-ending hell
there is no escape and therefore no healing, and so the infliction of punishment in such a hell is pointless and immoral. This third understanding
of punishment, therefore, is incompatible with the notion of perpetual

16   *On First Principles* 2.10.6; tr. Butterworth, 143.
17   *On First Principles* 2.10.6; tr. Butterworth, 144.

torment in hell; it requires us, rather, to think in terms of some kind of purgatory after death. But in that case this purgatory should be envisaged as a house of healing, not a torture chamber; as a hospital, not a prison.[18] Here, in his grand vision of God as the cosmic physician, Origen is at his most convincing.

An uncondemned universalist

Origen's longing for the salvation of all had already brought him under suspicion in his own lifetime.[19] Yet there were some among his spiritual descendants who kept alive this universal hope. The two most notable examples are to be found at the end of the fourth century: Evagrius of Pontus, monk in the Egyptian desert, and St Gregory of Nyssa, the younger brother of St Basil the Great. Evagrius upheld and perhaps hardened the full Origenist teaching concerning the preexistence of souls, the precosmic fall, and the final *apocatastasis*; and for this he was condemned along with Origen in 553. Gregory of Nyssa, on the other hand, abandoned Origen's speculations concerning preexistence and the precosmic fall,[20] while holding fast to his belief in an ultimate restoration; and, significantly, he has never been anathematized for this, either in 553 or in more recent times. In expressing his hope that all will be saved, Gregory of Nyssa is fully as confident as Origen. His words recall the great

18 It is true that Orthodox theologians usually express reservations about the doctrine of purgatory as developed in medieval and post-medieval Roman Catholic teaching; but at the same time most of them allow for some sort of purging or purification after death. See my book (published under the name Timothy Ware), *Eustratios Argenti: A Study of the Greek Church Under Turkish Rule* (Oxford: Clarendon Press, 1964), 139-60. Elsewhere I have suggested that Catholic and Orthodox views on the "middle state" after death are less sharply opposed than appears at first. See my article "'One Body in Christ': Death and the Communion of Saints," *Sobornost* 3:2 (1981), 179-91.

19 For attacks on Origen in his lifetime, see Joseph Wilson Trigg, *Origen: The Bible and Philosophy in the Third-Century Church* (London: SCM Press, 1983), 206-208; for fourth-century disputes, see Elizabeth A. Clark, *The Origenist Controversy: The Cultural Construction of an Early Christian Debate* (Princeton: Princeton Univ. Press, 1992); also Guillaumont, *Les "Képhalaia Gnostica."*

20 In *On the Making of humanity*, written ca. 380, Gregory of Nyssa advances a complex theory concerning what is sometimes called "double creation" of the human race (see especially §§16-17), but this is not at all the same as Origen's doctrine of the preexistence of souls, which elsewhere Gregory specifically repudiates (*On the Soul and the Resurrection*, PG 46:109B-113B; tr. Roth, 90-92).

affirmation of Paul, "and thus God will be all in all" (1 Cor 15:28). "When, through these long and circuitous methods," writes Gregory, "the wickedness which is now mingled and consolidated with our nature has been finally expelled from it, and when all those things that are now sunk down in evil are restored to their original state, there will ascend from the entire creation a united hymn of thanksgiving... All this is contained in the great mystery of the Divine Incarnation."[21] This final restoration, Gregory clearly states, will embrace even the devil.

Despite this bold claim, Gregory of Nyssa has never been condemned as a heretic, but on the contrary he is honored as a saint. Why should this be so? Perhaps he escaped reprobation because he was Basil's brother. Yet if he was treated differently from his master Origen, perhaps it was because, while retaining Origen's hope in the eventual triumph of good over evil, he abandoned the notion of preexistence and so avoided the circularity of the Origenist scheme. Whatever the explanation, the fact that Gregory has not been anathematized is certainly significant. It suggests that, if dissociated from speculations about a precosmic fall, a carefully qualified expression of universal hope is acceptable, even within the bounds of strict orthodoxy.

St Gregory of Nyssa is one of the patrons of the house of ecumenical studies to which I am attached in Oxford; and personally I am delighted that this should be so.

The scourgings of love

A third patristic author who dared to hope for the salvation of all was St Isaac of Nineveh, honored and loved throughout the Christian East as "Isaac the Syrian." Although he lived some three generations after the Fifth Ecumenical Council, he was unaffected by the anti-Origenist anathemas associated with it; for, as a member of the Church of the East,[22] dwelling in Mesopotamia far outside the bounds of the Byzantine Empire, he owed no allegiance to the Emperor at Constantinople and did not recognize the Council held in 553 as ecumenical. Possibly he was altogether unaware of its decrees.

---

21 *Catechetical Oration* 26: ed. Mühlenberg, 67.7-11, 13-15.
22 Often styled "the Nestorian Church," but this is an inaccurate and misleading designation.

Particularly striking is Isaac's understanding of hell. He insists that the texts in the New Testament about fire, the worm, outer darkness, and the gnashing of teeth are not to be understood literally and in a physical sense. He speaks of hell or Gehenna as "noetic" or "intelligible."[23] Hell is an "effect," not a "substance,"[24] while the "outer darkness" is not a place but "the state without any delight in true knowledge and communion with God."[25] "There will be psychic weeping and grinding of teeth," says Isaac, "which is a grief more hard to endure than fire."[26] The teeth-gnashing in the Age to come, then, so far from being physical and material, signifies an inner and spiritual anguish. I am reminded of the story of the preacher who, in his sermons on hell, dwelt with particular relish upon the gnashing of teeth. Eventually an elderly member of the congregation could bear it no more. "But I have no teeth," she exclaimed—to which the preacher replied severely, "Teeth will be provided."

Isaac had a better answer. In his view, the real torment in hell consists, not in burning by material fire, nor in any physical pain, but in the pangs of conscience that a person suffers on realizing that he or she has rejected the love of God:

> Also I say that even those who are scourged in hell are tormented with the scourgings of love.

> The scourges that result from love—that is, the scourges of those who have become aware that they have sinned against love—are harder and more bitter than the torments which result from fear.

> The pain which gnaws the heart as the result of sinning against love is sharper than all other torments that there are.

> It is wrong to imagine that the sinners in hell are deprived of the love of God... [But] the power of love works in two ways: it torments those who have sinned, just as happens among friends here on earth; but to those who have observed its duties, love gives delight.

> So it is in hell: the contrition that comes from love is the harsh torment.[27]

23 *Homilies* 65(64) and 76 (alias Appendix A, §5): tr. Wensinck, 306, 350; tr. Miller, 313, 395.
24 *Homily* 26(27): tr. Miller, 133; Wensinck, 128, renders less clearly, "...facts, not persons."
25 *Homily* 76 (alias Appendix A, §5): tr. Wensinck, 350-51; tr. Miller, 396.
26 *Homily* 6: tr. Wensinck, 60. In Miller (tr.), 57, the word "psychic" does not occur.
27 *Homily* 27(28): tr. Wensinck, 136; tr. Miller, 141. For the most part I follow here the translation of Sebastian Brock in A. M. Allchin (ed.), *The Heart of Compassion: Daily Readings with St*

When I first came across this passage as a student more than forty years ago, I said to myself: That is the only view of hell that makes any sense to me. God is love, St Isaac tells us, and this divine love is unchanging and inexhaustible. God's love is everywhere and embraces everything: "If I go down to hell, Thou art there also" (Ps 138 [139]:8). Thus even those in hell are not cut off from the love of God. Love acts, however, in a twofold way: it is joy to those who accept it but torture to those who shut it out. In the words of George MacDonald, "The terror of God is but the other side of His love; it is love outside, that would be inside."[28]

Thus those in hell feel as agonizing pain that which the saints feel as unending delight. God does not inflict torment upon those in hell, but it is they who torment themselves through their willful refusal to respond to His love. As Georges Bernanos observes, "Hell is not to love any more."[29] "The love of God," writes Vladimir Lossky, "will be an intolerable torment to those who have not acquired it within themselves."[30] From this it follows that those in hell are self-enslaved, self-imprisoned. Ultimately, states C. S. Lewis,

> there are only two kinds of people…those who say to God, "Thy will be done," and those to whom God says, in the end, "*Thy* will be done." All that are in Hell, choose it. Without that self-choice there could be no Hell… The doors of hell are locked on the *inside*.[31]

Now if all this is true—if, as Isaac says, those in hell are not cut off from the love of God, and if, as Lewis asserts, they are self-imprisoned—then may it not be that they still have some hope of redemption? (Indeed, the Orthodox Church says a special prayer for them at Vespers on the Sunday of Pentecost.)[32] If divine love is constantly knocking on the door of their heart, and if that door is locked on the inside, may not the time come when at long last they respond to love's invitation and open the door? If the reason for their suffering is that they recognize how grievously they

Isaac of Syria, "Enfolded in Love" Series (London: Darton, Longman & Todd, 1989), 53. For a similar view of hell, see Origen, *On First Principles* 2.10.4-5; tr. Butterworth, 141-43.

28 Cited in C. S. Lewis, *George MacDonald: An Anthology* (London: Geoffrey Bles, 1946), 49 (§84).

29 *Journal d'un curé de campagne* (Paris: Plon, Le Livre de Poche, 1961), 142.

30 *The Mystical Theology of the Eastern Church*, 234.

31 *The Great Divorce: A Dream* (London: Geoffrey Bles, 1945), 66-67; *The Problem of Pain*, 115.

32 See above, 35.

have sinned against love, does this not imply that there is still within them some spark of goodness, some possibility of repentance and restoration?

Isaac, for his part, definitely believed that this was so. In the second part of his *Homilies* (previously thought to have been lost, but rediscovered in 1983 by Dr. Sebastian Brock) Isaac speaks of a "wonderful outcome" that God will bring to pass at the end of history:

> I am of the opinion that He is going to manifest some wonderful outcome, a matter of immense and ineffable compassion on the part of the glorious Creator, with respect to the ordering of this difficult matter of [Gehenna's] torment: out of it the wealth of His love and power and wisdom will become known all the more—and so will the insistent might of the waves of His goodness.
>
> It is not [the way of] the compassionate Maker to create rational beings in order to deliver them over mercilessly to unending affliction.[33]

Isaac has two main reasons for affirming with such confidence his expectation of a "wonderful outcome." First, even more passionately than Origen, he rejects any suggestion that God is vengeful and vindictive. This he sees as blasphemy: "Far be it, that vengeance could ever be found in that Fountain of love and Ocean brimming with goodness!" When God punishes us, or appears to do so, the purpose of this punishment is never retributive and retaliatory, but exclusively reformative and therapeutic:

> God chastises with love, not for the sake of revenge—far be it!—but seeking to make whole His image… Love's chastisement is for correction, but it does not aim at retribution.[34]

As Isaac insists in the second part, "God is not one who requites evil, but He sets aright evil… The Kingdom and Gehenna are matters belonging to mercy."[35] Gehenna is nothing else than a place of purging and purification which helps to bring about God's master plan "that all should be saved and come to the knowledge of the truth" (1 Tim 2:4).

Second, and more fundamentally, Isaac is convinced that "many waters cannot quench love" (Song 8:7). "Not even the immense wickedness of the demons can overcome the measure of God's goodness," he writes,

33 *Homily* 39.6: tr. Brock, 165.
34 *Homily* 45(48): tr. Wensinck, 216; tr. Miller, 230.
35 *Homily* 39.15, 22; tr. Brock, 170, 172.

quoting Diodore of Tarsus.[36] Unquenchable and limitless as it is, God's love will eventually triumph over evil: "There exists with Him a single love and compassion which is spread out over all creation, [a love] which is without alteration, timeless and everlasting... No part belonging to any single one of [all] rational beings will be lost."[37] Here, then, in distant Mesopotamia is one who is not afraid to affirm with Julian of Norwich and T. S. Eliot, "All shall be well, and all manner of thing shall be well."

Love and freedom

Within the tradition of the Christian East, then, we have identified three powerful witnesses who dare to hope for the salvation of all. Other witnesses could certainly be cited from the West, particularly among the Anabaptists, Moravians, and Christadelphians. Yet it has to be admitted that in East and West alike—but more particularly in the West because of the influence of St Augustine of Hippo—the voices raised in favor of universal salvation remain a small minority. Most Christians, at any rate until the twentieth century, have assumed that the main part of the human race will end up in an everlasting hell: "For many are called, but few are chosen" (Mt 22:14). How far is such an assumption justified? Having looked at Scripture and tradition, let us now invoke reason. Drawing together all that has been said so far, let us marshal three arguments in favor of universalism and four against.

In favor of universal hope

The power of divine love. As a God of infinite compassion, it is argued, the Creator is not grudging in His mercy and forgiveness but immeasurably patient. He compels no one, but He will in fact wait until each and every one of His rational creatures voluntarily responds to His love. Divine love is stronger than all the forces of darkness and evil within the universe, and in the end it will prevail. "Love never fails" (1 Cor 13:8); it is never exhausted, never comes to an end. This appeal to the invincibility of divine love is the strongest argument in favor of universal hope.

---

36 *Homily* 39.13: tr. Brock, 169. Isaac also appeals to Theodore of Mopsuestia (39.8: tr. Brock, 166-67).
37 *Homily* 40.1, 7: tr. Brock, 174, 176.

The essence of hell. This is basically a restatement of the first argument. As we noted when citing St Isaac the Syrian, hell is not God's rejection of humankind but humankind's refusal of God. It is not a punishment which God inflicts upon us, but a state of mind in which we punish ourselves. God does not shut the door against those in hell; He does not withdraw His love from them, but it is they who deliberately harden their hearts against that love. Since, then, those in hell are still enfolded in divine love, it remains possible that they may some day open their hearts to this omnipresent compassion; and, when they do, they will find that God has not stopped loving them. "If we are faithless, He remains faithful; for He cannot deny himself" (2 Tim 2:13). His nature is love, and He cannot cease to be that which He is.

The non-reality of evil. This is an argument that we have not so far had occasion to discuss. "I am He who is," says God to Moses at the burning bush in the Septuagint version of Ex 3:14; "I am the Existing One" (*ego eimi ho on*). God is Being and Reality, and He is the sole source of all existence. Evil, on the other hand, is in the strict sense non-being and unreality. Evil and sin have no substantive existence, for they are not a "thing" that God has made; they are a distortion of the good, a parasite—not a noun but an adjective. This was clearly shown to Julian of Norwich, who states in her *Thirteenth Revelation*: "I did not see sin, for I believe that it has no kind of substance, no share in being, nor can it be recognized except by the pains which it causes."[38]

Existence, then, is good, for it is a gift from God; and everything that exists, by the very fact of existing, retains some link with God, who is the only source of existence. From this it follows that nothing that exists can be entirely and utterly evil. To posit something totally evil would be a non-sense, a contradiction in terms; for such a thing would be altogether unreal and could not actually exist. Even the devil, because he exists, still has a continuing relationship with God. Thus where there is existence, there is hope—even for the devil.

A possible conclusion from this third line of argument is not universal salvation but conditional immortality. At the end God will indeed be "all in all," not because all rational creatures have been saved but because at a

---

38 *Showings*, ed. Edmund Colledge and James Walsh, The Classics of Western Spirituality (New York/Ramsey/Toronto: Paulist Press, 1978), 148.

certain point the radically wicked have simply ceased to be. Cut off from God, the unique source of existence, they have lapsed into non-being. At the end-time, that is to say, there will be a resurrection to eternal life, but no resurrection to eternal death; or, rather, there will be resurrection to a death that is final but not continuing, for it will entail annihilation.

This notion of conditional immortality has much to be said in its favor. It is an attractive way of avoiding the need to choose between universal salvation and an unending hell. But, although it was held by the fourth-century African author Arnobius of Sicca, it has otherwise little support in earlier tradition. The objection commonly advanced against the "conditionalist" standpoint is that God's gift of existence is stable and changeless. It is something that He will never withdraw: "For the *charismata* and the calling of God are irrevocable" (Rom 11:29). Within each rational being endowed with free will, there is something unique and unrepeatable; God never does the same thing twice. Shall this uniqueness disappear forever from the universe?

Against universal hope

The argument from free will. Because humans are free, it is argued, they are at liberty to reject God. His gifts are irrevocable; He will never take away from us our power of voluntary choice, and so we are free to go on saying "No" to Him through all eternity. Such unending rejection of God is precisely the essence of hell. Because free will exists, there must exist also the possibility of hell as a place of everlasting suffering. Take away hell, and you deny freedom. None can be forced to enter heaven against their will. As the Russian theologian Paul Evdokimov observes, God can do anything except compel us to love him; for love is free, and thus where there is no liberty of choice there is no love.[39] Whereas the appeal to the power of divine love constitutes the strongest argument in favor of universal salvation, this appeal to free will is certainly the strongest argument on the other side. Significantly, both parties in the debate, although in different ways, seek their main support from the fact that God is love.

The point of no return. But, it may be rejoined, does not this argument from free will prove too much? If God never takes away from us our lib-

---

39 *L'Orthodoxie* (Neuchâtel/Paris: Delachaux et Niestlé, 1959), 60.

erty of choice, and if those in hell therefore retain free will, then is not the possibility of repentance a continuing option for them? To this the anti-universalists commonly reply that there is a point of no return, after which repentance becomes impossible. God does not deprive the damned of their freedom, but the misuse of their freedom becomes eventually so deeply rooted in them that they cannot thereafter change, and thus they remain fixed forever in their attitude of rejection. God has not ceased to love them, but they have rendered themselves incapable of ever again responding to that love.

A parallel can thus be drawn between the saints in heaven and the damned in hell. The saints in heaven have not lost their freedom, but it is no longer possible for them ever again to turn away from God and to lapse into sin. They still have liberty of choice, but all their choices are good. In a similar way the damned in hell still retain a residual freedom of choice, for they have not ceased to be persons. But all their choices are bad, and it is no longer possible for them to ascend to the divine realm. The devil possesses freedom—but not the freedom to repent. In this way, after the Last Judgment there will be a "great divorce," and the chasm between heaven and hell will remain forever impassable.

The argument from justice. It is contrary to divine justice, so it is often alleged, that the wicked should enjoy the same reward as the righteous; the moral harmony of the universe will be impaired if evildoers do not receive their just recompense. I find this argument far less strong than the two previous arguments. As St Isaac the Syrian rightly insists, our human notions of retributive justice are altogether inapplicable to God.[40] He is a God not of vengeance but of forgiving love; His justice is nothing other than His love. When He punishes, His purpose is not to requite but to heal.

The moral and pastoral argument. Finally, on the anti-universalist side it is often said that universalism deprives the Christian message of its sense of urgency and underestimates the note of insistent warning present throughout the New Testament. Christ begins His public preaching with the word "Today" (Lk 4:21). "See, now is the acceptable time," states Paul; "see, now is the day of salvation" (2 Cor 6:2). *Today, now*: it is this present

40 Compare also the parable of the laborers in the vineyard (Mt 20:1-16). By conventional human criteria God is certainly *un*just!

life that is our moment of opportunity and decision, our time of crisis, the *kairos* when we make the choices that determine our eternal future. If, on the other hand, we are allowed an unlimited series of further chances after our death, and if in any case we shall all end up in the same place whatever we do in this present life, then where is the challenge in the preaching of the Christian message, and where is the need for conversion and repentance here and now? If the triumph of God's love is inevitable and there is ultimately nothing for us to choose between, does this not make our present acts of moral decision trivial and meaningless?

Origen is aware of this difficulty. The doctrine of *apocatastasis*, he advises, ought to be kept secret; for, if preached openly to the immature, it will lead them to become careless and indifferent.[41] No doubt it is for this reason that the nineteenth-century Pietist theologian Christian Gottlieb Barth remarks, "Anyone who does not believe in the universal restoration is an ox, but anyone who teaches it is an ass."[42] St Isaac the Syrian deals with the problem in a different way. It makes an immeasurable difference to us, he points out, whether we respond to divine love here and now or only after countless aeons. Even though the torment of hell is not everlasting, it remains truly appalling: "Nevertheless [Gehenna] is grievous, even if it is thus limited in its extent: who can [possibly] bear it?"[43]

If the strongest argument in favor of universal salvation is the appeal to divine love, and if the strongest argument on the opposite side is the appeal to human freedom, then we are brought back to the dilemma with which we started: how are we to bring into concord the two principles *God is love* and *Human beings are free*? For the time being we cannot do more than hold fast with equal firmness to both principles at once, while admitting that the manner of their ultimate harmonization remains a mystery beyond our present comprehension. What St Paul said about the reconciliation of Christianity and Judaism is applicable also to the final

---

41 *Against Celsus* 6.26; tr. Chadwick, 341. Thus for Origen the notion of an eternal hell has a certain usefulness as a deterrent, though only in the case of persons at a low spiritual level.

42 Quoted in Jaroslav Pelikan, *The Melody of Theology: A Philosophical Dictionary* (Cambridge, MA: Harvard University Press, 1988), 5. I am grateful to Professor Donald Paul Burgo of Fontbonne College, St Louis, for drawing my attention to this passage. He rightly adds that the ox and the ass were already at the stable in Bethlehem before the wise men had found their way to it.

43 *Homily* 40.7: tr. Brock, 176.

reconciliation of the total creation: "O the depth of the riches and wisdom and knowledge of God! How unsearchable are His judgments and how inscrutable His ways!" (Rom 11:33).

When I am waiting at Oxford Station for the train to London, sometimes I walk up to the northernmost stretch of the long platform until I reach a notice: "Passengers must not proceed beyond this point. Penalty: £50." In discussion of the future hope, we need a similar notice: "Theologians must not proceed beyond this point"—Let my readers devise a suitable penalty. Doubtless, Origen's mistake was that he tried to say too much. It is a fault that I admire rather than execrate, but it was a mistake nonetheless.

Our belief in human freedom means that we have no right to categorically affirm, "All *must* be saved." But our faith in God's love makes us dare to *hope* that all will be saved.

> Is there anybody there? said the traveler,
> Knocking on the moonlit door.

Hell exists as a possibility because free will exists. Yet, trusting in the inexhaustible attractiveness of God's love, we venture to express the hope—it is no more than a hope—that in the end, like Walter de la Mare's Traveller, we shall find that there is nobody there. Let us leave the last word, then, with St Silouan of Mount Athos: "Love could not bear that... We must pray for all."

BIBLIOGRAPHICAL NOTE

The texts included in the present volume originally appeared in the following publications:

"Strange Yet Familiar: My Journey to the Orthodox Church," in Thomas Doulis (ed.), *Toward the Authentic Church: Orthodox Christians Discuss Their Conversion* (Minneapolis: Light & Life, 1996), 145-68.

"'Go Joyfully': The Mystery of Death and Resurrection," in Dan Cohn-Sherbock and Christopher Lewis (eds.), *Beyond Death: Theological and Philosophical Reflections on Life After Death* (Basingstoke/London: Macmillan, 1995), 27-41.

"The Orthodox Experience of Repentance," in *Sobornost* 2:1 (1980), 18-28.

"The Theology of Worship," in *Sobornost* 5:10 (1970), 729-37.

"A Sense of Wonder," in Dan Cohn-Sherbock (ed.), *Tradition and Unity: Sermons Published in Honor of Robert Runcie* (London: Bellew, 1991), 79-83.

"Pray Without Ceasing: The Ideal of Continual Prayer in Eastern Monasticism," in *Eastern Churches Review* 2:3 (1969), 253-61.

"Silence in Prayer: The Meaning of Hesychia," in A. M. Allchin (ed.), *Theology and Prayer: Essays on Monastic Themes Presented at the Orthodox-Cistercian Conference, Oxford, 1973*, Studies Supplementary to *Sobornost* 3 ([London]: Fellowship of St Alban and St Sergius, 1975), 8-28; also in M. Basil Pennington (ed.), *One Yet Two: Monastic Tradition in East and West*, Cistercian Studies Series 29 (Kalamazoo, MI: Cistercian Publications, 1976), 22-47.

"The Seed of the Church: Martyrdom as a Universal Vocation," in *Sobornost* 5:1 (1983), 7-18; also issued separately (Witney, Oxford: St Stephen's Press, 1995).

"The Spiritual Guide in Orthodox Christianity," in John-David Robinson (ed.), "Word Out of Silence: A Symposium on World Spiritualities," *Cross Currents* 24: 2-3 (1974), 296-313; reprinted in Kevin G. Culligan (ed.), *Spiritual Direction: Contemporary Readings* (Locust Valley, NY: Living Flame Press, 1983), 20-40.

"The Fool in Christ as Prophet and Apostle," in *Sobornost* 6:2 (1984), 6-28.

"Time: Prison or Path to Freedom?" in *Fairacres Chronicle* 22:3 (1989), 5-15; reprinted in Jane Osborne and Sister Christine, SLG (eds.), *Wide as God's Love* (London/ Dublin/Edinburgh: New City, 1994), 108-19.

"Dare We Hope for the Salvation of All? Origen, St Gregory of Nyssa, and St Isaac the Syrian," in *Theology Digest* 45:4 (1998), 303-17.

INDEX PART I
Persons

A

Abraham, Abba (4th-5th cent.), 104
Afanassieff, Archpriest Nicolas (1893-1966), 16
Agapy, *Starets* of Valamo (ca. 19th cent.), 84
Alexander, King of Yugoslavia (1888-1934), 150
Allchin, Canon Donald (A. M.) (born 1930), 6, 73n.
Alonius, Abba (4th cent.), 102n.
Ambrose, Bishop of Milan, St (ca. 339-97), 94
Ammonas, Abba (4th cent.), 91, 110
Amphilochios of Patmos, Archimandrite (1889-1970), 149-50
Amvrosy of Optino, St (1812-91), 60
André (Scrima), Archimandrite (20th cent.), 144-145
Andrew of Constantinople, fool in Christ, St (7th or 9th-10th cent.), 157, 158, 165, 166, 173, 177, 178, 180
Andrew of Crete, St (ca. 660-740), 161
Anthony (Bloom), Metropolitan of Sourozh (born 1914), 22, 26, 99n., 103n., 108
Antiochus of St Sabas (7th cent.), 75
Antony of Egypt (the Great), St (ca. 251-356), 77-78, 86, 91, 94, 103, 104, 109, 110, 122, 128, 131-32, 133, 139, 142, 147, 166
Antony, monk of St Sabas (20th cent.), 84
Aquinas: *see* Thomas Aquinas
Aristotle (384-322 BC), 71n., 182
Arnobius of Sicca (4th cent.), 212
Arsenius, Abba (ca. 360-449), 91, 93, 165
Athanasius, Bishop of Alexandria, St (ca. 296-373), 122, 131
Athenagoras (Kokkinakis), Archbishop of Thyateira and Great Britain (1909-79), 22n.
Augustine, Bishop of Hippo, St (354-430), 12, 13, 168, 190, 210

B

Baker, Dom Augustine (1575-1641), 145
Balsamon, Theodore, Patriarch of Antioch (ca. 1130-after 1195), 179
Barker, Sir Ernest (1874-1960), 10
Barsanuphius of Gaza, St (6th cent.), 90, 91, 92, 99, 120, 122, 123, 139, 140, 145, 151
Barth, Christian Gottlieb (1799-1862), 214
Basil the Blessed of Moscow, fool in Christ, St (†1552), 159, 176
Basil the Great, Archbishop of Caesarea, St (ca. 330-79), 12, 52, 77n., 82, 93, 205, 206
  Liturgy of, 29, 30, 50
Basil (Krivocheine), Archbishop (1900-85), 5, 22, 104n.
Beausobre, Iulia de (Lady Namier) (1893-1977), 6, 32-33, 112-14, 116, 153, 175
Benedict of Nursia, St (ca. 480-ca. 550), 148
Berdyaev, Nicolas (1871-1948), 73, 187
Bernanos, Georges (1888-1948), 208
Blake, William (1757-1827), 140, 189
Bloom: *see* Anthony (Bloom)
Boris (Godunov), Tsar of Russia (1552-1605), 154
Boris, Price of Kiev, St (†1015), 13
Brianchaninov: *see* Ignaty (Brianchaninov)
Brock, Sebastian (born 1938), 209
Buber, Martin (1878-1965), 74, 117
Burgo, Professor Donald Paul, 214n.

C

Cabasilas: *see* Nicolas Cabasilas
Caiaphas, 178
Cassian: *see* John Cassian
Cheremeteff, Archpriest George (†1971), 22, 23
Chitty, Fr Derwas (1901-71), 6, 90n.
Chrysostom: *see* John Chrysostom
Cicero (106-43 BC), 124

INDEX PART 2
Subjects

1443.

9

51
54
55

1900.
244.95
100.

2700.

2749

5